P9-DNA-462

Welcome to

A POCKET Style Manual

EIGHTH EDITION

Faster and more reliable than a Google search, *A Pocket Style Manual* covers everything you need for college writing—especially researched writing. You can turn to it for help with finding, evaluating, integrating, and citing sources—as well as for advice on revising sentences for clarity, grammar, and punctuation. The following reference aids will help you find everything you need to be a successful college writer in any course.

- **The brief and detailed contents** inside the front and back covers allow you to quickly spot the help you need.

- **The index** at the back of the book includes plain-language entries like "*I* vs. *me*" to point to common problems like pronoun case.

- **Color-coded MLA, APA, *Chicago*, and CSE** sections give discipline-specific advice for working with sources. Directories at the beginning of each section list documentation models.

- **The glossaries** on pages 293–310 offer useful definitions and help with commonly confused or misused words such as *affect/effect*.

If your instructor has assigned a Hacker Handbooks media product, even more help is at your fingertips:

- **Nearly 300 exercises** help you improve your writing and effectively work with sources.

- **50 model papers** in 5 documentation styles provide guidance in writing and formatting your work in any course.

- **33 LearningCurve quizzes** offer game-like sentence-level practice and let you track your progress.

EIGHTH EDITION

A POCKET
Style Manual

Diana Hacker

Nancy Sommers
Harvard University

bedford/st.martin's
Macmillan Learning
Boston | New York

For Bedford/St. Martin's

Vice President, Editorial, Macmillan Learning Humanities: Edwin Hill
Senior Program Director for English: Leasa Burton
Senior Program Manager: Stacey Purviance
Executive Editor: Michelle M. Clark
Marketing Manager: Vivian Garcia
Director of Content Development: Jane Knetzger
Senior Editor: Mara Weible
Senior Media Editor: Barbara G. Flanagan
Senior Content Project Manager: Gregory Erb
Senior Media Project Manager: Allison Hart
Senior Workflow Manager: Jennifer Wetzel
Production Supervisor: Robert Cherry
Associate Editor: Stephanie Thomas
Copy Editor: Arthur Johnson
Indexer: Ellen Kuhl Repetto
Photo Editor: Martha Friedman
Permissions Manager: Kalina Ingham
Senior Art Director: Anna Palchik
Text Design: Claire Seng-Niemoeller
Cover Design: William Boardman
Composition: Cenveo Publisher Services
Printing and Binding: RR Donnelley

Printed in China.

2   1   0   9   8

f   e   d   c   b

For information, write: Bedford/St. Martin's, 75 Arlington Street, Boston, MA 02116

ISBN 978-1-319-05740-4

Acknowledgments

Clarity

1 Tighten wordy sentences.

Long sentences are not necessarily wordy, nor are short sentences always concise. A sentence is wordy if it can be tightened without loss of meaning.

1a Redundancies

Redundancies such as *cooperate together, yellow in color,* and *basic essentials* are a common source of wordiness. There is no need to say the same thing twice.

▶ **Daniel ~~is employed~~ [works] at a private rehabilitation center ~~working~~ as a physical therapist.**

Modifiers are redundant when their meanings are suggested by other words in the sentence.

▶ **Sylvia ~~very hurriedly~~ scribbled her name and phone number on the back of a greasy napkin.**

1b Empty or inflated phrases

An empty word or phrase can be cut with little or no loss of meaning. An inflated phrase can be reduced to a word or two.

▶ **~~In my opinion,~~ [T]their current immigration policy is misguided.**

▶ **Funds are limited ~~at this point in time.~~ [now.]**

INFLATED	CONCISE
along the lines of	like
at the present time	now, currently
because of the fact that	because
by means of	by
due to the fact that	because
for the reason that	because
in order to	to
in spite of the fact that	although, though
in the event that	if
until such time as	until

1c Needlessly complex structures

Simplifying sentences and using stronger verbs can help make writing clearer and more direct.

▶ Researchers ~~were involved in examining~~ the effect

  examined

  of classical music on unborn babies.

▶ ~~It is imperative that~~ all night managers follow

  A   must

  strict procedures when locking the safe.

▶ The financial analyst claimed that because of

  volatile market conditions she could not ~~make an~~

  estimate ~~of~~ the company's future profits.

2   Prefer active verbs.

As a rule, active verbs express meaning more vigor-ously than forms of the verb *be* or verbs in the passive voice. Forms of *be* (*be, am, is, are, was, were, being, been*) lack vigor because they convey no action. Passive verbs lack strength because their subjects receive the action instead of doing it.

  Forms of *be* and passive verbs have legitimate uses, but choose an active verb whenever possible.

BE VERB A surge of power *was* responsible for the destruction of the pumps.

PASSIVE The pumps *were destroyed* by a surge of power.

ACTIVE A surge of power *destroyed* the pumps.

2a When to replace *be* verbs

Not every *be* verb needs replacing. The forms of *be* (*be, am, is, are, was, were, being, been*) work well when you want to link a subject to a noun that clearly renames it or to an adjective that describes it: *Orchard House was the home of Louisa May Alcott. The harvest will be bounti-ful after the summer rains.*

  If using a *be* verb makes a sentence needlessly wordy, consider replacing it. Often a phrase following the verb

contains a noun or an adjective (such as *violation* or *resistant*) that suggests a more vigorous, active verb (*violate*,
resisted).

▶ Burying nuclear waste in Antarctica would ~~be in~~ violate
^

~~violation of~~ an international treaty.

▶ When Rosa Parks ~~was resistant to~~ resisted giving up her
^

seat on the bus, she became a civil rights hero.

NOTE: When used as helping verbs with present participles to express ongoing action, *be* verbs are fine: *She
was swimming when the whistle blew.* (See 11b.)

2b When to replace passive verbs

In the active voice, the subject of the sentence performs the action; in the passive, the subject receives
the action.

ACTIVE   The committee *reached* a decision.

PASSIVE   A decision *was reached* by the committee.

In passive sentences, the actor (in this case *committee*)
frequently does not appear: *A decision was reached.*

In most cases, you will want to emphasize the actor,
so you should use the active voice. To replace a passive
verb with an active one, make the actor the subject of
the sentence.

▶ ~~Samples were~~ collected daily from the stagnant
Investigators   samples
^   ^

pond.

▶ ~~The land was stripped of timber before the settlers~~
The settlers stripped the land of timber before realizing
^

~~realized~~ the consequences of their actions.

The passive voice is appropriate when you wish to
emphasize the receiver of the action or to minimize the
importance of the actor. In the following sentence, for
example, the writer intended to focus on the tobacco
plants, not on the people spraying them: *As the time for
harvest approaches, the tobacco plants are sprayed with a
chemical to retard the growth of suckers.*

3 Balance parallel ideas.

If two or more ideas are parallel, they should be expressed in parallel grammatical form.

A kiss can be a comma, a question mark, or an

exclamation point.   —Mistinguett

This novel is not to be tossed lightly aside, but to

be hurled with great force.   —Dorothy Parker

3a Items in a series

Balance all items in a series by presenting them in parallel grammatical form.

▶ Cross-training involves a variety of exercises,
                                    lifting
   such as running, swimming, and weights.
                                       ^

▶ Children who study music also learn confidence,
                          creativity.
   discipline, and ~~they are creative.~~
                  ^

▶ Racing to work, Sam drove down the middle of
                                ignored
   the road, ran one red light, and two stop signs.
                                   ^

3b Paired ideas

When pairing ideas, underscore their connection by expressing them in similar grammatical form. Paired ideas are usually connected in one of three ways: (1) with a coordinating conjunction such as *and*, *but*, or *or*; (2) with a correlative conjunction such as *either...or*, *neither...nor*, *not only...but also*, or *whether...or*; or (3) with a word introducing a comparison, usually *than* or *as*.

▶ Many states are reducing property taxes for home
                 extending
   owners and ~~extend~~ financial aid in the form of tax
             ^
   credits to renters.

   The coordinating conjunction *and* connects two *-ing* verb forms: *reducing...extending*.

▶ Thomas Edison was not only a prolific inventor

but also ~~was~~ a successful entrepreneur.

The correlative conjunction *not only . . . but also* connects
two noun phrases: *a prolific inventor* and *a successful
entrepreneur.*

▶ It is easier to speak in abstractions than ^{to ground} ~~grounding~~

one's thoughts in reality.

The comparative term *than* links two infinitive phrases:
to speak . . . to ground.

NOTE: Repeat function words such as prepositions (*by,
to*) and subordinating conjunctions (*that, because*) to
make parallel ideas easier to grasp.

▶ Our study revealed that left-handed students were

more likely to have trouble with classroom desks
^{that}
and rearranging desks for exam periods was useful.

4   Add needed words.

Sometimes writers leave out words intentionally, without affecting meaning. But the result is often a confusing or an ungrammatical sentence. Readers need to see
at a glance how the parts of a sentence are connected.

4a Words in compound structures

In compound structures, words are often omitted for
economy: *Tom is a man who means what he says and
[who] says what he means.* Such omissions are acceptable as long as the omitted words are common to both
parts of the compound structure.

If a sentence is ungrammatical because an omitted
word is not common to both parts of the compound
structure, the word must be put back in.

▶ Advertisers target customers whom they identify
                 who
  through demographic research or have purchased
                                    ^
  their product in the past.

    The word *who* must be included because *whom . . . have
    purchased* is not grammatically correct.

                         accepted
▶ Mayor Davidson never has and never will accept a
                                ^
  bribe.

    Has . . . accept is not grammatically correct.

                             in
▶ Many South Pacific tribes still believe and live by
                                   ^
  ancient laws.

    Believe . . . by is not idiomatic English.

4b The word *that*

Add the word *that* if there is any danger of misreading
without it.

▶ In his obedience experiments, psychologist Stanley
                         that
  Milgram discovered ordinary people were willing
                    ^
  to inflict physical pain on strangers.

    Milgram didn't discover people; he discovered that people
    were willing to inflict pain on strangers.

4c Words in comparisons

Comparisons should be between items that are alike.
To compare unlike items is illogical and distracting.

▶ The forests of North America are much more
                       those of
  extensive than Europe.
            ^

    Comparisons should be complete so that readers
will understand what is being compared.

INCOMPLETE   Brand X is less salty.

COMPLETE   Brand X is less salty than Brand Y.

Also, comparisons should leave no ambiguity about meaning. In the following sentence, two interpretations are possible.

AMBIGUOUS   Kai helped me more than my friend.

CLEAR   Kai helped me more than *he helped* my friend.

CLEAR   Kai helped me more than my friend *did*.

5 Eliminate confusing shifts.

5a Shifts in point of view

The point of view of a piece of writing is the perspective from which it is written: first person (*I* or *we*), second person (*you*), or third person (*he, she, it, one,* or *they*). The *I* (or *we*) point of view, which emphasizes the writer, is a good choice for writing based primarily on personal experience. The *you* point of view, which emphasizes the reader, works well for giving advice or explaining how to do something. The third-person point of view, which emphasizes the subject, is appropriate in most academic and professional writing.

Writers who have trouble settling on an appropriate point of view sometimes shift confusingly from one to another. The solution is to choose a suitable perspective and then stay with it. (See also 12a.)

▶ Our class practiced rescuing a victim trapped in a
   We   our
   wrecked car. ~~You~~ were graded on ~~your~~ speed and
              ^   ^
   skill in freeing the victim.

   You
▶ ~~Travelers~~ need a signed passport for trips abroad.
   ^
   You should also fill out the emergency information

   page in the passport.

5b Shifts in tense

Consistent verb tenses clearly establish the time of the actions being described. When a passage begins in one tense and then shifts without warning and for no reason to another, readers are distracted and confused.

▶ There was no way I could fight the current and
                                    jumped
  win. Just as I was losing hope, a stranger ~~jumps~~
                                                      ^
            swam
  off a passing boat and ~~swims~~ toward me.
                          ^

Writers often shift verb tenses when writing about
literature. The literary convention is to describe fictional
events consistently in the present tense. (See p. 29.)

6   Untangle mixed constructions.

A mixed construction contains sentence parts that do
not sensibly fit together. The mismatch may be a matter
of grammar or of logic.

6a Mixed grammar

You should not begin a sentence with one grammatical
plan and then switch without warning to another. Rethink-
ing the purpose of the sentence can help you revise.

        M
▶ For ~~most drivers who~~ have a blood alcohol level of
      ^
  .05 percent increase their risk of causing an accident.

  The prepositional phrase beginning with *For* cannot
  serve as the subject of the verb *increase*. The revision
  makes *drivers* the subject.

▶ Although the United States is a wealthy nation, ~~but~~

  more than 20 percent of our children live in poverty.

  The coordinating conjunction *but* cannot link a subordinate
  clause (*Although...*) with an independent clause (*more than
  20 percent...*).

6b Illogical connections

A sentence's subject and verb should make sense together.

            the double personal exemption for
▶ Under the revised plan, the elderly/ ~~who now receive~~
                                      ^
  ~~a double personal exemption,~~ will be abolished.

  The exemption, not the elderly, will be abolished.

> The court decided that ~~Tiffany's welfare~~ would not
> _{Tiffany}
>
> be safe living with her abusive parents.

Tiffany, not her welfare, would not be safe.

6c *Is when*, *is where*, and *reason...is because* constructions

In formal English, readers sometimes object to *is when*, *is where*, and *reason...is because* constructions on grammatical or logical grounds.

> Anorexia nervosa is ~~where people~~ think they are
> ^{a disorder suffered by people who}
>
> too fat and diet to the point of starvation.

Anorexia nervosa is a disorder, not a place.

> ~~The reason~~ Ʈhe experiment failed ~~is~~ because
>
> conditions in the lab were not sterile.

7 Repair misplaced and dangling modifiers.

Modifiers should point clearly to the words they modify. As a rule, related words should be kept together.

7a Misplaced words

Limiting modifiers such as *only*, *even*, *almost*, *nearly*, and *just* should appear in front of a verb only if they modify the verb. If they limit the meaning of some other word in the sentence, they should be placed in front of that word.

> Medical lasers ~~only~~ destroy the target, leaving the
> ^{only}
>
> surrounding healthy tissue intact.

> I couldn't ~~even~~ save a dollar out of my paycheck.
> ^{even}

When the limiting modifier *not* is misplaced, the sentence usually suggests a meaning the writer did not intend.

▶ In the United States in 1860, _{not} all black southerners

were ~~not~~ slaves.

The original sentence means that no black southerners were slaves. The revision makes the writer's real meaning clear.

7b Misplaced phrases and clauses

Although phrases and clauses can appear at some distance from the words they modify, make sure your meaning is clear. When phrases or clauses are oddly placed, absurd misreadings can result.

▶ *On the walls*
~~There~~ are many pictures of comedians who have

performed at Gavin's. ~~on the walls.~~

The comedians weren't performing on the walls; the pictures were on the walls.

▶ The robber was described as a *170-pound,* six-foot-tall man

with a mustache. ~~weighing 170 pounds.~~

The robber, not the mustache, weighed 170 pounds.

7c Dangling modifiers

A dangling modifier fails to refer logically to any word in the sentence. Dangling modifiers are usually introductory word groups (such as verbal phrases) that suggest but do not name an actor. When a sentence opens with such a modifier, readers expect the subject of the next clause to name the actor. If it doesn't, the modifier dangles.

DANGLING   Upon entering the doctor's office, a skeleton caught my attention.

This sentence suggests—absurdly—that the skeleton entered the doctor's office.

To repair a dangling modifier, you can revise the sentence in one of two ways:

1. Name the actor in the subject of the sentence.
2. Name the actor in the modifier.

▶ Upon entering the doctor's office, a skeleton.
    ^I noticed   ^
    ~~caught my attention.~~

▶ ~~Upon entering~~ the doctor's office, a skeleton
    ^As I entered

    caught my attention.

You cannot repair a dangling modifier simply by moving it: *A skeleton caught my attention upon entering the doctor's office.* The sentence still suggests that the skeleton entered the doctor's office.

▶ **Wanting to create checks and balances on power,**
    the framers of
    the Constitution divided the government into
    ^
    three branches.

    The framers (not the Constitution itself) wanted to create checks and balances.

▶ **After completing seminary training, ~~women's~~**
    women were often denied
    ^
    access to the priesthood. ~~was often denied~~
    ^

    The women (not their access to the priesthood) completed the training. The writer has revised the sentence by making *women* (not *women's access*) the subject.

7d Split infinitives

An infinitive consists of *to* plus a verb: *to think, to dance.* When a modifier appears between its two parts, an infinitive is said to be "split": *to slowly drive.* If a split infinitive is awkward, move the modifier to another position in the sentence.

▶ **Cardiologists encourage their patients to**
                                    more carefully.
    ~~more carefully~~ **watch their cholesterol levels.**
                                                        ^

Attempts to avoid split infinitives sometimes result in awkward sentences. When alternative phrasing sounds unnatural, most experts allow—and even encourage—splitting the infinitive. *We decided to actually enforce the law* is a natural construction in English. *We decided actually to enforce the law* is not.

8 Provide sentence variety.

Sentence variety can help keep readers interested in your writing. If most of your sentences are the same length or begin the same way, try combining them or varying sentence starters.

8a Combining choppy sentences

If a series of short sentences sounds choppy, consider combining sentences. Look for opportunities to tuck some of your ideas into subordinate clauses. A subordinate clause, which contains a subject and a verb, begins with a word such as *after, although, because, before, if, since, that, unless, until, when, where, which,* or *who.* (See p. 309.)

▶ We keep our use of insecticides to a minimum./
    because we
    ~~We~~ are concerned about the environment.
    ^

Also look for opportunities to tuck some of your ideas into phrases, word groups that lack a subject and a verb. You will usually see more than one way to combine choppy sentences; the method you choose should depend on the details you want to emphasize.

▶ The Chesapeake and Ohio Canal, ~~is~~ a 184-mile
    ^
    waterway constructed in the 1800s/. ~~It~~ was a major
    ^
    source of transportation for goods during the Civil War.

This revision emphasizes the significance of the canal during the Civil War. The first sentence, about the age of the canal, has been made into a phrase modifying *Chesapeake and Ohio Canal.*

    Used as a major source of transportation for goods
    during the Civil War, the
▶ ~~The~~ Chesapeake and Ohio Canal is a 184-mile
    ^
    waterway constructed in the 1800s. ~~It was a major~~

    ~~source of transportation for goods during the Civil War.~~

This revision emphasizes the age of the canal. The second sentence, about the canal's use for transportation of goods, has become a participial phrase modifying *Chesapeake and Ohio Canal.*

When short sentences contain ideas of equal importance, it is often effective to combine them with *and*, *but*, or *or*.

> Shore houses were flooded up to the first floor/, ^and^
>
> Brant's Lighthouse was swallowed by the sea.

8b Varying sentence openings

Most sentences in English begin with the subject, move to the verb, and continue to an object, with modifiers tucked in along the way or put at the end. For the most part, such sentences are fine. Put too many of them in a row, however, and they become monotonous.

Words, phrases, or clauses modifying the verb can often be inserted ahead of the subject.

> ^Eventually a^ ~~A~~ few drops of sap ~~eventually~~ began to trickle into
>
> the pail.

> ^Just as the sun was coming up, a^ ~~A~~ pair of black ducks flew over the pond. ~~just as~~
>
> ~~the sun was coming up.~~

Participial phrases (beginning with verb forms such as *driving* or *exhausted*) can frequently be moved to the start of a sentence without loss of clarity.

> ~~The committee,~~ ^D^discouraged by the researchers'
>
> ^the committee^ apparent lack of progress, nearly withdrew
>
> funding for the prizewinning experiments.

NOTE: In a sentence that begins with a participial phrase, the subject of the sentence must name the person or thing being described. If it doesn't, the phrase dangles. (See 7c.)

9 Find an appropriate voice.

An appropriate voice is one that suits your subject, engages your audience, and conforms to the conventions of the genre in which you are writing, such as lab reports, informal essays, research papers, business memos, and so on.

In academic and professional writing, certain language is generally considered inappropriate: jargon, clichés, slang, and sexist or biased language.

9a Jargon

Jargon is specialized language used among members of a trade, profession, or group. Use jargon only when readers will be familiar with it or when plain English will not do as well.

JARGON   We outsourced the work to an outfit in Ohio because we didn't have the bandwidth to tackle it in-house.

REVISED   We hired a company in Ohio because we had too few employees to do the work.

Broadly defined, jargon includes puffed-up language designed more to impress readers than to inform them. The following are common examples from business, government, higher education, and the military, with plain English translations in parentheses.

commence (begin)	indicator (sign)
components (parts)	optimal (best)
endeavor (try)	parameters (boundaries, limits)
facilitate (help)	prior to (before)
finalize (finish)	utilize (use)
impact (v.) (affect)	viable (workable)

Sentences filled with jargon are hard to read and often wordy.

▶ The CEO should ~~dialogue~~ talk with investors about ~~partnering~~ working with clients to buy land in ~~economically~~ poor ~~deprived zones.~~ neighborhoods.

▶ All ~~employees functioning in the capacity of~~ work-study students ~~are required to give evidence of~~ must prove that they are ~~current enrollment.~~ currently enrolled.

9b Clichés

The pioneer who first announced that he had "slept like a log" no doubt amused his companions with a fresh and unlikely comparison. Today, however, that comparison is a cliché, a saying that can no longer add emphasis or surprise. To see just how predictable clichés are, put your hand over the right-hand column below and then finish the phrases given on the left.

beat around the	bush
busy as a	bee, beaver
cool as a	cucumber
crystal	clear
light as a	feather
like a bull	in a china shop
playing with	fire
selling like	hotcakes
water under the	bridge
white as a	sheet, ghost
avoid clichés like the	plague

The solution for clichés is simple: Just delete them. Sometimes you can write around a cliché by adding an element of surprise. One student who had written that she had butterflies in her stomach revised her cliché like this:

> If all of the action in my stomach is caused by butterflies, there must be a horde of them, with horseshoes on.

The image of butterflies wearing horseshoes is fresh and unlikely, not predictable like the original cliché.

9c Slang

Slang is an informal and sometimes private vocabulary that expresses the solidarity of a group such as teenagers, rap musicians, or sports fans. Although it does have a certain vitality, slang is a code that not everyone understands, and it is too informal for most written work.

> When the server crashed, three hours of unsaved *we lost* data. ~~went down the tubes.~~

9d Sexist language

Sexist language excludes, stereotypes, or demeans women or men and should be avoided. Using nonsexist language shows respect for and sensitivity to your readers.

In your writing, avoid referring to any one profession as exclusively male or exclusively female (teachers as women or engineers as men, for example). Also avoid using different conventions when identifying women and men.

▶   All executives' ~~wives~~ *spouses* are invited to the picnic.

▶   Boris Stotsky, attorney, and ~~Mrs.~~ Cynthia Jones, *graphic designer,* ~~mother of three,~~ are running for city council.

Traditionally, *he, him,* and *his* were used to refer generically to persons of either sex: *A journalist is motivated by his deadline.* You can avoid such sexist usage in one of three ways: substitute a pair of pronouns (*he or she, his or her*); reword in the plural; or revise the sentence to avoid the problem.

▶   A journalist is motivated by his *or her* deadline.

▶   ~~A journalist is~~ *Journalists are* motivated by ~~his deadline.~~ *their deadlines.*

▶   A journalist is motivated by ~~his~~ *a* deadline.

Like *he* and *his,* the nouns *man* and *men* and related words were once used generically to refer to persons of either sex. Use gender-neutral terms instead.

INAPPROPRIATE	APPROPRIATE
chairman	chairperson, chair
congressman	representative, legislator
fireman	firefighter
mailman	mail carrier, postal worker
mankind	people, humans
to man	to operate, to staff
weatherman	meteorologist, forecaster

9e Offensive language

Your writing should be respectful and free of stereotypical, biased, or other offensive language. Be especially careful when describing or labeling people. When naming groups of people, choose labels that the groups currently use to describe themselves. For example, *Negro* is not an acceptable label for African Americans; instead of *Indian*, use *Native American* or, better, the name of the specific group.

▶ North Dakota takes its name from the ~~Indian~~ Lakota word

meaning "friend" or "ally."

▶ Many ~~Oriental~~ Asian immigrants have recently settled in

our small town.

Avoid stereotyping a person or a group even if you believe your generalization to be positive.

▶ It was no surprise that Greer, ~~a Chinese American,~~ an excellent math and science student,

was selected for the honors chemistry program.

Grammar

10   Make subjects and verbs agree.

In the present tense, verbs agree with their subjects in number (singular or plural) and in person (first, second, or third). The present-tense ending -s is used on a verb if its subject is third-person singular; otherwise the verb takes no ending. Consider, for example, the present-tense forms of the verb *give*.

	SINGULAR	PLURAL
FIRST PERSON	I give	we give
SECOND PERSON	you give	you give
THIRD PERSON	he/she/it gives	they give
	Yolanda gives	parents give

The verb *be* varies from this pattern; it has special forms in *both* the present and the past tense.

PRESENT-TENSE FORMS OF *BE*		PAST-TENSE FORMS OF *BE*	
I am	we are	I was	we were
you are	you are	you were	you were
he/she/it is	they are	he/she/it was	they were

This section describes particular situations that can cause problems with subject-verb agreement.

10a Words between subject and verb

Word groups often come between the subject and the verb. Such word groups, usually modifying the subject, may contain a noun that at first appears to be the subject. By mentally stripping away such modifiers, you can isolate the noun that is in fact the subject.

The *samples* on the tray in the lab *need* testing.

▶ High levels of air pollution damages the respiratory tract.

The subject is *levels*, not *pollution*.

▶ The slaughter of pandas for their pelts ~~have~~ has caused the panda population to decline drastically.

The subject is *slaughter*, not *pandas* or *pelts*.

NOTE: Phrases beginning with the prepositions *as well as, in addition to, accompanied by, together with,* and *along with* do not make a singular subject plural: *The governor as well as his press secretary was* [not *were*] *on the plane.*

10b Subjects joined with *and*

Compound subjects joined with *and* are nearly always plural.

▶   Bleach and ammonia creates a toxic gas when mixed.

EXCEPTION: If the parts of the subject form a single unit, you may treat the subject as singular: *Bacon and eggs is always on the menu.*

10c Subjects joined with *or* or *nor*

With compound subjects joined with *or* or *nor*, make the verb agree with the part of the subject nearer to the verb.

has
▶   If an infant or a child ~~have~~ a high fever, call a doctor.
                          ^

                                                    were
▶   Neither the lab assistant nor the students ~~was~~ able
                                                    ^

    to download the program.

10d Indefinite pronouns such as *someone*

Indefinite pronouns refer to nonspecific persons or things. The following indefinite pronouns are singular: *anybody, anyone, anything, each, either, everybody, everyone, everything, neither, nobody, no one, somebody, someone, something.*

                                          was
▶   Nobody who participated in the taste tests ~~were~~ paid.
                                              ^

    has
▶   Each of the essays ~~have~~ been graded.
                      ^

A few indefinite pronouns (*all, any, none, some*) may be singular or plural depending on the noun or pronoun they refer to: *Some of our luggage was lost. Some of the rocks were slippery. None of his advice makes sense. None of the eggs were broken.*

10e Collective nouns such as *jury*

Collective nouns such as *jury, committee, audience, crowd, class, family,* and *couple* name a group. In American English, collective nouns are usually treated as singular: They emphasize the group as a unit.

>   meets
> **The board of trustees ~~meet~~ in Denver twice a year.**
>   ^

Occasionally, to draw attention to the individual members of the group, a collective noun may be treated as plural: *The class are debating among themselves.* Many writers prefer to add a clearly plural noun such as *members: The class members are debating among themselves.*

NOTE: In general, when fractions or units of measurement are used with a singular noun, treat them as singular; when they are used with a plural noun, treat them as plural: *Three-fourths of the pie has been eaten. One-fourth of the drivers were texting.*

10f Subject after verb

Verbs ordinarily follow subjects. When this normal order is reversed, it is easy to be confused.

>   are
> **Of particular concern ~~is~~ penicillin and tetracycline,**
>   ^
> **antibiotics used to make animals more resistant**
> **to disease.**

The subject, *penicillin and tetracycline,* is plural.

The subject always follows the verb in sentences beginning with *there is* or *there are* (or *there was* or *there were*).

>   were
> **There ~~was~~ a turtle and a snake in the tank.**
>   ^

The subject, *turtle and snake,* is plural, so the verb must be *were.*

10g Who, which, and that

Like most pronouns, the relative pronouns *who, which,* and *that* have antecedents, nouns or pronouns to which they refer. Relative pronouns used as subjects of subordinate clauses take verbs that agree with their antecedents.

ANT PN   V
Take a *train that arrives* before 6:00.

Constructions such as *one of the students who* (or *one of the things that*) may cause problems for writers. Do not assume that the antecedent must be *one*. Instead, consider the logic of the sentence.

▶ Our ability to use language is one of the things
that ~~sets~~ us apart from animals.
     set
     ^

The antecedent of *that* is *things*, not *one*. Several things set us apart from animals.

When the phrase *the only* comes before *one*, you are safe in assuming that *one* is the antecedent of the relative pronoun.

▶ Carmen is the only one of my friends who ~~live~~
                                           lives
                                            ^
in my building.

The antecedent of *who* is *one*, not *friends*. Only one friend lives in the building.

10h Plural form, singular meaning

Words such as *athletics, economics, mathematics, physics, politics, statistics, measles,* and *news* are usually singular, despite their plural form.

▶ Politics ~~are~~ among my mother's favorite pastimes.
           is
           ^

EXCEPTION: Occasionally some of these words, especially *economics, mathematics, politics,* and *statistics,* have plural meanings: *Office politics often affect decisions about hiring and promotion. The economics of the building plan are prohibitive.*

10i Titles, company names, and words mentioned as words

Titles, company names, and words mentioned as words are singular.

▶ *Lost Cities* describe the discoveries of fifty ancient
   describes

civilizations.

▶ Delmonico Brothers ~~specialize~~ in organic produce
   specializes

and additive-free meats.

▶ *Controlled substances* ~~are~~ a euphemism for illegal
   is

drugs.

11 Be alert to other problems with verbs.

Section 10 deals with subject-verb agreement. This section describes a few other potential problems with verbs.

11a Irregular verbs

For all regular verbs, the past-tense and past-participle
forms are the same, ending in *-ed* or *-d*, so there is no
danger of confusion. This is not true, however, for
irregular verbs, such as the following.

BASE FORM	PAST TENSE	PAST PARTICIPLE
break	broke	broken
fly	flew	flown
go	went	gone

The past-tense form, which never has a helping
verb, expresses action that occurred entirely in the past.
The past participle is used with a helping verb—either
with *has, have,* or *had* to form one of the perfect tenses
or with *be, am, is, are, was, were, being,* or *been* to form
the passive voice.

PAST TENSE   Last July, we *went* to Beijing.

PAST PARTICIPLE   We have *gone* to Beijing twice.

When you aren't sure which verb form to choose
(*went* or *gone, broke* or *broken,* and so on), consult the list
that begins at the bottom of the next page. Choose the
past-tense form if your sentence doesn't have a helping
verb; choose the past-participle form if it does.

saw
▶ Yesterday we ~~seen~~ a film about rain forests.
        ^

Because there is no helping verb, the past-tense form *saw*
is required.

fallen
▶ By the end of the day, the stock market had ~~fell~~

two hundred points.
        ^

Because of the helping verb *had*, the past-participle form
fallen is required.

Distinguishing between *lie* and *lay*   Writers often
confuse the forms of *lie* (meaning "to recline or rest on a
surface") and *lay* (meaning "to put or place something").
The intransitive verb *lie* does not take a direct object:
The tax forms lie on the table. The transitive verb *lay*
takes a direct object: *Please lay the tax forms on the table*.

In addition to confusing the meanings of *lie* and
lay, writers are often unfamiliar with the Standard
English forms of these verbs.

BASE FORM	PAST TENSE	PAST PARTICIPLE	PRESENT PARTICIPLE
lie	lay	lain	lying
lay	laid	laid	laying

Elizabeth was so exhausted that she *lay* down for a
nap. [Past tense of *lie*, meaning "to recline"]

The prosecutor *laid* the photograph on a table close
to the jurors. [Past tense of *lay*, meaning "to place"]

Letters dating from the Civil War were *lying* in the
corner of the chest. [Present participle of *lie*]

The patient had *lain* in an uncomfortable position all
night. [Past participle of *lie*]

Common irregular verbs

BASE FORM	PAST TENSE	PAST PARTICIPLE
arise	arose	arisen
awake	awoke, awaked	awaked, awoke
be	was, were	been
beat	beat	beaten, beat
become	became	become
begin	began	begun
bend	bent	bent

BASE FORM	PAST TENSE	PAST PARTICIPLE
bite	bit	bitten, bit
blow	blew	blown
break	broke	broken
bring	brought	brought
build	built	built
burst	burst	burst
buy	bought	bought
catch	caught	caught
choose	chose	chosen
cling	clung	clung
come	came	come
cost	cost	cost
deal	dealt	dealt
dig	dug	dug
dive	dived, dove	dived
do	did	done
draw	drew	drawn
dream	dreamed, dreamt	dreamed, dreamt
drink	drank	drunk
drive	drove	driven
eat	ate	eaten
fall	fell	fallen
fight	fought	fought
find	found	found
fly	flew	flown
forget	forgot	forgotten, forgot
freeze	froze	frozen
get	got	gotten, got
give	gave	given
go	went	gone
grow	grew	grown
hang (execute)	hanged	hanged
hang (suspend)	hung	hung
have	had	had
hear	heard	heard
hide	hid	hidden
hurt	hurt	hurt
keep	kept	kept
know	knew	known
lay (put)	laid	laid
lead	led	led

BASE FORM	PAST TENSE	PAST PARTICIPLE
lend	lent	lent
let (allow)	let	let
lie (recline)	lay	lain
lose	lost	lost
make	made	made
prove	proved	proved, proven
read	read	read
ride	rode	ridden
ring	rang	rung
rise (get up)	rose	risen
run	ran	run
say	said	said
see	saw	seen
send	sent	sent
set (place)	set	set
shake	shook	shaken
shoot	shot	shot
shrink	shrank	shrunk, shrunken
sing	sang	sung
sink	sank	sunk
sit (be seated)	sat	sat
slay	slew	slain
sleep	slept	slept
speak	spoke	spoken
spin	spun	spun
spring	sprang	sprung
stand	stood	stood
steal	stole	stolen
sting	stung	stung
strike	struck	struck, stricken
swear	swore	sworn
swim	swam	swum
swing	swung	swung
take	took	taken
teach	taught	taught
throw	threw	thrown
wake	woke, waked	waked, woken
wear	wore	worn
win	won	won
wring	wrung	wrung
write	wrote	written

11b Tense

Tenses indicate the time of an action in relation to the time of the speaking or writing about that action. The most common problem with tenses—shifting from one tense to another—is discussed in 5b. Other problems with tenses are detailed in this section, after the following survey of tenses.

Survey of tenses   Tenses are classified as present, past, and future, with simple, perfect, and progressive forms for each.

The simple tenses indicate relatively simple time relations. The *simple present* tense is used primarily for actions occurring at the time they are being discussed or for actions occurring regularly. The *simple past* tense is used for actions completed in the past. The *simple future* tense is used for actions that will occur in the future. In the following table, the simple tenses are given for the regular verb *walk*, the irregular verb *ride*, and the highly irregular verb *be*.

SIMPLE PRESENT

SINGULAR		PLURAL	
I	walk, ride, am	we	walk, ride, are
you	walk, ride, are	you	walk, ride, are
he/she/it	walks, rides, is	they	walk, ride, are

SIMPLE PAST

SINGULAR		PLURAL	
I	walked, rode, was	we	walked, rode, were
you	walked, rode, were	you	walked, rode, were
he/she/it	walked, rode, was	they	walked, rode, were

SIMPLE FUTURE

I, you, he/she/it, we, they	will walk, ride, be

A verb in one of the perfect tenses (a form of *have* plus the past participle) expresses an action that was or will be completed at the time of another action.

PRESENT PERFECT

I, you, we, they	have walked, ridden, been
he/she/it	has walked, ridden, been

PAST PERFECT

I, you, he/she/it, we, they	had walked, ridden, been

FUTURE PERFECT

I, you, he/she/it, we, they   will have walked, ridden, been

Each of the six tenses has a progressive form used to describe actions in progress. A progressive verb consists of a form of *be* followed by the present participle.

PRESENT PROGRESSIVE

I	am walking, riding, being
he/she/it	is walking, riding, being
you, we, they	are walking, riding, being

PAST PROGRESSIVE

| I, he/she/it | was walking, riding, being |
| you, we, they | were walking, riding, being |

FUTURE PROGRESSIVE

I, you, he/she/it, we, they   will be walking, riding, being

PRESENT PERFECT PROGRESSIVE

| I, you, we, they | have been walking, riding, being |
| he/she/it | has been walking, riding, being |

PAST PERFECT PROGRESSIVE

| I, you, he/she/it, we, they | had been walking, riding, being |

FUTURE PERFECT PROGRESSIVE

| I, you, he/she/it, we, they | will have been walking, riding, being |

Special uses of the present tense   Use the present tense when writing about literature or when expressing general truths.

▶   The scarlet letter ~~was~~ a punishment placed on
                ^*is*
       Hester's breast by the community, and yet it ~~was~~
                                                       ^*is*

       an imaginative product of Hester's own needlework.

▶   Galileo taught that the earth ~~revolved~~ around the sun.
                                             ^*revolves*

The past perfect tense   The past perfect tense is used for an action already completed by the time of

another past action. This tense consists of a past participle preceded by *had* (*had worked*, *had gone*).

▶ We built our cabin forty feet above an abandoned
     had been
 quarry that ~~was~~ flooded in 1920 to create a lake.
       ^

▶ By the time dinner was served, the guest of honor
 had
 left.
 ^

11c Mood

There are three moods in English: the *indicative*, used for
facts, opinions, and questions; the *imperative*, used for
orders or advice; and the *subjunctive*, used to express
wishes, requests, or conditions contrary to fact. For
many writers, the subjunctive is especially challenging.

 For wishes and in *if* clauses expressing conditions
contrary to fact, the subjunctive is the past-tense form
of the verb; in the case of *be*, it is always *were* (not *was*),
even if the subject is singular.

 I wish that Jamal *drove* more slowly late at night.

 If I *were* a member of Congress, I would vote for the bill.

TIP: Do not use the subjunctive mood in *if* clauses
expressing conditions that exist or may exist: *If Danielle
passes* [not *passed*] *the test, she will become a lifeguard.*

 Use the subjunctive mood in *that* clauses following
verbs such as *ask, insist, recommend,* and *request.* The
subjunctive in such cases is the base form of the verb.

 Dr. Chung insists that her students *be* on time.

 We recommend that Dawson *file* form 1050 soon.

12 Use pronouns with care.

Pronouns are words that substitute for nouns: *he, it,
them, her, me,* and so on. Pronoun errors are typically
related to the four topics discussed in this section:

a. pronoun-antecedent agreement (singular vs. plural)
b. pronoun reference (clarity)

c. pronoun case (personal pronouns such as *I* vs. *me*)
d. pronoun case (*who* vs. *whom*)

12a Pronoun-antecedent agreement

The antecedent of a pronoun is the word the pronoun refers to. A pronoun and its antecedent agree when they are both singular or both plural.

SINGULAR The *doctor* finished *her* rounds.

PLURAL The *doctors* finished *their* rounds.

Indefinite pronouns Indefinite pronouns refer to nonspecific persons or things. Even though some of the following indefinite pronouns may seem to have plural meanings, treat them as singular in formal English: *anybody, anyone, anything, each, either, everybody, everyone, everything, neither, nobody, no one, nothing, somebody, someone, something.*

In this class *everyone* performs at *his or her* [not *their*] own fitness level.

When *they* or *their* refers mistakenly to a singular antecedent such as *everyone*, you will usually have three options for revision:

1. Replace *they* with *he or she* (or *their* with *his or her*).
2. Make the antecedent plural.
3. Rewrite the sentence to avoid the problem.

▶ If anyone wants to audition, ~~they~~ he or she should sign up.

▶ If ~~anyone wants~~ singers want to audition, they should sign up.

▶ ~~If anyone~~ Anyone who wants to audition/ ~~they~~ should sign up.

Because the *he or she* construction is wordy, often the second or third revision strategy is more effective.

NOTE: The traditional use of *he* (or *his*) to refer to persons of either sex is now widely considered sexist. (See p. 17.)

Generic nouns A generic noun represents a typical member of a group, such as *a student*, or any member of a group, such as *any lawyer*. Although generic nouns may seem to have plural meanings, they are singular.

> Every *runner* must train rigorously if *he or she wants*
> [not *they want*] to excel.

When a plural pronoun refers mistakenly to a generic noun, you will usually have the same revision options as for indefinite pronouns.

▶ A medical student must study hard if ~~they want~~ to

    he or she wants

succeed.

▶ ~~A medical student~~ must study hard if they want to

    Medical students

succeed.

▶ A medical student must study hard ~~if they want~~ to

succeed.

Collective nouns Collective nouns such as *jury, committee, audience, crowd, family,* and *team* name a group. In American English, collective nouns are usually singular because they emphasize the group functioning as a unit.

> The planning *committee* granted *its* [not *their*]
> permission to build.

If the members of the group function individually, however, you may treat the noun as plural: *The family put their signatures on the document.* Or you might add a plural antecedent such as *members* to the sentence: *The family members put their signatures on the document.*

12b Pronoun reference

In the sentence *When Andrew got home, he went straight to bed*, the noun *Andrew* is the antecedent of the pronoun *he*. A pronoun should refer clearly to its antecedent.

Ambiguous reference   Ambiguous reference occurs when the pronoun could refer to two possible antecedents.

▶ The cake collapsed when Aunt Harriet put it
~~When Aunt Harriet put the cake~~ on the table/. ~~it~~
^   ^
~~collapsed.~~

▶ "You have
Tom told James, ~~that he had~~ won the lottery."
^   ^

What collapsed—the cake or the table? Who won the lottery—Tom or James? The revisions eliminate the ambiguity.

Implied reference   A pronoun must refer to a specific antecedent, not to a word that is implied but not actually stated.

▶ the braids
After braiding Ann's hair, Sue decorated ~~them~~ with
^
ribbons.

Vague reference of *this*, *that*, or *which*   The pronouns *this*, *that*, and *which* should ordinarily refer to specific antecedents rather than to whole ideas or sentences. When a pronoun's reference is too vague, either replace the pronoun with a noun or supply an antecedent to which the pronoun clearly refers.

▶ Television advertising has created new demands
the ads
for prescription drugs. People respond to ~~this~~ by
^
asking for drugs they may not need.

▶ Romeo and Juliet were both too young to have
a fact
acquired much wisdom, ~~and~~ that accounts for
^
their rash actions.

Indefinite reference of *they*, *it*, or *you*   The pronoun *they* should refer to a specific antecedent. Do not use *they* to refer indefinitely to persons who have not been specifically mentioned.

▶ The board
~~They~~ announced an increase in sports fees for all
^
student athletes.

The word *it* should not be used indefinitely in constructions such as *In the article, it says that*...

> The
> ▶ ~~In the~~ encyclopedia, ~~it~~ states that male moths can
>   ^
>
> smell female moths from several miles away.

The pronoun *you* is appropriate only when the writer is addressing the reader directly: *Once you have kneaded the dough, let it rise in a warm place.* Except in informal contexts, however, *you* should not be used to mean "anyone in general." Use a noun instead, as in the following example.

> ▶ Ms. Pickersgill's *Guide to Etiquette* stipulates that
>   a guest
>   ~~you~~ should not arrive at a party too early or leave
>   ^
>
> too late.

12c Case of personal pronouns (*I* vs. *me* etc.)

The personal pronouns in the following chart change what is known as *case form* according to their grammatical function in a sentence. Pronouns functioning as subjects or subject complements appear in the *subjective* case; those functioning as objects appear in the *objective* case; and those showing ownership appear in the *possessive* case.

	SUBJECTIVE CASE	OBJECTIVE CASE	POSSESSIVE CASE
SINGULAR	I	me	my
	you	you	your
	he/she/it	him/her/it	his/her/its
PLURAL	we	us	our
	you	you	your
	they	them	their

Pronouns in the subjective and objective cases are frequently confused. Most of the rules in this section specify when to use one or the other of these cases (*I* or *me*, *he* or *him*, and so on).

Compound word groups You may sometimes be confused when a subject or an object appears as part of a compound structure. To test for the correct pronoun, mentally strip away all of the compound structure except the pronoun in question.

▶ While diving for pearls, Ikiko and ~~her~~ *she* found a

sunken boat.

> *Ikiko and she* is the subject of the verb *found*. Strip away the words *Ikiko and* to test for the correct pronoun: *she found* [not *her found*].

▶ The most traumatic experience for her father and
~~I~~ *me* occurred long after her operation.

> *Her father and me* is the object of the preposition *for*. Strip away the words *her father and* to test for the correct pronoun: *for me* [not *for I*].

When in doubt about the correct pronoun, some writers try to evade the choice by using a reflexive pronoun such as *myself*. Using a reflexive pronoun in such situations is nonstandard.

▶ The cabdriver gave my husband and ~~myself~~ *me* some

good tips on traveling in New Delhi.

> *My husband and me* is the indirect object of the verb *gave*.

Appositives   Appositives are noun phrases that rename nouns or pronouns. A pronoun used as an appositive has the same function (usually subject or object) as the word(s) it renames.

▶ The chief strategists, Dr. Bell and ~~me,~~ *I,* could not

agree on a plan.

> The appositive *Dr. Bell and I* renames the subject, *strategists*. Test: *I could not agree on a plan* [not *me could not agree on a plan*].

▶ The reporter interviewed only two witnesses, the
shopkeeper and ~~I.~~ *me.*

> The appositive *the shopkeeper and me* renames the direct object, *witnesses*. Test: *interviewed me* [not *interviewed I*].

Subject complements   Use subjective-case pronouns for subject complements, which rename or describe the subject and usually follow *be, am, is, are, was, were, being,* or *been.*

▶   During the Lindbergh trial, Bruno Hauptmann
                                  he.
   repeatedly denied that the kidnapper was ~~him.~~
                                          ^

> If *kidnapper was he* seems too stilted, rewrite the sentence: *During the Lindbergh trial, Bruno Hauptmann repeatedly denied that he was the kidnapper.*

We or us before a noun   When deciding whether *we* or *us* should precede a noun, choose the pronoun that would be appropriate if the noun were omitted.

   We
▶   ~~Us~~ tenants would rather fight than move.
   ^

> Test: *We would rather fight* [not *Us would rather fight*].

                                   us
▶   Management is shortchanging ~~we~~ tenants.
                                     ^

> Test: *Management is shortchanging us* [not *Management is shortchanging we*].

Pronoun after than or as   When a comparison begins with *than* or *as*, your choice of pronoun will depend on your meaning. To test for the correct pronoun, finish the sentence.

                                       I.
▶   My brother is six years older than ~~me.~~
                                       ^

> Test: *older than I* [*am*].

▶   We respected no other candidate for city council as
               her.
   much as ~~she.~~
         ^

> Test: *as much as* [*we respected*] *her.*

Pronoun before or after an infinitive   An infinitive is the word *to* followed by a verb. Both subjects and objects of infinitives take the objective case.

                               me
▶   Ms. Wilson asked John and ~~I~~ to drive the senator
   her   ^
   and ~~she~~ to the airport.
   ^

> *John and me* is the subject and *senator and her* is the object of the infinitive *to drive.*

Pronoun or noun before a gerund   If a pronoun modifies a gerund, use the possessive case: *my, our, your, his, her, its, their.* A gerund is a verb form ending in *-ing* that functions as a noun.

▶   The chances of ~~you~~ being hit by lightning are

about two million to one.

(*your* above *you*)

Nouns as well as pronouns may modify gerunds. To form the possessive case of a noun, use an apostrophe and *-s* (*victim's*) for a singular noun or just an apostrophe (*victims'*) for a plural noun. (See also 19a.)

▶   The old order in France paid a high price for the
~~aristocracy~~ exploiting the lower classes.

(*aristocracy's* above *aristocracy*)

12d *Who* vs. *whom*

Who, a subjective-case pronoun, is used for subjects and subject complements. *Whom*, an objective-case pronoun, is used for objects. The words *who* and *whom* appear primarily in subordinate clauses or in questions.

In subordinate clauses   When deciding whether to use *who* or *whom* in a subordinate clause, check for the word's function within the clause.

▶   He tells that story to ~~whomever~~ will listen.

(*whoever* above *whomever*)

   Whoever is the subject of *will listen.* The entire subordinate clause *whoever will listen* is the object of the preposition *to.*

▶   You will work with our senior engineers, ~~who~~ you

will meet later.

(*whom* above *who*)

   Whom is the direct object of the verb *will meet.* This becomes clear if you restructure the clause: *you will meet whom later.* Some writers test by substituting *he* for *who* and *him* for *whom: you will meet him later.*

In questions   When deciding whether to use *who* or *whom* in a question, check for the word's function within the question.

Who
▶ ~~Whom~~ was responsible for creating that computer
  ^
virus?

Who is the subject of the verb *was*.

Whom
▶ ~~Who~~ would you nominate for council president?
  ^

Whom is the direct object of the verb *would nominate*.
This becomes clear if you restructure the question: *You
would nominate whom?*

13   Use adjectives and adverbs appropriately.

Adjectives modify nouns or pronouns; adverbs modify
verbs, adjectives, or other adverbs.

Many adverbs are formed by adding *-ly* to adjectives
(*formal, formally*). But don't assume that all words ending in *-ly* are adverbs or that all adverbs end in *-ly*. Some
adjectives end in *-ly* (*lovely, friendly*), and some adverbs
don't (*always, here*). When in doubt, consult a dictionary.

13a   Adjectives

Adjectives ordinarily precede the nouns they modify.
But they can also function as subject complements
following linking verbs (usually a form of *be*: *be, am,
is, are, was, were, being, been*). When an adjective functions as a subject complement, it describes the subject.

Justice is *blind*.

Verbs such as *smell, taste, look, appear, grow,* and
feel may also be linking. If the word following one of
these verbs describes the subject, use an adjective; if
the word modifies the verb, use an adverb.

ADJECTIVE   The detective looked *cautious*.

ADVERB   The detective looked *cautiously* for the
              fingerprints.

Linking verbs usually suggest states of being, not
actions. For example, to look *cautious* suggests the state
of being cautious, whereas to look *cautiously* is to per-
form an action in a cautious way.

▶ Lori looked ~~well~~ ^*good*^ in her new raincoat.

▶ All of us on the debate team felt ~~badly~~ ^*bad*^ about our

performance.

The verbs *looked* and *felt* suggest states of being, not actions, so they should be followed by adjectives.

13b Adverbs

Use adverbs to modify verbs, adjectives, and other adverbs. Adverbs usually answer one of these questions: When? Where? How? Why? Under what conditions? How often? To what degree?

Adjectives are often used incorrectly in place of adverbs in casual or nonstandard speech.

▶ The manager must ensure that the office runs
^*smoothly*^ ~~smooth~~ and ~~efficient.~~ ^*efficiently.*^

▶ The chance of recovering any property lost in the
fire looks ~~real~~ ^*really*^ slim.

The incorrect use of the adjective *good* in place of the adverb *well* is especially common in casual or non-standard speech.

▶ We were delighted that Nomo had done so ~~good~~ ^*well*^

on the exam.

13c Comparatives and superlatives

Most adjectives and adverbs have three forms: the positive, the comparative, and the superlative.

POSITIVE	COMPARATIVE	SUPERLATIVE
soft	softer	softest
fast	faster	fastest
careful	more careful	most careful
bad	worse	worst
good	better	best

Comparative vs. superlative   Use the comparative to compare two things, the superlative to compare three or more.

▶ Which of these two brands of toothpaste is ~~best?~~ $\overset{better?}{\wedge}$

▶ Jia is the ~~more~~ $\overset{most}{\wedge}$ qualified of the three applicants.

Forms of comparatives and superlatives   To form comparatives and superlatives of one-syllable adjectives, use the endings *-er* and *-est*: *smooth, smoother, smoothest*. For adjectives with three or more syllables, use *more* and *most* (or *less* and *least*): *exciting, more exciting, most exciting*. Two-syllable adjectives form comparatives and superlatives in both ways: *lovely, lovelier, loveliest; helpful, more helpful, most helpful*.

     Some one-syllable adverbs take the endings *-er* and *-est* (*fast, faster, fastest*), but longer adverbs and all of those ending in *-ly* use *more* and *most* or *less* and *least* (*carefully, less carefully, least carefully*).

Double comparatives or superlatives   When you have added *-er* or *-est* to an adjective or an adverb, do not also use *more* or *most* (or *less* or *least*).

▶ All the polls indicated that Gore was more ~~likelier~~ $\overset{likely}{\wedge}$

    to win than Bush.

Absolute concepts   Do not use comparatives or superlatives with absolute concepts such as *unique* or *perfect*. Either something is unique or it isn't. It is illogical to suggest that absolute concepts come in degrees.

▶ That is the most ~~unique~~ $\overset{unusual}{\wedge}$ wedding gown I have

    ever seen.

14   Repair sentence fragments.

As a rule, do not treat a piece of a sentence as if it were a sentence. When you do, you create a fragment. To be a sentence, a word group must consist of at least one full independent clause. An independent clause includes a subject and a verb, and it either stands alone as a sentence or could stand alone.

You can repair a fragment in one of two ways: Either pull the fragment into a nearby sentence, punctuating the new sentence correctly, or rewrite the fragment as a complete sentence.

14a Fragmented clauses

A subordinate clause is patterned like a sentence, with both a subject and a verb, but it begins with a word that tells readers it cannot stand alone—a word such as *after, although, because, before, if, so that, that, though, unless, until, when, where, which,* or *who.* (For a longer list, see p. 309.)

Most fragmented clauses beg to be pulled into a sentence nearby.

▶ We fear the Zika virus./ ~~Because~~ *because* it is transmitted by

the common mosquito.

If a fragmented clause cannot be attached to a nearby ~~sentence, try rewriting it.~~ The simplest way to turn a fragmented clause into a sentence is to delete the opening word or words that mark it as subordinate.

▶ Uncontrolled development is taking a deadly toll

on the environment. ~~So that in~~ *In* many parts of the

world, fragile ecosystems are collapsing.

14b Fragmented phrases

Like subordinate clauses, certain phrases are sometimes mistaken for sentences. They are fragments if they lack a subject, a verb, or both. Often a fragmented phrase may simply be pulled into a nearby sentence.

▶ The archaeologists worked slowly./, ~~Examining~~ *examining* and

labeling hundreds of pottery shards.

The word group beginning with *Examining* is a verbal phrase, not a sentence.

▶ Many adults suffer silently from agoraphobia/. A^a

fear of the outside world.

A fear of the outside world is an appositive phrase, not a
sentence.

▶ It has been said that there are only three indigenous
   American art forms/: J̶a̶z̶z̶,_{jazz,} musical comedy, and

soap operas.

The list is not a sentence. Notice how easily a colon
corrects the problem. (See 18b.)

If the fragmented phrase cannot be attached to a
nearby sentence, turn the phrase into a sentence. You
may need to add a subject, a verb, or both.

▶ Jamie explained how to access the database. A̶l̶s̶o̶ ^{She also taught us}

how to submit reports and request vendor payments.

The revision turns the fragmented phrase into a sentence
by adding a subject and a verb.

14c Acceptable fragments

Skilled writers occasionally use sentence fragments for
emphasis. Although fragments are sometimes appropriate, writers and readers do not always agree on when
they are appropriate. Therefore, you will find it safer to
write in complete sentences.

15 Revise run-on sentences.

Run-on sentences are independent clauses that have not
been joined correctly. An independent clause is a word
group that can stand alone as a sentence. When two or
more independent clauses appear in one sentence, they
must be joined in one of these ways:

• with a comma and a coordinating conjunction
  (*and, but, or, nor, for, so, yet*)

• with a semicolon (or occasionally a colon or a dash)

There are two types of run-on sentences. When a writer puts no mark of punctuation and no coordinating conjunction between independent clauses, the result is a *fused sentence*.

FUSED

Air pollution poses risks to all humans it can be deadly for people with asthma.

A far more common type of run-on sentence is the *comma splice*—two or more independent clauses joined with a comma but without a coordinating conjunction. In some comma splices, the comma appears alone.

COMMA SPLICE

Air pollution poses risks to all humans, it can be deadly for people with asthma.

In other comma splices, the comma is accompanied by a joining word, such as *however*, that is not a coordinating conjunction. (See 15b.)

COMMA SPLICE

Air pollution poses risks to all humans, however, it can be deadly for people with asthma.

To correct a run-on sentence, you have four choices:

1. Use a comma and a coordinating conjunction.
2. Use a semicolon (or, if appropriate, a colon or a dash).
3. Make the clauses into separate sentences.
4. Restructure the sentence, perhaps by subordinating one of the clauses.

CORRECTED WITH COMMA AND COORDINATING CONJUNCTION

Air pollution poses risks to all humans, but it can be deadly for people with asthma.

CORRECTED WITH SEMICOLON

Air pollution poses risks to all humans; it can be deadly for people with asthma.

CORRECTED WITH SEPARATE SENTENCES

Air pollution poses risks to all humans. It can be deadly for people with asthma.

CORRECTED BY RESTRUCTURING

Although air pollution poses risks to all humans, it can be deadly for people with asthma.

One of these revision techniques will usually work better than the others for a particular sentence. The fourth technique, the one requiring the most extensive revision, is often the most effective.

15a Revision with a comma and a coordinating conjunction

When a coordinating conjunction (*and*, *but*, *or*, *nor*, *for*, *so*, *yet*) joins independent clauses, it is usually preceded by a comma.

▶ Most of his friends had made plans for their
                but
retirement, Tom had not.
         ^

15b Revision with a semicolon (or a colon or a dash)

When the independent clauses are closely related and their relation is clear without a coordinating conjunction, a semicolon is an acceptable method of revision.

▶ Tragedy depicts the individual confronted with

the fact of death/; comedy depicts the adaptability
             ^

of human society.

A semicolon is required between independent clauses that have been linked with a conjunctive adverb such as *however* or *therefore* or a transitional phrase such as *in fact* or *on the contrary*. (See p. 63 for longer lists.)

▶ The timber wolf looks like a large German shepherd/;
                                            ^

however, the wolf has longer legs, larger feet, and

a wider head.

If the first independent clause introduces a quoted sentence, use a colon.

► Scholar and crime writer Carolyn Heilbrun says this
about the future/: "Today's shocks are tomorrow's
^
conventions."

Either a colon or a dash may be appropriate when
the second clause summarizes or explains the first. (See
18b and 21d.)

15c Revision by separating sentences

If both independent clauses are long—or if one is a
question and the other is not—consider making them
separate sentences.

► Why should we spend money on space exploration/ ?
   We   ^
   ~~we~~ have enough underfunded programs here on
   ^
   Earth.

15d Revision by restructuring the sentence

For sentence variety, consider restructuring the run-on
sentence, perhaps by turning one of the independent
clauses into a subordinate clause or a phrase.

► One of the most famous advertising slogans is
                                           which
   Wheaties cereal's "Breakfast of Champions," ~~it~~
                                                ^
   was penned in 1933.

► Mary McLeod Bethune, ~~was~~ the seventeenth child
   of former slaves, ~~she~~ founded the National Council
   of Negro Women in 1935.

16 Consider grammar topics for multilingual writers.

16a Verbs

This section offers a brief review of English verb forms
and tenses and the passive voice.

Verb forms   Every main verb in English has five forms (except *be*, which has eight). These forms are used to create all of the verb tenses in Standard English. The following list shows these forms for the regular verb *help* and the irregular verbs *give* and *be*.

	REGULAR (*HELP*)	IRREGULAR (*GIVE*)	IRREGULAR (*BE*)*
BASE FORM	help	give	be
PAST TENSE	helped	gave	was, were
PAST PARTICIPLE	helped	given	been
PRESENT PARTICIPLE	helping	giving	being
***-S* FORM**	helps	gives	is

*Be also has the forms *am* and *are*, which are used in the present tense. (See also p. 28.)

Verb tense   Here are descriptions of the tenses and progressive forms in Standard English. See also 11b.

The simple tenses show general facts, states of being, and actions that occur regularly.

Simple present tense (base form or -s form) expresses general facts, constant states, habitual or repetitive actions, or scheduled future events: *The sun rises in the east. The plane leaves tomorrow at 6:30.*

Simple past tense (base form + -ed or -d or irregular form) is used for actions that happened at a specific time or during a specific period in the past or for repetitive actions that have ended: *She drove to Montana three years ago. When I was young, I walked to school.*

Simple future tense (will + base form) expresses actions that will occur at some time in the future and promises or predictions of future events: *I will call you next week.*

The simple progressive forms show continuing action.

Present progressive (am, is, are + present participle) shows actions in progress that are not expected to remain constant or future actions (with verbs such as *go, come,* or *move*): *We are building our house at the shore. They are moving tomorrow.*

Past progressive (was, were + present participle) shows actions in progress at a specific past time or a continuing action that was interrupted: *Roy was driving his new* *car yesterday. When she walked in, we were planning her party.*

Future progressive (*will* + *be* + present participle) expresses actions that will be in progress at a certain time in the future: *Nan will be flying home tomorrow.*

TIP: Certain verbs are not normally used in the progressive: *appear, believe, belong, contain, have, hear, know, like, need, see, seem, taste, think, understand,* and *want.* There are exceptions, however, that you must notice as you encounter them: *We are thinking of buying a summer home.*

The perfect tenses show actions that happened or will happen before another time.

Present perfect tense (*have, has* + past participle) expresses actions that began in the past and continue to the present or actions that happened at an unspecific time in the past: *She has not spoken of her grandfather in a long time. They have traveled to Africa twice.*

Past perfect tense (*had* + past participle) expresses an action that began or occurred before another time in the past: *By the time Hakan was fifteen, he had learned to drive. I had just finished my walk when my brother drove up.* (See also p. 28.)

Future perfect tense (*will* + *have* + past participle) expresses actions that will be completed before or at a specific future time: *By the time I graduate, I will have taken five film study classes.*

The perfect progressive forms show continuous past actions before another present or past time.

Present perfect progressive (*have, has* + *been* + present participle) expresses continuous actions that began in the past and continue to the present: *My sister has been living in Oregon since 2008.*

Past perfect progressive (*had* + *been* + present participle) conveys actions that began and continued in the past until some other past action: *By the time I moved to Georgia, I had been supporting myself for five years.*

Future perfect progressive (*will* + *have* + *been* + present participle) expresses actions that are or will be in progress before another specified time in the future: *By the* *time we reach the cashier, we will have been waiting in line for an hour.*

Modal verbs The nine modal verbs—*can, could, may, might, must, shall, should, will*, and *would*—are used with the base form of verbs to show certainty, necessity, or possibility. Modals do not change form to indicate tense.

▶ The art museum will ~~launches~~ its fundraising
                         launch
campaign next month.

▶ We could ~~spoke~~ Portuguese when we were young.
             speak

Passive voice When a sentence is written in the passive voice, the subject receives the action instead of doing it. To form the passive voice, use a form of *be*—*am, is, are, was, were, being, be*, or *been*—followed by the past participle of the main verb. (For appropriate uses of the passive voice, see 2b.)

▶ *Dreaming in Cuban* was ~~writing~~ by Cristina García.
                          written

▶ Senator Dixon will defeated
                    be

NOTE: Verbs that do not take direct objects—such as *occur, happen, sleep, die*, and *fall*—do not form the passive voice.

16b Articles (*a, an, the*)

Articles and other noun markers Articles (*a, an, the*) are part of a category of words known as *noun markers* or *determiners*. Noun markers identify the nouns that follow them. Besides articles, noun markers include possessive nouns (*Elena's, child's*); possessive pronoun/ adjectives (*my, your, their*); demonstrative pronoun/ adjectives (*this, that*); quantifiers (*all, few, neither, some*); and numbers (*one, twenty-six*).

       ART N
Felix is reading a book about mythology.

       ART ADJ   N
We took an exciting trip to Alaska last summer.

When to use *a* or *an* Use *a* or *an* with singular count nouns that refer to one unspecific item (not a whole category). *Count nouns* refer to persons, places, things, or ideas that can be counted: *one girl, two girls; one city, three cities; one goose, four geese.*

▶ My professor asked me to bring ^a dictionary to class.

▶ We want to rent ^{an} apartment close to the lake.

When to use *the* Use *the* with most nouns that the reader can identify specifically. Usually the identity will be clear to the reader for one of the following reasons.

1. The noun has been previously mentioned.

▶ A truck cut in front of our van. When ^{the} truck skidded

a few seconds later, we almost crashed into it.

2. A phrase or clause following the noun restricts its identity.

▶ Bryce warned me that ^{the} GPS in his car was not working.

3. A superlative adjective such as *best* or *most intelligent* makes the noun's identity specific. (See also 13c.)

▶ Brita had ^{the} best players on her team.

4. The noun describes a unique person, place, or thing.

▶ During an eclipse, one should not look directly at ^{the} sun.

5. The context or situation makes the noun's identity clear.

▶ Please don't slam ^{the} door when you leave.

6. The noun is singular and refers to a class or category of items (most often animals, musical instruments, and inventions).

▶ ^{The tin} ~~Tin~~ whistle is common in traditional Irish music.

When not to use articles Do not use *a* or *an* with non-count nouns. *Noncount nouns* refer to things or abstract ideas that cannot be counted or made plural: *salt, silver,* *air, furniture, patience, knowledge.* (See the chart at the bottom of this page.)

To express an approximate amount of a noncount noun, use a quantifier such as *some* or *more*: *some water, enough coffee, less violence.*

▶ Ava gave us ~~an~~ information about the Peace Corps.

▶ Claudia said she had ~~a~~ ^{some} news that would surprise

her parents.

Do not use articles with nouns that refer to all of something or something in general.

▶ ~~The kindness~~ ^{Kindness} is a virtue.

▶ In some parts of the world, ~~the~~ rice is preferred to

all other grains.

Commonly used noncount nouns

Food and drink
beef, bread, butter, candy, cereal, cheese, cream, meat, milk, pasta, rice, salt, sugar, wine

Nonfood substances
air, cement, coal, dirt, gasoline, gold, paper, petroleum, plastic, rain, silver, snow, soap, steel, wood, wool

Abstract nouns
advice, anger, beauty, confidence, courage, employment, fun, happiness, health, honesty, information, intelligence, knowledge, love, poverty, satisfaction, wealth

Other
biology (and other areas of study), clothing, equipment, furniture, homework, jewelry, luggage, machinery, mail, money, news, poetry, pollution, research, scenery, traffic, transportation, violence, weather, work

NOTE: A few noncount nouns can also be used as count nouns: *He had two loves: music and archery.*

When to use articles with proper nouns Do not use articles with most singular proper nouns: *Prime Minister Trudeau, Jamaica, Lake Huron, Ivy Street, Mount Everest.* Use *the* with most plural proper nouns: *the McGregors, the Bahamas, the Finger Lakes, the United States.* Also use *the* with large regions, oceans, rivers, and mountain ranges: *the Sahara, the Indian Ocean, the Amazon River, the Rocky Mountains.*

There are, however, many exceptions, especially with geographic names. Note exceptions when you encounter them or consult a native speaker or an ESL dictionary.

16c Sentence structure

This section focuses on the major challenges that multilingual students face when writing sentences in English.

Omitted verbs Some languages do not use linking verbs (*am, is, are, was, were*) between subjects and complements (nouns or adjectives that rename or describe the subject). Every English sentence, however, must include a verb.

▶ Jim ^is^ intelligent.

▶ Many streets in San Francisco ^are^ very steep.

Omitted subjects Some languages do not require a subject in every sentence. Every English sentence, however, needs a subject.

▶ Your aunt is very energetic. ^She seems^ ~~Seems~~ young for her age.

EXCEPTION: In commands, the subject *you* is understood but not present in the sentence: *Give me the book.*

The word *it* is used as the subject of a sentence describing the weather or temperature, stating the time, indicating distance, or suggesting an environmental fact. Do not omit *it* in such sentences.

It is raining in the valley and snowing in the mountains.

It is 9:15 a.m.

It is three hundred miles to Chicago.

In July, *it* is very hot in Arizona.

In some English sentences, the subject comes after the verb, and a placeholder (called an expletive)—*there* or *it*—comes before the verb.

EXP V ┌── S ──┐   ┌── S ── V
There are many people here today. (Many people are here today.)

EXP V   ┌─ S ─┐   ┌─ S ─┐   V
It is important to study daily. (To study daily is important.)

                   there are
▶ As you know, ╷ many religious sects in India.
                 ^

Repeated subjects, objects, and adverbs English does not allow a subject to be repeated in its own clause.

▶ The doctor ~~she~~ advised me to cut down on salt.

Do not add a pronoun even when a word group comes between the subject and the verb.

▶ The car that had been stolen ~~it~~ was found.

Do not repeat an object or an adverb in an adjective clause. Adjective clauses begin with relative pronouns (*who, whom, whose, which, that*) or relative adverbs (*when, where*). Relative pronouns usually serve as subjects or objects in the clauses they introduce; another word in the clause cannot serve the same function. Relative adverbs should not be repeated by other adverbs later in the clause.

▶ The cat ran under the car that ~~it~~ was parked on

the street.

The relative pronoun *that* is the subject of the adjective clause, so the pronoun *it* cannot be added as the subject.

If the clause begins with a relative adverb, do not use another adverb with the same meaning later in the clause.

▶ The office where I work ~~there~~ is close to home.

The adverb *there* cannot repeat the relative adverb *where*.

16d Prepositions showing time and place

The chart on this page is limited to three prepositions that show time and place: *at, on,* and *in.* Not every possible use is listed in the chart, so don't be surprised when you encounter exceptions and idiomatic uses that you must learn one at a time. For example, in English, we ride *in* a car but *on* a bus, plane, train, or subway.

At, on, and *in* to show time and place

Showing time

AT *at* a specific time: *at* 7:20, *at* dawn, *at* dinner

ON *on* a specific day or date: *on* Tuesday, *on* June 4

IN *in* a part of a day: *in* the afternoon, *in* the daytime [but *at* night]

    in a year or month: *in* 1999, *in* July

    in a period of time: finished *in* three hours

Showing place

AT *at* a meeting place or location: *at* home, *at* the club

    at a specific address: living *at* 10 Oak Street

    at the edge of something: sitting *at* the desk

    at the corner of something: turning *at* the intersection

    at a target: throwing the snowball *at* Lucy

ON *on* a surface: placed *on* the table, hanging *on* the wall

    on a street: the house *on* Spring Street

    on an electronic medium: *on* television, *on* the Internet

IN *in* an enclosed space: *in* the garage, *in* an envelope

    in a geographic location: *in* San Diego, *in* Texas

    in a print medium: *in* a book, *in* a magazine

Punctuation

17 The comma

The comma was invented to help readers. Without it, sentence parts can collide into one another unexpectedly, causing misreadings.

CONFUSING   If you cook Elmer will do the dishes.

CONFUSING   While we were eating a rattlesnake approached our campsite.

Add commas in the logical places (after *cook* and *eating*), and suddenly all is clear. No longer is Elmer being cooked, the rattlesnake being eaten.

Various rules have evolved to prevent such misreadings and to guide readers through complex grammatical structures. Those rules are detailed in sections 17a–17i. (Section 17j explains when not to use a comma.)

17a Before a coordinating conjunction joining independent clauses

When a coordinating conjunction connects two or more independent clauses—word groups that could stand alone as separate sentences—a comma must come before the conjunction. There are seven coordinating conjunctions in English: *and*, *but*, *or*, *nor*, *for*, *so*, and *yet*.

A comma tells readers that one independent clause has come to a close and that another is about to begin.

▶ Jake has no talent for numbers, so he hires
                                ^
someone to prepare his taxes.

EXCEPTION: If the two independent clauses are short and there is no danger of misreading, the comma may be left out.

The plane took off and we were on our way.

TIP: As a rule, do *not* use a comma with a coordinating conjunction that joins only two words, phrases, or subordinate clauses. (See 17j. See also 17c for commas with coordinating conjunctions joining three or more elements.)

17b After an introductory word group

Use a comma after an introductory clause or phrase. A comma tells readers that the introductory word group has come to a close and that the main part of the sentence is about to begin. The most common introductory word groups are adverb clauses, prepositional phrases, and participial phrases.

▶ When Arthur ran his first marathon, he was

pleased to finish in under four hours.

▶ During the past decade, scientists have made

important discoveries about how humans form

memories.

▶ Buried under layers of younger rocks, the earth's

oldest rocks contain no fossils.

EXCEPTION: The comma may be omitted after a short clause or phrase if there is no danger of misreading.

In no time we were at 2,800 feet.

NOTE: Other introductory word groups include transitional expressions and absolute phrases (see 17f).

17c Between items in a series

In a series of three or more items (words, phrases, or clauses), use a comma between all items, including the last two.

▶ Langston Hughes's poetry is concerned with pride,

social justice, and the African American experience.

Although some writers view the last comma in a series as optional, most experts advise using it because its omission can result in ambiguity or misreading.

17d Between coordinate adjectives

Use a comma between coordinate adjectives, those that each modify a noun separately.

▶ Should patients with severe, irreversible brain

                           ^

    damage be put on life support systems?

Adjectives that can be connected with *and* are coordinate: *severe and irreversible.*

NOTE: Do not use a comma between cumulative adjectives, those that do not each modify the noun separately.

    Three large gray shapes moved slowly toward us.

Cumulative adjectives cannot be joined with *and* (not *three and large and gray shapes*).

17e To set off a nonrestrictive element, but not a restrictive element

A *restrictive* element defines or limits the meaning of the word it modifies; it is therefore essential to the meaning of the sentence and is not set off with commas. A *nonrestrictive* element describes a word whose meaning is clear without it. Because it is not essential to the meaning of the sentence, it is set off with commas.

RESTRICTIVE (NO COMMAS)

The campers need clothes *that are durable.*

NONRESTRICTIVE (WITH COMMAS)

The campers need sturdy shoes, *which are expensive.*

If you remove a restrictive element from a sentence, the meaning changes significantly, becoming more general than intended. The writer of the first sample sentence does not mean that the campers need clothes in general. The meaning is more restricted: The campers need *durable* clothes.

If you remove a nonrestrictive element from a sentence, the meaning does not change significantly. Some information may be lost, but the defining characteristics of the person or thing described remain the same: The campers need *sturdy shoes*, and these happen to be expensive.

Elements that may be restrictive or nonrestrictive include adjective clauses, adjective phrases, and appositives.

Adjective clauses   Adjective clauses, which usually follow the noun or pronoun they describe, begin with a relative pronoun (*who, whom, whose, which, that*) or with a relative adverb (*when, where*). When an adjective clause is nonrestrictive, set it off with commas; when it is restrictive, omit the commas.

NONRESTRICTIVE CLAUSE (WITH COMMAS)

▶ The Kyoto Protocol, which was adopted in 1997, aims to reduce greenhouse gases.

RESTRICTIVE CLAUSE (NO COMMAS)

▶ The giant panda/ that was born at the San Diego Zoo in 2003/ was sent to China in 2007.

NOTE: Use *that* only with restrictive clauses. Many writers use *which* only with nonrestrictive clauses, but usage varies.

Adjective phrases   Prepositional or verbal phrases functioning as adjectives may be restrictive or nonrestrictive. Nonrestrictive phrases are set off with commas; restrictive phrases are not.

NONRESTRICTIVE PHRASE (WITH COMMAS)

▶ The helicopter, with its million-candlepower spotlight illuminating the area, circled above.

RESTRICTIVE PHRASE (NO COMMAS)

▶ One corner of the attic was filled with newspapers/ dating from the 1920s.

Appositives   An appositive is a noun or pronoun that renames a nearby noun. Nonrestrictive appositives are set off with commas; restrictive appositives are not.

NONRESTRICTIVE APPOSITIVE (WITH COMMAS)

▶ Darwin's most important book, *On the Origin of Species*, was the result of many years of research.

RESTRICTIVE APPOSITIVE (NO COMMAS)

▶ Selections from the book/ *Democracy and Education*/

were read aloud in class.

17f To set off transitional and parenthetical expressions, absolute phrases, and word groups expressing contrast

Transitional expressions Transitional expressions serve as bridges between sentences or parts of sentences. They include conjunctive adverbs such as *however, therefore,* and *moreover* and transitional phrases such as *for example* and *as a matter of fact*. For more examples, see page 63.

When a transitional expression appears between independent clauses in a compound sentence, it is preceded by a semicolon and usually followed by a comma.

▶ Minh did not understand our language; moreover,
∧
he was unfamiliar with our customs.

When a transitional expression appears at the beginning of a sentence or in the middle of an independent clause, it is usually set off with commas.

▶ In fact, stock values rose after the company's press
∧
release.

▶ Natural foods are not always salt-free; celery, for
∧
example, is relatively high in sodium.
∧

Parenthetical expressions Expressions that provide only supplemental information and interrupt the flow of a sentence should be set off with commas.

▶ Evolution, so far as we know, doesn't work this way.
∧   ∧

Absolute phrases An absolute phrase consists of a noun followed by a participle or participial phrase. It modifies the whole sentence and should be set off with commas.

```
┌─────── ABSOLUTE PHRASE ───────┐
│        N  PARTICIPLE          │
```
The sun appearing for the first time all week, we were

at last able to begin the archaeological dig.

Word groups expressing contrast Sharp contrasts
beginning with words such as *not* and *unlike* are set off
with commas.

▶ Unlike Robert, Celia loved poetry slams.
               ∧

17g To set off nouns of direct address, the words *yes* and *no*, interrogative tags, and mild interjections

▶ Forgive me, Angela, for forgetting our meeting.
              ∧   ∧

▶ Yes, the loan will probably be approved.
       ∧

▶ The film was faithful to the book, wasn't it?
                                    ∧

▶ Well, cases like this are difficult to decide.
        ∧

17h To set off direct quotations introduced with expressions such as *he said*

▶ Gladwell asserts, "Those who are successful . . .
                   ∧
   are most likely to be given the kinds of special

   opportunities that lead to further success" (30).

17i With dates, addresses, and titles

Dates In dates, set off the year from the rest of the
sentence with a pair of commas.

▶ On December 12, 1890, orders were sent out for
                  ∧   ∧
   the arrest of Sitting Bull.

EXCEPTIONS: Commas are not needed if the date is
inverted or if only the month and year are given: *The
15 April 2018 deadline is approaching. May 2016 was a
surprisingly cold month.*

Addresses The elements of an address or a place
name are separated by commas. A zip code, however, is
not preceded by a comma.

▶ The teen group met at 708 Spring Street, Washington,
                                          ∧   ∧
  IL 61571.

Titles If a title follows a name, set off the title with a
pair of commas.

▶ Sandra Barnes, MD, was appointed to the board.
              ∧   ∧

17j Misuses of the comma

Do not use commas unless you have good reasons for
using them. In particular, avoid using commas in the
following situations.

**WITH A COORDINATING CONJUNCTION JOINING ONLY TWO
WORDS, PHRASES, OR SUBORDINATE CLAUSES**

▶ Marie Curie discovered radium/ and later applied
  her work on radioactivity to medicine.

TO SEPARATE A VERB FROM ITS SUBJECT

▶ Zoos large enough to give the animals freedom to
  roam/ are becoming more popular.

BETWEEN CUMULATIVE ADJECTIVES (See p. 57.)

▶ We found an old/ maroon hatbox.

TO SET OFF RESTRICTIVE ELEMENTS (See pp. 57–59.)

▶ Drivers/ who think they own the road/ make
  cycling a dangerous sport.

▶ Margaret Mead's book/ *Coming of Age in Samoa*/
  caused controversy when it was published.

AFTER A COORDINATING CONJUNCTION

▶ TV talk shows are sometimes performed live, but/
  more often they are taped.

AFTER *SUCH AS* OR *LIKE*

▶ Bacterial infections such as/ methicillin-resistant
Staphylococcus aureus (MRSA) have become a
serious concern in hospitals.

BEFORE *THAN*

▶ Touring Crete was more thrilling for us/ than
visiting the Greek islands frequented by the rich.

BEFORE A PARENTHESIS

▶ At InterComm, Sylvia began at the bottom/ (with
only a cubicle and a swivel chair), but within
three years she had been promoted to supervisor.

TO SET OFF AN INDIRECT (REPORTED) QUOTATION

▶ Samuel Goldwyn once said/ that a verbal contract
isn't worth the paper it's written on.

WITH A QUESTION MARK OR AN EXCLAMATION POINT

▶ "Why don't you try it?/" she coaxed.

18 The semicolon and the colon

18a The semicolon

The semicolon is used between independent clauses
not joined with a coordinating conjunction. It can
also be used between items in a series containing
internal punctuation.

The semicolon is never used between elements of
unequal grammatical rank.

Between independent clauses When two independent clauses appear in one sentence, they are usually
linked with a comma and a coordinating conjunction (*and, but, or, nor, for, so, yet*). The coordinating

conjunction signals the relation between the clauses. If the relation is clear without a conjunction, a writer may choose to connect the clauses with a semicolon instead.

> In film, a low-angle shot makes the subject look powerful; a high-angle shot does just the opposite.

A writer may also connect the clauses with a semicolon and a conjunctive adverb such as *however* or a transitional phrase such as *for example*.

> Many corals grow very gradually; in fact, the creation of a coral reef can take centuries.

CONJUNCTIVE ADVERBS

accordingly, also, anyway, besides, certainly, consequently, conversely, finally, furthermore, hence, however, incidentally, indeed, instead, likewise, meanwhile, moreover, nevertheless, next, nonetheless, now, otherwise, similarly, specifically, still, subsequently, then, therefore, thus

TRANSITIONAL PHRASES

after all, as a matter of fact, as a result, at any rate, at the same time, even so, for example, for instance, in addition, in conclusion, in fact, in other words, in the first place, on the contrary

NOTE: A semicolon must be used whenever a coordinating conjunction does not appear between independent clauses. To use merely a comma — or to use a comma and a conjunctive adverb or transitional expression — creates an error known as a *comma splice*. (See 15.)

Between items in a series containing internal punctuation Three or more items in a series are usually separated by commas. If one or more of the items contain internal punctuation, a writer may use semicolons for clarity.

> Science suggests that you can improve your memory by sleeping seven to eight hours a day; using mnemonics, self-testing, and visualization techniques; and including water, berries, and fish in your diet.

Misuses of the semicolon Do not use a semicolon in the following situations.

18b

BETWEEN AN INDEPENDENT CLAUSE AND A SUBORDINATE CLAUSE

▶ The media like to portray my generation as lazy⫽,
  although polls show that we work as hard as the
  twentysomethings before us.

BETWEEN AN APPOSITIVE AND THE WORD IT REFERS TO

▶ We were fascinated by the species *Argyroneta*
  aquatica⫽, a spider that lives underwater.

TO INTRODUCE A LIST

▶ Some birds are flightless⫽ : emus, penguins, and
  ostriches.

**BETWEEN INDEPENDENT CLAUSES JOINED BY *AND*, *BUT*, *OR*,
NOR, *FOR*, *SO*, OR *YET***

▶ Five of the applicants had used spreadsheets⫽,
  but only one was familiar with databases.

18b The colon

Main uses of the colon A colon can be used after an
independent clause to direct readers' attention to a list,
an appositive, or a quotation.

A LIST

The routine includes the following: twenty knee bends,
fifty leg lifts, and five minutes of running in place.

AN APPOSITIVE

My roommate lives on two things: snacks and social
media.

A QUOTATION

Consider the words of Benjamin Franklin: "There
never was a good war or a bad peace."

For other ways of introducing quotations, see pages 70–71.

A colon may also be used between independent
clauses if the second clause summarizes or explains the
first clause.

Faith is like love: It cannot be forced.

When an independent clause follows a colon, begin the independent clause with a capital letter. Some disciplines use a lowercase letter; see 34a, 39a, and 44a for variations.

Conventional uses   Use a colon after the salutation in a formal letter, to indicate hours and minutes, to show proportions, between a title and a subtitle, to separate city and publisher in bibliographic entries, and between chapter and verse in citations of sacred texts.

Dear Editor:

5:30 p.m.

The ratio of women to men was 2:1.

Alvin Ailey: A Life in Dance

Boston: Bedford/St. Martin's, 2016

Luke 2:14, Qur'an 67:3

NOTE: MLA recommends a period in citations of sacred texts: Luke 2.14, Qur'an 67.3.

Misuses of the colon   A colon must be preceded by an independent clause. Therefore, avoid using it in the following situations.

BETWEEN A VERB AND ITS OBJECT OR COMPLEMENT

▶   Some important vitamins found in vegetables are⫻

vitamin A, thiamine, niacin, and vitamin C.

BETWEEN A PREPOSITION AND ITS OBJECT

▶   The heart's two pumps each consist of⫻ an upper

chamber, or atrium, and a lower chamber, or

ventricle.

AFTER *SUCH AS*, *INCLUDING*, OR *FOR EXAMPLE*

▶   The NCAA regulates college sports, including⫻

basketball, softball, and football.

19 The apostrophe

The apostrophe indicates possession and marks contractions. In addition, it has a few conventional uses.

19a To indicate possession

The apostrophe is used to indicate that a noun or an indefinite pronoun is possessive. Possessives usually indicate ownership, as in *Tim's hat, the writer's desk,* or *someone's gloves.* Frequently, however, ownership is only loosely implied: *the tree's roots, a day's work.* If you are not sure whether a word is possessive, try turning it into an *of* phrase: *the roots of the tree, the work of a day.*

When to add -'s Add -'s if the noun does not end in -s or if the noun is singular and ends in -s or an s sound.

> Luck often propels a rock musician's career.

> Thank you for refunding the children's money.

> Lois's sister spent last year in India.

> Her article presents an overview of Marx's teachings.

EXCEPTION: If pronunciation would be awkward with an apostrophe and an -s, some writers use only the apostrophe: *Sophocles'.*

When to add only an apostrophe If the noun is plural and ends in -s, add only an apostrophe.

> Both diplomats' briefcases were searched by guards.

Joint possession To show joint possession, use -'s (or -s') with the last noun only; to show individual possession, make all nouns possessive.

> Have you seen Joyce and Greg's new camper?

> Hernando's and Maria's expectations were quite different.

Compound nouns If a noun is compound, use -'s (or -s') with the last element.

> Her father-in-law's sculpture won first place.

Indefinite pronouns such as *someone* Use -'s to indicate that an indefinite pronoun is possessive. Indefinite pronouns refer to no specific person or thing: *anyone, everyone, someone, no one,* and so on.

This diet will improve almost anyone's health.

NOTE: Possessive pronouns (*its, his,* and so on) do not use an apostrophe. (See 19d.)

19b To mark contractions

In a contraction, an apostrophe takes the place of missing letters.

It's a shame that Frank can't go on the tour.

It's stands for *it is, can't* for *cannot*.
The apostrophe is also used to mark the omission of the first two digits of a year (*the class of '13*) or years (*the '60s generation*).

19c Conventional uses

An apostrophe typically is not used to pluralize numbers, abbreviations, letters, or words mentioned as words. Note the few exceptions and be consistent in your writing.

Plural numbers and abbreviations Do not use an apostrophe in the plural of any numbers (including decades) or of any abbreviations.

Peggy skated nearly perfect figure 8s.

DVDs first became available in the 1990s.

Plural letters Italicize the letter and use roman (regular) font style for the -*s* ending.

Two large *J*s were painted on the door.

To avoid misreading, you may use an apostrophe with some letters: *A*'s.

Plural of words mentioned as words Italicize the word and use roman (regular) font style for the -*s* ending.

We've heard enough *maybe*s.

Words mentioned as words may also appear in quotation marks. When you choose this option, use the apostrophe.

> We've heard enough "maybe's."

19d Misuses of the apostrophe

Do not use an apostrophe in the following situations.

WITH NOUNS THAT ARE PLURAL BUT NOT POSSESSIVE

▶ Some ~~outpatient's~~ *outpatients* have special parking permits.
        ^

IN THE POSSESSIVE PRONOUNS *ITS*, *WHOSE*, *HIS*, *HERS*, *OURS*, *YOURS*, AND *THEIRS*

▶ Each area has ~~it's~~ *its* own conference room.
           ^

▶ We attended a reading by Junot Díaz, ~~who's~~ *whose* work
                   ^

focuses on the Dominican immigration experience.

It's means "it is"; *who's* means "who is" (see 19b). Possessive pronouns such as *its* and *whose* contain no apostrophes.

20 Quotation marks

Quotation marks are used to enclose direct quotations. They are also used around some titles and to set off words used as words.

20a To enclose direct quotations

Direct quotations of a person's words, whether spoken or written, must be in quotation marks.

> "The contract negotiations are stalled," the mediator told reporters, "but I'll bring both sides together."

Use single quotation marks to enclose a quotation within a quotation.

> Marshall notes that Peabody's school focused on "not merely 'teaching' but 'educating children morally and spiritually as well as intellectually from the first'" (107).

EXCEPTIONS: Do not use quotation marks around indirect quotations, which report what a person said without using the person's exact words: *The mediator pledged to find a compromise even though negotiations had broken down.*

When a long quotation has been set off from the text by indenting, quotation marks are not needed. (See pp. 129, 187, and 243–44.)

20b Around titles of short works

Use quotation marks around titles of short works such as articles, poems, short stories, songs, television and radio episodes, and chapters or subdivisions of long works.

> Nirvana's song "All Apologies" is a classic.

NOTE: Titles of long works such as books, plays, television and radio programs, films, magazines, and so on are put in italics. (See pp. 82–83.)

20c To set off words used as words

Although words used as words are ordinarily italicized (see p. 83), quotation marks are also acceptable. Use one method or the other consistently.

> The words "affect" and "effect" are frequently confused.

20d Other punctuation with quotation marks

This section describes the conventions to observe in placing various marks of punctuation inside or outside quotation marks. It also explains how to punctuate when introducing quoted material.

Periods and commas Place periods and commas inside quotation marks.

> "I'm here for my service-learning project," I told the teacher. "I'd like to become a reading specialist."

This rule applies to single and double quotation marks, and it applies to quotation marks around words, phrases, and clauses.

EXCEPTION: In MLA and APA parenthetical in-text citations, the period follows the citation in parentheses. MLA:
*According to Cole, "The instruments of science have vastly
extended our senses" (53).* APA: *According to Cole (1999),
"The instruments of science have vastly extended our senses"
(p. 53).*

Colons and semicolons   Put colons and semicolons
outside quotation marks.

> Harold wrote, "I regret that I cannot attend the
> fundraiser for AIDS research"; his letter, however,
> contained a contribution.

Question marks and exclamation points   Put question marks and exclamation points inside quotation
marks unless they apply to the whole sentence.

> Professor Abrams asked us on the first day of class,
> "What are your three goals for the course?"

> Have you heard the old proverb "Do not climb the
> hill until you reach it"?

In the first sentence, the question mark applies only to
the quoted question. In the second sentence, the question mark applies to the whole sentence.

Introducing quoted material   After a word group
introducing a quotation, choose a colon, a comma, or no
punctuation at all, whichever is appropriate in context.

If a quotation has been formally introduced, a colon
is appropriate. A formal introduction is a full independent clause, not just an expression such as *he said* or *she
writes.*

> Thomas Friedman provides a challenging yet optimistic
> view of the future: "We need to get back to work on
> our country and on our planet. The hour is late, the
> stakes couldn't be higher, the project couldn't be
> harder, the payoff couldn't be greater" (25).

If a quotation is introduced or followed by an
expression such as *he said* or *she writes*, use a comma.

> About New England's weather, Mark Twain once
> declared, "In the spring I have counted one hundred
> and thirty-six different kinds of weather within four
> and twenty hours" (55).

"Unless another war is prevented it is likely to bring destruction on a scale never before held possible," Einstein wrote in the aftermath of the atomic bomb (29).

When you blend a quotation into your own sentence, use either a comma or no punctuation, depending on the way the quotation fits into your sentence structure.

The future champion could, as he put it, "float like a butterfly and sting like a bee."

Virginia Woolf wrote in 1928 that "a woman must have money and a room of her own if she is to write fiction" (4).

If a quotation appears at the beginning of a sentence, use a comma after it unless the quotation ends with a question mark or an exclamation point.

"I've always thought of myself as a reporter," American poet Gwendolyn Brooks stated (162).

"What is it?" she asked, bracing herself.

If a quoted sentence is interrupted by explanatory words, use commas to set off the explanatory words.

"With regard to air travel," Stephen Ambrose notes, "Jefferson was a full century ahead of the curve" (53).

If two successive quoted sentences from the same source are interrupted by explanatory words, use a comma before the explanatory words and a period after them.

"Everyone agrees journalists must tell the truth," Bill Kovach and Tom Rosenstiel write. "Yet people are befuddled about what 'the truth' means" (37).

20e Misuses of quotation marks

Avoid using quotation marks in the following situations.

FAMILIAR SLANG, TRITE EXPRESSIONS, OR HUMOR

▶ The economist emphasized that 5 percent was a "ballpark figure."

INDIRECT QUOTATIONS

▶ After finishing the exam, Chuck said that "he was due for a coffee break."

21 Other marks

21a The period

Use a period to end all sentences except direct questions or genuine exclamations.

> The therapist asked whether the session was beneficial.

A period is conventionally used with personal titles, Latin abbreviations, and designations for time.

Mr.	i.e.	a.m. (or AM)
Ms.	e.g.	p.m. (or PM)
Dr.	etc.	

NOTE: If a sentence ends with a period marking an abbreviation, do not add a second period.

A period is not used for most other abbreviations.

CA	UNESCO	FCC	NATO	BS	BC
NY	AFL-CIO	IRS	USA	PhD	BCE

21b The question mark

Use a question mark after a direct question.

> What is the horsepower of a 747 engine?

NOTE: Use a period, not a question mark, after an indirect question, one that is reported rather than asked directly.

> He asked me who was teaching the geography course.

21c The exclamation point

Use an exclamation point after a sentence that expresses exceptional feeling or deserves special emphasis.

> When Gloria entered the room, I turned on the lights, and we all yelled, "Surprise!"

Do not overuse the exclamation point.

▶ In the fisherman's memory, the fish lives on,

increasing in length and weight each year, until it

is big enough to shade a fishing boat!.
                                      ^

This sentence doesn't need to be pumped up with an exclamation point. It is emphatic enough without it.

21d The dash

The dash may be used to set off parenthetical material that deserves special emphasis. When typing, use two hyphens to form a dash (- -), with no spaces before or after the dash. If your word processing program has what is known as an "em-dash" (—), you may use it instead, with no space before or after it.

Use a dash to introduce a list, to signal a restatement or an amplification, or to indicate a striking shift in tone or thought.

> Along the wall are the bulk liquids — sesame seed oil, honey, safflower oil, and half-liquid peanut butter.

> Peter decided to focus on his priorities — applying to graduate school, getting financial aid, and finding a roommate.

> Kiere took a few steps back, came running full speed, kicked a mighty kick — and missed the ball.

In the first two examples, the writer could also use a colon. (See 18b.) The colon is more formal than the dash and not quite as dramatic.

Use a pair of dashes to set off parenthetical material that deserves special emphasis or to set off an appositive that contains commas.

> Everything in the classroom — from the pencils on the desks to the books on the shelves — was in perfect order.

> In my hometown, people's basic needs — food, clothing, and shelter — are less costly than in Denver.

TIP: Unless you have a specific reason for using the dash, avoid it. Unnecessary dashes create a choppy effect.

21e Parentheses

Parentheses have several conventional uses.

Use parentheses to enclose supplemental material, minor digressions, and afterthoughts.

> Nurses record patients' vital signs (temperature, pulse, and blood pressure) several times a day.

Use parentheses around an abbreviation following the spelled-out form the first time you mention a term. Use the abbreviation alone in subsequent references.

> Data from the Uniform Crime Reports (UCR) indicate that homicide rates have been declining. Because most murders are reported to the police, the data from the UCR are widely viewed as a valid indicator of homicide rates.

Use parentheses to enclose letters or numbers labeling items in a series.

> Freudians recognize three parts to a person's psyche: (a) the unconscious id, where basic drives reside; (b) the ego, which controls many of our conscious decisions; and (c) the superego, which regulates behavior according to internalized societal expectations.

Parentheses are used around page numbers in in-text citations and, in APA style, around dates in in-text citations and the reference list. (See also 33a, 38a, and 38b.)

TIP: Do not overuse parentheses. Often a sentence reads more gracefully without them.

▶ Research shows that seventeen million ~~(estimates~~
                    from   to
~~run as high as~~ twenty-three million) Americans

have diabetes.

21f Brackets

Use brackets to enclose any words or phrases you have inserted into an otherwise word-for-word quotation.

> *Audubon* reports that "if there are not enough young to balance deaths, the end of the species [California condor] is inevitable" (4).

The *Audubon* article did not contain the words *California condor* in the sentence quoted.

The Latin word "sic" in brackets indicates that an error in a quoted sentence appears in the original source.

> According to the review, the book was "an important contribution to gender studies, suceeding [sic] where others have fallen short."

NOTE: APA and *Chicago* use italics for the word "sic" (but not for the brackets). MLA uses regular (roman) font. See pages 187, 243, and 120, respectively.

21g The ellipsis mark

Use an ellipsis mark, three spaced periods, to indicate that you have deleted material from an otherwise word-for-word quotation.

> Harmon (2011) noted, "During hibernation, heart rate would drop to nine beats per minute between breaths . . . and then speed up with each inhale."

If you delete a full sentence or more in the middle of a quoted passage, use a period before the three ellipsis dots.

NOTE: Do not use the ellipsis mark at the beginning of a quotation; do not use it at the end of a quotation unless you have cut some words from the end of the final sentence quoted.

21h The slash

Use the slash to separate two or three lines of poetry that have been run into your text. Add a space both before and after the slash. (For more than three lines of poetry, see p. 121.)

> In the opening lines of "Jordan," George Herbert pokes fun at popular poems of his time: "Who says that fictions only and false hair / Become a verse? Is there in truth no beauty?"

Use the slash sparingly, if at all, to separate options: *pass/fail, producer/director.* Put no space around the slash. Avoid using expressions such as *he/she* and *his/her* and the awkward construction *and/or.*

Mechanics

22 Capitalization

In addition to the following guidelines, a good dictionary can tell you when to use capital letters.

22a Proper vs. common nouns

Proper nouns and words derived from them are capitalized; common nouns are not. Proper nouns name specific persons, places, and things. All other nouns are common nouns.

The following types of words are usually capitalized: names of deities, religions, religious followers, and sacred books; words of family relationship used as names; particular places; nationalities and their languages, races, and tribes; educational institutions and departments and specific courses; government departments and organizations and political parties; historical movements, periods, events, and documents; and trade names.

PROPER NOUNS	COMMON NOUNS
God (used as a name)	a god
Book of Common Prayer	a sacred book
Uncle Pedro	my uncle
Dad (used as a name)	my dad
Lake Superior	a large lake
the South	a southern state
Wrigley Field	a baseball stadium
University of Wisconsin	a state university
Geology 101	a geology course
Veterans Administration	a federal agency
Phi Kappa Psi	a fraternity
the Democratic Party	a political party
the Enlightenment	the eighteenth century
Advil	a painkiller

Months, holidays, and days of the week are capitalized: *May, Labor Day, Monday.* The seasons and numbers of the days of the month are not: *summer, the fifth of June.*

Names of school subjects are capitalized only if they are names of languages: *geology, history, English, French.* Names of particular courses are capitalized: *Geology 101, Principles of Economics.*

Capitalization varies widely for terms such as *web, Internet,* and so on, so check with your instructor about whether you should follow the guidelines for MLA, APA, or *Chicago* style (34, 39, or 44, respectively).

NOTE: Do not capitalize common nouns to make them seem important: *Our company is currently hiring technical support staff* [not *Company, Technical Support Staff*].

22b Titles with proper names

Capitalize a title when used as part of a proper name but usually not when used alone.

> Prof. Margaret Burnes; Dr. Sinyee Sein; John Scott Williams Jr.; Anne Tilton, LLD

> District Attorney Mill was ruled out of order.

> The district attorney was elected for a two-year term.

Usage varies when the title of an important public figure is used alone: *The president* [or *President*] *vetoed the bill.*

22c Titles of works

In the text of a paper, major words—nouns, pronouns, verbs, adjectives, and adverbs—should be capitalized in both titles and subtitles. Minor words—articles, prepositions, and coordinating conjunctions—are not capitalized unless they are the first or last word of a title or subtitle. (In APA style, also capitalize all words of four or more letters in titles. See 39a.)

> *The Impossible Theater: A Manifesto*

> "Man in the Middle"

> "I Want to Hold Your Hand"

Titles of works are handled differently in the APA reference list. See "Preparing the list of references" in 39a.

22d First word of a sentence or quoted sentence

The first word of a sentence should be capitalized. Capitalize the first word of a quoted sentence but not a quoted phrase.

Loveless writes, "If failing schools are ever to be turned around, much more must be learned about how schools age as institutions" (25).

Russell Baker has written that sports are "the opiate of the masses" (46).

If a quoted sentence is interrupted by explanatory words, do not capitalize the first word after the interruption.

"When we all think alike," he said, "no one is thinking."

When a sentence appears within parentheses, capitalize the first word unless the parentheses appear within another sentence.

Early detection of breast cancer increases survival rates. (See table 2.)

Early detection of breast cancer increases survival rates (see table 2).

22e First word following a colon

Capitalize the first word after a colon if it begins an independent clause.

Clinical trials revealed problems: A high percentage of participants reported severe headaches.

NOTE: Preferences vary among academic disciplines. See 34a, 39a, and 44a.

Always use lowercase for a list or an appositive that follows a colon.

Students were divided into two groups: residents and commuters.

22f Abbreviations

Capitalize abbreviations for departments and agencies of government, other organizations, and corporations; capitalize trade names and the call letters of radio and television stations.

EPA, FBI, DKNY, IBM, WERS, KNBC-TV

23 Abbreviations, numbers, and italics

23a Abbreviations

Use abbreviations only when they are clearly appropriate.

Appropriate abbreviations   Use standard abbreviations for titles immediately before and after proper names.

TITLES BEFORE PROPER NAMES	TITLES AFTER PROPER NAMES
Ms. Nancy Linehan	Thomas Hines Jr.
Mr. Raphael Zabala	Anita Lor, PhD
Dr. Margaret Simmons	Robert Simkowski, MD
Rev. John Stone	Mia Chin, LLD

Do not abbreviate a title if it is not used with a proper name: *My history professor* [not *prof.*] *was an expert on naval warfare.*

Familiar abbreviations for the names of organizations, corporations, and countries are also acceptable: *CIA, FBI, NAACP, EPA, YMCA, NBC, USA.*

When using an unfamiliar abbreviation (such as *NAB* for National Association of Broadcasters) throughout a paper, write the full name followed by the abbreviation in parentheses at the first mention of the name. Then use just the abbreviation throughout the rest of the paper.

Other commonly accepted abbreviations include *BC, AD, a.m., p.m., No.,* and *$.* The abbreviation *BC* ("before Christ") follows a date, and *AD* ("*anno Domini*") precedes a date. Acceptable alternatives are *BCE* ("before the common era") and *CE* ("common era").

40 BC (or 40 BCE)   4:00 a.m. (or AM)   No. 12 (or no. 12)
AD 44 (or 44 CE)   6:00 p.m. (or PM) $150

Inappropriate abbreviations   In formal writing, abbreviations for the following are not commonly accepted.

DAYS OF THE WEEK   Monday (*not* Mon.)

HOLIDAYS   Christmas (*not* Xmas)

MONTHS   January, February (*not* Jan., Feb.)

COURSES OF STUDY political science (*not* poli. sci.)

STATES AND COUNTRIES Florida (*not* FL or Fla.)

Use abbreviations for units of measurement when they are preceded by numerals, as in most scientific writing (*13 cm, 5 ft*). Do not abbreviate them when they are used alone (*The results were measured in millimeters*) or when they appear with spelled-out numbers (*The plant grew five inches in one week*). (See also 23b.)

Although Latin abbreviations are appropriate in footnotes and bibliographies and in informal writing, use the appropriate English phrases in formal writing.

e.g. (Latin *exempli gratia*, "for example")

et al. (Latin *et alii*, "and others")

etc. (Latin *et cetera*, "and so forth")

i.e. (Latin *id est*, "that is")

N.B. (Latin *nota bene*, "note well")

23b Numbers

Spell out numbers of one or two words. Use numerals for numbers that require more than two words to spell out.

▶ The 1980 eruption of Mount St. Helens blasted
  ~~16~~ sixteen miles into the sky and devastated ~~two hundred thirty~~ 230 square miles of land.

If a sentence begins with a number, spell out the number or rewrite the sentence.

▶ One hundred fifty
  ~~150~~ children in our program need expensive dental treatment.

Academic styles vary for handling numbers in the text of a paper. In the humanities, MLA and *Chicago* spell out numbers below 101 and large round numbers (*forty million*); they use numerals for specific numbers above one hundred (*234*). In the social sciences and the sciences, APA and CSE spell out the numbers one through nine and use numerals for all other numbers.

Generally, numerals are acceptable for the following.

DATES   July 4, 1776; 56 BC; AD 30

ADDRESSES   77 Latches Lane, 519 West 42nd Street

PERCENTAGES   55 percent (or 55%)

FRACTIONS, DECIMALS $^7/_8$, 0.047

SCORES   7 to 3, 21–18

STATISTICS   average age 37

SURVEYS   4 out of 5

EXACT AMOUNTS OF MONEY $105.37

DIVISIONS OF BOOKS   volume 3, chapter 4, page 189

DIVISIONS OF PLAYS   act 3, scene 3 (or act III, scene iii)

TIME OF DAY   4:00 p.m., 1:30 a.m.

23c Italics

This section describes conventional uses for italics: for titles of works; names of ships, aircraft, and spacecraft; foreign words; and words as words.

Titles of works   Titles of the following types of works are italicized.

TITLES OF BOOKS   *The Color Purple, The Round House*

MAGAZINES   *Time, Scientific American, Slate*

NEWSPAPERS   the *Baltimore Sun,* the *Orlando Sentinel*

PAMPHLETS   *Common Sense, Facts about Marijuana*

LONG POEMS   *The Waste Land, Paradise Lost*

PLAYS   *King Lear, Wicked*

FILMS   *Casablanca, Argo*

TELEVISION PROGRAMS   *The Voice, Frontline*

RADIO PROGRAMS   *All Things Considered*

MUSICAL COMPOSITIONS   *Porgy and Bess*

CHOREOGRAPHIC WORKS   *Brief Fling*

WORKS OF VISUAL ART   *American Gothic*

VIDEO GAMES   *Dragon Age, Call of Duty*

DATABASES [MLA]   *Academic Search Premier*

WEBSITES [MLA]   *Salon, Google*

COMPUTER SOFTWARE OR APP [MLA]   *Photoshop, Instagram*

Sometimes guidelines for italics vary among the style guides (MLA, APA, and *Chicago*). See also the style section your instructor has assigned.

The titles of other works, such as short stories, essays, songs, and short poems, are enclosed in quotation marks. (See 20b.)

NOTE: Do not use italics when referring to the Bible; the titles of books in the Bible (Genesis, not *Genesis*); the titles of legal documents (the Constitution, not the *Constitution*); or the titles of your own papers.

Names of ships, aircraft, spacecraft   Italicize names of specific ships, aircraft, and spacecraft.

Queen Mary 2, Wright Flyer, Endeavour

Foreign words   Italicize foreign words used in an English sentence.

I wished my German teacher a *gute Reise* before his flight.

EXCEPTION: Do not italicize foreign words that have become part of the English language — "laissez-faire," "fait accompli," "modus operandi," and "per diem," for example.

Words as words etc.   Italicize words used as words, letters mentioned as letters, and numbers mentioned as numbers.

Tomás assured us that the chemicals could probably be safely mixed, but his *probably* stuck in our minds.

Some toddlers have trouble pronouncing the letters *f* and *s*.

A big *3* was painted on the stage door.

NOTE: Quotation marks may be used instead of italics to set off words mentioned as words. (See 20c.)

Inappropriate italics   Italicizing to emphasize words or ideas is often ineffective and should be used sparingly.

24 Spelling and the hyphen

24a Spelling

A spell checker is a useful tool, but it has limitations. It won't catch words commonly confused (*accept, except*) or some typographical errors (*won* for *own*). You still need to proofread, and you may need to turn to the dictionary or to the glossary of usage at the back of this book.

Major spelling rules If you need to improve your spelling, review the following rules and exceptions.

1. In general, use *i* before *e* except after *c* and except when sounded like "ay," as in *neighbor* and *weigh*.

I BEFORE E	relieve, believe, sieve, niece, fierce, frieze
E BEFORE I	receive, deceive, sleigh, freight, eight
EXCEPTIONS	seize, either, weird, height, foreign, leisure

2. Generally, drop a final silent *-e* when adding a suffix that begins with a vowel. Keep the final *e* if the suffix begins with a consonant.

desire, desiring	achieve, achievement
remove, removable	care, careful

EXCEPTIONS changeable, judgment, argument, truly

3. When adding *-s* or *-ed* to words ending in *-y*, ordinarily change *-y* to *-i* when the *-y* is preceded by a consonant but not when it is preceded by a vowel.

comedy, comedies	monkey, monkeys
dry, dried	play, played

With proper names ending in *-y*, however, do not change the *-y* to *-i* even if it is preceded by a consonant: *the Dougherty family, the Doughertys*.

4. If a final consonant is preceded by a single vowel and the consonant ends a one-syllable word or a stressed syllable, double the consonant when adding a suffix beginning with a vowel.

bet, betting   occur, occurrence
commit, committed

5. Add -s to form the plural of most nouns; add -es to singular nouns ending in -s, -sh, -ch, and -x.

table, tables   church, churches
paper, papers   dish, dishes

Ordinarily add -s to nouns ending in -o when the -o is preceded by a vowel. Add -es when the -o is preceded by a consonant.

radio, radios   hero, heroes
video, videos   tomato, tomatoes

To form the plural of a hyphenated compound word, add the -s to the chief word even if it does not appear at the end.

mother-in-law, mothers-in-law

NOTE: English words derived from other languages such as Latin, Greek, or French sometimes form the plural as they would in their original language.

medium, media   chateau, chateaux
criterion, criteria

Spelling variations   Following is a list of some common words spelled differently in American and British English. Consult a dictionary for others.

AMERICAN	BRITISH
canceled, traveled	cancelled, travelled
color, humor	colour, humour
judgment	judgement
check	cheque
realize, apologize	realise, apologise
defense	defence
anemia, anesthetic	anaemia, anaesthetic
theater, center	theatre, centre
fetus	foetus
mold, smolder	mould, smoulder

AMERICAN	BRITISH
civili<u>z</u>ation	civili<u>s</u>ation
conne<u>ct</u>ion, infle<u>ct</u>ion	conne<u>x</u>ion, infle<u>x</u>ion

24b The hyphen

In addition to the following guidelines, a dictionary will help you make decisions about hyphenation.

Compound words   The dictionary will tell you whether to treat a compound word as a hyphenated compound (*water-repellent*), as one word (*waterproof*), or as two words (*water table*). If the compound word is not in the dictionary, treat it as two words.

Words functioning together as an adjective   When two or more words function together as an adjective before a noun, connect them with a hyphen. Generally, do not use a hyphen when such compounds follow the noun.

▶   Pat Hobbs is not yet a well-known candidate
                                          ^

▶   After our television campaign, Pat Hobbs will be

   well/known.

Do not use a hyphen to connect *-ly* adverbs to the words they modify.

▶   A slowly/moving truck tied up traffic.

NOTE: In a series of hyphenated adjectives modifying the same noun, hyphens are suspended: *Do you prefer first-, second-, or third-class tickets?*

Conventional uses   Hyphenate the written form of fractions and of compound numbers from twenty-one to ninety-nine. Also use a hyphen with the prefixes *all-*, *ex-*, and *self-* and with the suffix *-elect*.

▶   One-fourth of my income goes for rent.
       ^

▶   The charity is funding more self-help projects.
                                          ^

Hyphenation at ends of lines   Only words that already contain a hyphen may break at the end of a line of text. If your writing software automatically breaks words at the ends of lines, disable that setting.

Email addresses, URLs, and DOIs need special attention when they occur at the end of a line of text or in a bibliographic citation. Do not insert a hyphen. Break an email address after the @ symbol or before a period. For URLs and DOIs, consult the guidelines for MLA, APA, *Chicago*, or CSE style (34a, 39a, 44a, or 46b, respectively).

Research

A college research assignment asks you to pose questions worth exploring, read widely in search of possible answers, interpret what you read, draw reasoned conclusions, and support those conclusions with valid and well-documented evidence. It asks you to enter a research conversation by responding to the ideas of other writers and thinkers who have explored your topic. As you listen to and learn from the voices already in the conversation, you'll find entry points where you can add your own insights.

This section and the color-coded sections that follow—MLA (blue), APA (green), *Chicago* (purple), and CSE (turquoise)—will help you write your paper and properly document your sources in the style your instructor requires.

25 Posing a research question

Every research project starts with questions. Working within the guidelines of your assignment, pose a few preliminary questions that seem worth researching—questions that you want to explore, that you feel would engage your audience, and about which there is a substantial debate. Try using a journalist's questions—*What? When? Where? Who? Why?* and *How?*—to formulate research questions for your project.

As you draft possible questions, choose those that are focused (not too broad), challenging (not just factual), and grounded (not too speculative) as entry points in a research conversation.

25a Choosing a focused question

If your initial question is too broad, given the length of the paper you plan to write, look for ways to restrict your focus. Here, for example, is how two students refined their initial questions.

TOO BROAD	FOCUSED
What are the benefits of stricter auto emissions standards?	How will stricter auto emissions standards create new auto industry jobs and make US carmakers more competitive in the world market?

TOO BROAD	**FOCUSED**
What causes depression?	How has the widespread use of antidepressant drugs affected teenage suicide rates?

25b Choosing a challenging question

Your research paper will be more interesting to both you and your audience if you base it on an intellectually challenging line of inquiry. Try to draft questions that provoke thought and engage readers in a debate.

TOO FACTUAL	**CHALLENGING**
Is autism on the rise?	Why is autism so difficult to treat?
Where is wind energy being used?	What makes wind farms economically viable?

You may need to address a factual question in the course of answering a more challenging one, but a factual question is too limited to be the focus for an entire paper.

25o Choosing a grounded question

Make sure that your research question is grounded and not too speculative. Although speculative questions—such as those that address morality or beliefs—are worth asking in a research paper, they are unsuitable central questions. For most college courses, the central argument of a research paper should be grounded in evidence, not beliefs.

TOO SPECULATIVE	**GROUNDED**
Is it wrong to share pornographic personal photos by cell phone?	What role should the US government play in regulating mobile content?
Do medical scientists have the right to experiment on animals?	How have technological breakthroughs made medical experiments on animals increasingly unnecessary?

25d Testing a research question

As you draft possible research questions, explore your topic from multiple perspectives, and let your curiosity drive your project. You may find that your research leads you in unexpected directions and challenges your

Enter a research conversation

A college research project asks you to be in conversation with writers and researchers who have studied your topic—to respond to their ideas and positions and contribute your own insights to move the conversation forward. As you pose preliminary research questions, you may wonder where and how to step into a research conversation.

1 **Identify the experts and ideas in the conversation.** Who are the major writers and most influential people researching your topic? What positions have they taken? How and why do they disagree?

2 **Identify gaps in the conversation.** What questions haven't been asked yet? What arguments need to be challenged?

3 **Try using an orienting statement** to help you find an entry point.

* *On one side of the debate is position X, on the other side is Y, but there is a middle position, Z.*

* *The conventional view about the problem needs to be challenged because...*

* *Key details in this debate that have been overlooked are...*

* *Researchers have drawn conclusion X from the evidence, but one could also draw conclusion Y.*

initial assumptions. As your ideas evolve, keep testing your research question.

- Does the question allow you to enter into a research conversation that you care about?
- Can you show your audience why the question needs to be asked and why the answer matters?
- Is the question flexible enough to allow for many possible answers?
- Is the question focused, challenging, and grounded?

26 Finding appropriate sources

Before you begin looking for sources, think about what types of print and electronic sources will be appropriate for your paper. For example, if your research question addresses a historical issue, you might focus on scholarly books and articles and on primary sources, such as speeches. If your question addresses a current political issue, you might turn to government publications, research reports from think tanks, and magazine articles.

Considering the kinds of sources you need will help you develop a research strategy—a systematic plan for locating sources. Keep in mind that no single search strategy works for every topic. Effective researchers often use a combination of library databases and the web when looking for sources.

26a Using the library

The website hosted by your college library links to databases and other references, where you will find articles, studies, and reports from scholarly journals and other widely respected sources. Use your library's resources to find helpful, reliable sources written by the key writers and researchers debating your topic. Many libraries offer one-on-one help from research librarians, who can tell you what resources are available and suggest ways to improve your search.

Savvy searchers cut down on the clutter of a broad search by adding additional search terms, limiting a search to recent publications, or clicking on a database option to look at only one type of source, such as peer-reviewed articles. When looking for books, use your

---

Tips for smart searching

For currency. If your topic demands recent articles, try searching news outlets such as the *New York Times* and the BBC, think tanks, government agencies, and advocacy groups.

For authority. Look for experts being cited in sources you examine. Following the trail of citation may help you locate a network of relevant research related to your topic.

For scholarship. Use a library database to look for reports of original research written by the people who conducted it. Read abstracts to see whether the sources are worth further investigation.

For context. Books often provide context that articles cannot. You may find a single chapter or even a few pages that are just what you need to gain a deeper perspective.

---

library's online catalog to help you identify the books you need and to locate them within the library.

26b Using the web

When conducting searches, use terms that are as specific as possible, and enclose search phrases in quotation marks. You can refine your search by date or domain; for example, *autism site:.gov* will search for information about autism on government websites.

As you examine a site, look for an "about" link to learn about the site's author or sponsoring agency. Examine the URL for clues. Avoid sites that provide information but no explanation of who the authors are or why the site was created. For more on evaluating web sources, see page 101.

26c Using bibliographies and citations

Scholarly books and articles list the works the author has cited, usually at the end. These lists are useful shortcuts to additional reliable sources on your topic. Scholarly articles, for example, contain citations to related research studies, which can help you identify influential authors contributing to your research conversation. Even popular sources such as news articles, videos, and TED talks may refer to additional relevant sources that could be worth tracking down.

HOW TO Go beyond a Google search

Good research involves going beyond the information available from a quick Google search. You might start with Google to gain an overview of your topic, but relying on Google to find and choose your sources isn't a research strategy. To locate reliable, authoritative sources, be strategic about *how* and *where* you search.

1 **Familiarize yourself with the debate.** What is the current debate about the topic? Who are the most influential writers and researchers in the debate? Which experts or sources are cited repeatedly in the research conversation? In which disciplines, organizations, or governmental agencies is the debate taking place?

2 **Generate keywords to focus your search.** Start with two to four words that describe your topic. Be flexible and try new words and phrases as you encounter them in your research. Add words such as *debate*, *disagreements*, *controversies*, *proponents*, or *opponents* to your search terms to track down various positions in the research conversation.

3 **Search discipline-specific databases** available through your school library to locate carefully chosen scholarly (peer-reviewed) content that doesn't appear in search results on the open web. Use databases such as JSTOR and Academic Search Premier, designed for academic researchers.

4 **Try *CQ Researcher*,** available through most college libraries, if your topic has been in the news. This resource's brief articles provide pro/con arguments on current controversies in criminal justice, law, the environment, technology, health, and education.

5 **Explore the Pew Research Center online** for original research and nonpartisan discussions of findings and trends in a wide range of academic fields.

27 Evaluating sources

You can often locate far more potential sources for your topic than you will have time to read. Your challenge will be to determine what kinds of sources you need—and what you need these sources to do—and to select a reasonable number of trustworthy sources.

Keeping the following criteria in mind will help you evaluate sources and judge their usefulness to your research project.

Relevance   Is the source clearly related to your topic and your argument? Make sure your readers will understand *why* you've included the source in your paper. For example, you may disagree with the author's position, but citing and refuting the author's ideas should help you clarify or support your own position.

Currency   Check the publication date. How recent is the source? If you're writing about a current issue that changes rapidly, avoid sources with outdated information. If your paper is about something like technological innovations of World War I, a mix of older and newer sources may be appropriate.

Credibility   Where does the source come from? Who created it? Check for the author's credentials—what education or experience makes the author qualified to discuss your topic? If the source is authored by an organization rather than an individual, what research has the organization done to support its claims?

Length and depth   If the source is very short, it may not cover the topic thoroughly enough to be useful. If you find an abstract (a citation and summary of a text) that looks promising, use the citation to find the complete text. In most cases, abstracts themselves are not suitable sources.

27a Selecting sources

Determining how sources contribute to your writing
How you plan to use sources will affect how you evaluate them. Sources can have a range of functions in a paper.

You can use them to

- provide background information or context for your topic
- explain terms or concepts that your readers might not understand
- provide evidence for your argument
- lend authority to your argument
- offer counterevidence and alternative interpretations your argument should address

For examples of how student writers use sources for a variety of purposes, see 31, 37, and 42.

Evaluating search results   This section explains how to scan through search results for the most useful and reliable sources.

Databases   Most databases provide at least the following information, which can help you decide if a source is relevant, current, and scholarly.

Title and brief description (How relevant?)

Date (How current?)

Name of publication in which the source appears (How scholarly?)

Length (How extensive in coverage?)

Determining whether a source is scholarly

Many college assignments require you to use scholarly sources. Written by experts for a knowledgeable audience, these sources often go into more depth than books and articles written for a general audience. To determine whether a source is scholarly, look for the following:

- Formal language and presentation
- Authors who are academics or scientists
- Footnotes or a bibliography documenting the works cited in the source
- Original research and interpretation (rather than a summary of other people's work)
- Quotations from and analysis of primary sources (in the humanities)
- A description of research methods or a review of related research (in the sciences or social sciences)

See pages 98–99 for a sample scholarly source and popular source.

NOTE: In some databases, searches can be limited to refereed or peer-reviewed journals.

Library catalogs   The library's catalog usually lists enough basic information about resources in the library's collection to give you a first impression. If details such as the subject matter, currency, and length of a potential source look appropriate, it's probably worth taking a look at the source itself.

Web search engines   Reliable and unreliable sources live side-by-side on the web. Look for the following clues about the probable relevance, currency, and reliability of a potential source. (See also p. 94 for help with going beyond a Google search.)

> Title, keywords, and lead-in text (How relevant?)
>
> Date (How current?)
>
> Indication of the source's sponsor or purpose (How reliable?)
>
> URL, especially the domain name extension: for example, .com, .edu, .gov, or .org (How relevant? How reliable?)

27b Reading with an open mind and a critical eye

As you begin reading the sources you have chosen, keep an open mind. Do not let your personal beliefs prevent you from listening to new ideas and opposing viewpoints. Be curious about the wide range of positions in the research conversation you are entering. Your research question should guide you as you read your sources.

When you read critically, you are not necessarily judging an author's work harshly; you are simply examining the work's assumptions, assessing the evidence, and weighing the conclusions. Reading critically means

- reading carefully (*What does the source say?*),
- reading skeptically (*Are any of the author's points or conclusions problematic?*), and
- reading evaluatively (*How does this source help me make my argument?*).

For a checklist on evaluating sources, see page 100.

Common features of a scholarly source

1 Formal presentation with abstract and research methods

2 Includes review of previous research studies

3 Reports original research

4 Includes references

5 Multiple authors with academic credentials

FIRST PAGE OF ARTICLE

Cyberbullying: Using Virtual Scenarios to Educate and Raise Awareness

Vivian H. Wright, Joy J. Burnham, Christopher T. Inman, and Heather N. Ogorchock

Abstract

This study examined cyberbullying in three distinct phases to facilitate a multifaceted understanding of cyberbullying. The phases included (a) a quantitative survey, (b) a qualitative focus group, and (c) development of educational scenarios/simulations (within the Second Life virtual environment). Phase III was based on adolescent feedback about cyberbullying from Phases I and II of this study. In all three phases, adolescent reactions to cyberbullying were examined and reported to raise awareness and to educate others about cyberbullying. Results from scenario development indicate that simulations created in a virtual environment are engaging and have the potential to be a powerful tool in helping schools address problems such as cyberbullying education and prevention. (Keywords: cyberbullying, virtual worlds, Second Life, teacher education, counselor education)

Introduction

Cyberbullying has gained attention and recognition in recent years (Beale & Hall, 2007; Carney, 2008; Casey-Canon, Hayward, & Gowen, 2001; Kowalski & Limber, 2007; Li, 2007; Shariff, 2005). The increased interest and awareness of cyberbullying relates to such factors as the national media attention after several publicized cyberbullying tragedies (Maag, 2007; Stelter, 2008; Zifcak, 2006), the attenuation of communication [...] technology use among yo[...] ogy and the easy acces[...] youth, pickedly, deter inem[...] cyberbullying and its possibl[...] it come to be held in adoleni[...] systems (i.e., home, school, an[...] "school professionals" (Li, 2007, p. 1778), and mental health providers must not only be made aware of cyberbullying and its consequences, but must also have access to ways to deal with this growing concern.

Two years ago, cyberbullying was considered to be a "new territory" for exploration (Li, 2007, p. 1778) because there was limited information about bullying through "electronic means" (Li, p. 1780). In contrast, today studies on cyberbullying, including some descriptions of the worst cyberbullying incidences (Maag, 2007; Beale & Hall, 2007; Carney, 2008; Kowalski & Limber, 2007; Li, 2007). At this time, there is a need to raise awareness about the effects of cyberbullying and to create educational opportunities to serve multiple audiences (i.e., teachers, teacher educators, school administrators, school counselors, mental health professionals, students, parents) in the quest to identify and hopefully prevent cyberbullying in the future. Consequently, to facilitate a multifaceted understanding of

cyberbullying, this study sought to examine cyberbullying through three phases: (a) a quantitative survey, (b) a qualitative focus group, and (c) development of the educational scenarios/simulations (i.e., using virtual world avatars similar to those used in Linden Lab's (1993) Second Life (SL; http://secondlife.com) based on adolescent feedback from Phases I and II of this study. Adolescent reactions to cyberbullying in all three phases of this study were examined and reported with two aims in mind: (a) to raise awareness of cyberbullying, and (b) to educate others about cyberbullying.

Defining Cyberbullying

Cyberbullying has been described as a traumatic experience that can lead to physical, cognitive, emotional, and social consequences (Carney, 2008; Casey-Canon et al., 2001; Patchin & Hinduja, 2006). Cyberbullying has been defined as "bullying through the e-mail, instant messaging, in a chat room, on a website, or though digital messages or images sent to a cell phone" (Kowalski & Limber, 2007, p. 822). There are numerous methods to engage in cyberbullying, including e-mail, instant messaging, online gaming, chat rooms, and text messaging (Beale & Hall, 2007; Li, 2007). In addition, cyberbullying appears in different forms than traditional bullying. For example, Beale and Hall (2007), Mason (2007), and Willard (2008) found that at least seven different types of cyberbullying exist, including:

• [...]
• Exclusion: excluding someone purposefully

Research suggests that cyberbullying has distinct gender and age differences. According to the literature, girls are more likely to be online and to cyberbully (Beale & Hall, 2007; Kowalski & Limber, 2007; Li, 2006, 2007). This finding is "opposite of what happens off-line," where boys are more likely to bully than girls (Beale & Hall, p. 8). Age also appears to be a factor in cyberbullying. Cyberbullying increases in the elementary years, peaks during the middle school years, and declines in the high school years (Beale & Hall). Based on the literature, cyberbullying is a growing concern among middle school-aged children (Beale & Hall; Hinduja & Patchin, 2008; Kowalski & Limber, 2007; Li, 2007; Pellegrini & Bartini, 2000; Smith, Mahdavi, Carvalho, & Tippett, 2006; Williams & Guerra, 2006). Of the middle school grades, 6th grade students are usually the

2 Research suggests that cyberbullying has distinct gender and age differences. According to the literature, girls are more likely to be online and to cyberbully (Beale & Hall, 2007; Kowalski & Limber, 2007; Li, 2006, 2007) This finding is "opposite of what happens off-line," where boys are [...] information.

Volume 26/ Number 1 Fall 2009   Journal of Computing in Teacher Education   35

Copyright © 2009 ISTE (International Society for Technology in Education), 800.336.5191 (U.S. & Canada) or 541.302.3777 (Int'l), iste@iste.org, www.iste.org

© 2009 ISTE (International Society for Technology in Education).

EXCERPTS FROM OTHER PAGES

3 Table 2: Percentage of Students Who Experienced Cyberbullying through Various Methods

	E-mail	Facebook	MySpace	Cell Phone	Online Video	Chat Rooms
Victim	35.3%	11.8%	52.9%	50%	14.7%	11.8%
Bully	17.6%	0%	70.6%	47.1%	11.8%	5.9%

4 ## References

Bainbridge, W. S. (2007, July). The scientific research potential of virtual worlds. *Science, 317,* 472–476.

Beale, A., & Hall, K. (2007, September/October). Cyberbullying:
W[...]
8[...]

5 *Vivian H. Wright is an associate professor of instructional technology at the University of Alabama. In addition to teaching in the graduate program, Dr. Wright works with teacher educators on innovative ways to infuse technology in the curriculum to*

Common features of a popular source

1 Eye-catching title
2 Written by a staff reporter, not an expert
3 Presents anecdotes about the topic
4 Sources are named, but no formal works cited list appears
5 Presents a summary of research but no original research

ONLINE ARTICLE

CNN Health

Home TV & Video U.S. World Politics Justice Entertainment Tech Health Living Travel Opinion iReport Money Sports

Part of complete coverage on
Bullying

SPECIAL REPORT: BULLYING

When bullying goes high-tech **1**

by **Elizabeth Landau**, CNN **2**
updated 2:12 PM EDT, Mon April 15, 2013

STORY HIGHLIGHTS
- **As many as 25% of teenagers have experienced cyberbullying**
- **Among young people, it's rare that an online bully will be a total stranger**
- **Researchers are working on apps and algorithms to detect and report bullying online**

(CNN) -- Brandon Turley didn't have friends in sixth grade. He would often eat alone at lunch, having recently switched to his school without knowing anyone. **3**

While browsing MySpace one day, he saw that someone from school had posted a bulletin -- a message visible to multiple people -- declaring that Turley was a "fag." Students he had never even spoken with wrote on it, too, saying they agreed.

EXCERPT FROM A LATER SECTION

A pervasive problem
As many as 25% of teenagers have experienced cyberbullying at some point, said Justin W. Patchin, who studies the phenomenon at the University of Wisconsin-Eau Claire. He and colleagues have conducted formal surveys of 15,000 middle and high school students throughout the United States, and found that about 10% of teens have been victims of cyberbullying in the last 30 days. **4**   **5**

Evaluating all sources

Checking for signs of bias

- Does the author or publisher endorse political or religious views that could affect objectivity?
- Is the author or publisher associated with a special-interest group, such as PETA or the National Rifle Association, that might present only one side of an issue?
- Does the author present opposing views and treat them fairly?
- Does the author's language show signs of bias?

Assessing an argument

- What is the author's central claim or thesis?
- How does the author support this claim—with relevant and sufficient evidence or with anecdotes or emotional examples?
- Are statistics accurate and used fairly? Does the author explain where the statistics come from?
- Are any of the author's assumptions questionable?
- Does the author consider opposing arguments and refute them persuasively?

27c Assessing web sources with special care

Before using a web source in your paper, make sure you know who created the material and for what purpose. Sources with reliable information can stand up to scrutiny.

Even if you decide a particular web source isn't credible, current, or relevant enough for your paper, it may contain links to sources that might be more suitable. For example, many instructors do not consider wikis, such as *Wikipedia*, to be appropriate sources for college research. Authorship on many wikis is not limited to experts—entries may be written or changed by anyone—and information is often general rather than critical or in-depth. Most wiki entries include a references section, however, that can point you to books, articles, and websites that may contain valuable information and ideas from credible sources.

Evaluating web sources

Authorship

- Is there an author? You may need to do some clicking and scrolling to find the author's name. Check the home page or an "about this site" link.
- Can you tell whether the author is knowledgeable and credible? If the author's qualifications aren't listed on the site, look for links to the author's home page, which may provide evidence of his or her expertise.

Sponsorship

- Who, if anyone, sponsors the site? The sponsor of a site is often named and described on the home page.
- What does the URL tell you? The domain name extension often indicates the type of group hosting the site: commercial (.com), educational (.edu), nonprofit (.org), governmental (.gov), military (.mil), or network (.net). A domain extension may also indicate a country of origin: .uk (United Kingdom) or .jp (Japan), for instance.

Purpose and audience

- Why was the site created: To argue a position? To sell a product? To inform readers?
- Who is the site's intended audience?

Currency

- How current is the site? Check for the date of publication or the date of the latest update.
- How current are the site's links? If many of the links to other sites no longer work, the site may be too dated for your purposes.

27d Constructing an annotated bibliography

An annotated bibliography gives you an opportunity to summarize, evaluate, and record publication information for your sources before drafting your research paper. You summarize each source to understand its main ideas; you evaluate each source for accuracy and relevance and to assess how the source contributes to

---

> ### Key features of an annotated bibliography
>
> - **An organized list of sources arranged in alphabetical order by author** (or by title for works with no author) includes complete bibliographic information for each source.
>
> - **A brief entry for each source** is typically one hundred to two hundred words and written in paragraph form.
>
> - **A summary** of each source states the work's main ideas and key points and identifies the author's qualifications. The summary is in the third person and the present tense.
>
> - **An evaluation** of the source's role and usefulness includes an assessment of the source's strengths and limitations, the author's qualifications and expertise, and the function of the source in the research project.

your research project; and you record publication information for each source to make sure that you can cite the source if you use it in your paper.

Constructing an annotated bibliography focuses your attention on the most promising sources you've located, providing you with an opportunity to reflect on *how* and *why* these sources will help you answer your research question. In summarizing a source, you check to make sure you understand its main ideas. In evaluating a source, you consider the role of the source—to provide background information, explain a term, provide evidence, lend authority, offer a counterposition—and you distinguish the source's ideas from your own.

SAMPLE ANNOTATED BIBLIOGRAPHY ENTRY (MLA STYLE)

Resnik, David. "Trans Fat Bans and Human Freedom." *American Journal of Bioethics*, vol. 10, no. 3, Mar. 2010, pp. 27-32.

In this scholarly article, bioethicist David Resnik **1** argues that bans on unhealthy foods threaten our personal freedom. He claims that researchers don't **2** have enough evidence to know whether banning trans fats will save lives or money; all we know is that such bans restrict dietary choices. Resnik explains why most

Americans oppose food restrictions, noting our multiethnic
and regional food traditions as well as our resistance
to government limitations on personal freedoms. He
acknowledges that few people would miss eating trans
3
fats, but he fears that bans on such substances could lead
to widespread restrictions on red meat, sugary sodas, and
other foods known to have harmful effects. Resnik offers
a well-reasoned argument, but he goes too far by insisting
that all proposed food restrictions will do more harm than
good. This article contributes important perspectives on
4
American resistance to government intervention in food
choice and counters arguments in other sources that
support the idea of food legislation to advance public
health.

1 Annotations should be three to seven sentences long.
2 Summarize the source using present tense.
3 Evaluate the source for bias and relevance.
4 Evaluate the source for its contribution to the research project.

28 Managing information; avoiding plagiarism

An effective researcher is a good record keeper. Whether
you decide to keep records on paper or on your computer or another device, you will need methods for
managing information: keeping track of source materials, taking notes without plagiarizing your sources,
and maintaining a working bibliography. (For more on
avoiding plagiarism, see 30 for MLA style, 36 for APA
style, and 41 for *Chicago* style.)

28a Keeping track of source materials

Save a copy of each potential source as you conduct your
research. Many database services allow you to email,
save, or print citations or full texts, and you can easily
download, copy, or take screen shots of information
from the web.

28b

Working with photocopies, printouts, or electronic files—as opposed to relying on memory or hastily written notes—lets you annotate the source as you read. You also reduce the chances of unintentional plagiarism, since you will be able to compare your use of a source with the actual source, not just with your notes.

28b Taking notes responsibly: avoiding unintentional plagiarism

Plagiarism is often accidental. With so much time spent thinking about a topic and with so many potential sources to consider, you may forget where a helpful idea came from or that it wasn't yours to begin with. When you take notes, be very careful to put quotation marks around any borrowed words or phrases. Even if you half-copy the author's sentences—either by mixing the author's phrases with your own without using quotation marks or by plugging your synonyms into the author's sentence structure—you are committing plagiarism.

Summarizing and paraphrasing ideas and quoting exact language are three ways of taking notes. Make sure that any summary, paraphrase, or quotation in your notes includes information about where the words and ideas came from so that you can easily integrate and document the source in later stages of your writing. The box on page 105 can help you protect yourself against unintentional plagiarism, particularly when working with online sources.

28c Maintaining a working bibliography

Keep a record of each source you read or view. This record, called a *working bibliography*, will help you keep track of publication information for any sources you might use so that you can refer to them throughout your research and writing process and cite them accurately if you use them in your final paper. The format for citations in your working bibliography depends on the documentation style you are using. (For MLA style, see 33b; for APA style, see 38b; for *Chicago* style, see 43c; for CSE style, see 45c.)

Avoid plagiarizing from online sources

1 Keep in mind what plagiarism is. When you use another author's intellectual property—language, visuals, or ideas—in your writing without giving proper credit, you commit a kind of academic theft called *plagiarism.*

2 Treat online sources the same way you treat print sources. Language, data, or images that you find in an online source must be cited, even if the material is in the public domain (older works no longer protected by copyright law) or is publicly accessible on free sites, personal sites or social media accounts, or sites sponsored by federal, state, or municipal governments (.gov sites) or by nonprofit organizations (.org sites).

3 Keep track of words and ideas borrowed from sources. When you copy and paste passages from online sources, put quotation marks around any words that you have copied. Develop a system for distinguishing your own words and ideas from anything you've summarized, paraphrased, or quoted.

4 Build in time for note taking. If you're rushing, you're more likely to copy and paste something from a source without taking careful notes on where the material came from. Deciding that you'll take care of that part later leaves you vulnerable to accidental plagiarism.

Integrating and citing sources to avoid plagiarism

Source text

Our language is constantly changing. Like the Mississippi, it keeps forging new channels and abandoning old ones, picking up debris, depositing unwanted silt, and frequently bursting its banks. In every generation there are people who deplore changes in the language and many who wish to stop its flow. But if our language stopped changing it would mean that American society had ceased to be dynamic, innovative, pulsing with life—that the great river had frozen up.

— Robert MacNeil and William Cran, *Do You Speak American?*, p. 1

NOTE: The examples in this chart follow MLA style (see 33). For information on APA, *Chicago*, and CSE styles, see 38, 43, and 45, respectively.

If you are using an exact sentence from a source, with no changes...	→	... put quotation marks around the sentence. Use a signal phrase and include a page number in parentheses.
		MacNeil and Cran write, "Our language is constantly changing" (1).
If you are using a few exact words from the source but not an entire sentence...	→	... put quotation marks around the exact words that you have used from the source. Use a signal phrase and include a page number in parentheses.
		Some people, according to MacNeil and Cran, "deplore changes in the language" (1).
If you are using near-exact words from the source but changing some word forms (*I* to *she*, *walk* to *walked*) or adding words to clarify and make the quotation flow with your own text...	→	... put quotation marks around the quoted words and put brackets around the changes you have introduced. Include a signal phrase and follow the quotation with the page number in parentheses.
		MacNeil and Cran compare the English language to the Mississippi River, which "forg[es] new channels and abandon[s] old ones" (1).

MacNeil and Cran write, "In every generation there are people who deplore changes in the [English] language and many who wish to stop its flow" (1).

If you are paraphrasing or summarizing the source, using the author's ideas but not any of the author's exact words . . .   →   . . . introduce the ideas with a signal phrase and put the page number at the end of your sentence. Do not use quotation marks. (See 30, 36, and 41.)

MacNeil and Cran argue that changes in the English language are natural and that they represent cultural progress (1).

If you have used the source's sentence structure but substituted a few synonyms for the author's words . . .   →   STOP! This is a form of plagiarism even if you use a signal phrase and a page number. Change your sentence by using one of the techniques given in this chart or in 31, 37, or 42.

PLAGIARIZED

MacNeil and Cran claim that, like a river, English creates new waterways and discards old ones.

INTEGRATED AND CITED CORRECTLY

MacNeil and Cran claim, "Like the Mississippi, [English] keeps forging new channels and abandoning old ones" (1).

MLA
Papers

In English and other humanities courses, you may be asked to use the Modern Language Association (MLA) system of citations described in section 33. When writing an MLA paper based on sources, you face three main challenges: (1) supporting a thesis, (2) citing your sources and avoiding plagiarism, and (3) integrating quotations and other source material.

29 Supporting a thesis

Most research assignments ask you to form a thesis, or main idea, and to support that thesis with well-organized evidence.

29a Forming a working thesis

Once you have read a variety of sources and considered your subject from different perspectives, you are ready to form a working thesis—a one-sentence (or occasionally a two-sentence) statement of your central idea. The thesis expresses your informed, reasoned answer to your research question—an answer about which people might disagree. Usually your thesis will appear at the end of the first paragraph (see p. 174).

As you learn more about your subject, your ideas may change, and your working thesis will evolve, too. You can revise your working thesis as you draft.

In a research paper, your thesis will answer the central question that you pose, as in the following examples.

PUBLIC POLICY QUESTION

Should the state government enact laws to regulate healthy eating choices?

POSSIBLE THESIS

State governments have the responsibility to advance health policies and regulate healthy eating choices because of the rise of chronic diseases.

LITERATURE QUESTION

What does Stephen Crane's short story "The Open Boat" reveal about the relationship between humans and nature?

Test your thesis

When drafting and revising a thesis statement, make sure that it's suitable for your writing purpose and that you can successfully develop it with the sources available to you. The following guidelines will help you develop an effective thesis statement.

1 Make sure your thesis answers your research question and takes a position that needs to be argued and supported. Your thesis should not be a fact or a description.

2 Keep the scope of your project in mind. If your thesis is too broad, explore a subtopic of your original topic. If your thesis is too narrow, ask a research question that has more than one answer.

3 Avoid vague words such as *interesting* or *good*. Use concrete language, and make sure your thesis is focused and lets readers know your position.

4 Make sure your thesis stands up to the "So what?" test. Ask yourself why readers should be interested in your essay and should care about your thesis. If your thesis matters to you, your readers are more likely to find your ideas engaging.

POSSIBLE THESIS

In Stephen Crane's gripping tale "The Open Boat," four men lost at sea discover not only that nature is indifferent to their fate but also that their own particular talents make little difference as they struggle for survival.

MEDIA STUDIES QUESTION

How does the shift from print to online news change the way readers engage with the news?

POSSIBLE THESIS

The shift from print to online news provides opportunities for readers to become more engaged with the news, to hold journalists accountable, and to participate as producers, not simply as consumers.

Each of these thesis statements takes a stand on a debatable issue—an issue about which intelligent, well-meaning people might disagree. Each writer needs to convince such people that his or her view is worth taking seriously.

29b Organizing your ideas

The body of your paper will consist of evidence in support of your thesis. To get started, list your key points in the order you think you'll write about them, as student writer Sophie Harba did in this informal outline.

- Debates about the government's role in regulating food have a long history in the United States.

- Some experts argue that we should focus on the dangers of unhealthy eating habits and on preventing chronic diseases linked to diet.

- But food regulations are not a popular solution because many Americans object to government restrictions on personal choice.

- Food regulations designed to prevent chronic disease don't ask Americans to give up their freedom; they ask Americans to see health as a matter of public good.

After you have written a rough draft, a more formal outline can help you test and fine-tune the organization of your argument.

29c Using sources to inform and support your argument

The source materials you have gathered will help you develop and support your argument. Sources can play several different roles:

Providing background information or context   You can describe a study or offer a statistic to help readers grasp the significance of your topic or understand generalizations about it.

Explaining terms or concepts   Explain words, phrases, or ideas that might be unfamiliar to your readers. Quoting or paraphrasing a source can help you define terms and concepts in accessible language.

Supporting your claims   Back up your assertions with facts, examples, and other evidence from your research.

Lending authority to your argument   Expert opinion can give weight to your argument. But don't rely on experts to make your argument for you. Construct your argument in your own words and cite authorities in the field to support your position.

Anticipating and countering objections   Do not ignore sources that seem to contradict your position or that offer arguments different from your own. Instead, use them to give voice to opposing points of view and to state potential objections to your argument before you counter them.

29d Getting feedback

Once you have developed a thesis, identified useful sources, and begun drafting your paper, seek out a classmate or a writing center consultant to provide feedback on your work in progress. Feedback gives you perspective on what's working and what's not working in your draft and keeps the expectations of your readers in mind.

To help your reviewer respond with useful comments, provide a copy of the assignment and, if possible, copies of any sources you used to write your draft. You might also share your purpose for writing, why your topic matters to you, and what you hope

---

Getting feedback on a draft

Focus

- Is the thesis stated clearly? Can readers easily identify it? (29a, 29b)
- Do all major points support the thesis? (29c)

Organization

- Can readers easily follow the structure? (29b)
- Do topic sentences signal new ideas?
- Do any ideas seem misplaced or disconnected from the rest of the draft?

Use of sources

- Is the role of each source (as background, support, authority, counterargument) clear? Do your sources serve a variety of purposes? (29c)
- Do you clearly introduce sources with signal phrases? (31c)
- Do you analyze sources in your own words and connect them to your own ideas? (31d)
- Are your own ideas easy to identify and understand, with or without your sources?
- Is there language that doesn't sound like you and perhaps needs quotation marks or a citation?

---

to accomplish in your draft. To encourage relevant, focused feedback, tell your reviewer about any specific questions or concerns you have. The chart above offers some guiding questions you and your reader can use to review your writing.

30 Avoiding plagiarism

In a research paper, you draw on the work of other writers, and you must document their contributions by citing your sources. When you acknowledge your sources, you avoid plagiarism, a serious academic offense. In general, these three acts are considered plagiarism: (1) failing to cite quotations and borrowed ideas, (2) failing to enclose borrowed language in quotation marks, and (3) failing to put summaries and paraphrases in your own words.

30a Citing quotations and borrowed ideas

When you cite sources, you give credit to writers from whom you've borrowed words and ideas. You also let your readers know where your information comes from so that they can find and read the original sources. You must cite anything you borrow from a source, including direct quotations; statistics and other specific facts; visuals such as cartoons, graphs, and diagrams; and any ideas you present in a summary or a paraphrase.

The only exception is common knowledge—information your readers likely already know or could easily find in general sources. When you have seen information repeatedly in your reading, you don't need to cite it. However, when information has appeared in only one or two sources, when it is highly specific (as with statistics), or when it is controversial, you should cite the source. If you're not sure whether you need to cite something, check with your instructor.

30b Using the MLA citation system to lead readers to your sources

A writer might express an argument in a blog post, develop that argument in a TED talk, and publish it as an article in a print journal; that article might then appear in a database. Each location might offer a slightly different experience of the author's language and ideas, and those differences can affect how you and your readers think about the source. It's important to help readers identify the specific version you're referencing in your work.

To help readers find the exact source you used, MLA recommends a system of in-text citations paired with a list of all the sources you've cited. Here, briefly, is how the MLA citation system usually works:

1. The source is introduced by a signal phrase that names its author.
2. The material being cited is followed by a page number in parentheses (unless the source is unpaginated).
3. At the end of the paper, a list of works cited, arranged alphabetically by authors' last names (or by titles for works with no authors), gives complete publication information for the source.

IN-TEXT CITATION

Bioethicist David Resnik emphasizes that such policies "open the door to excessive government control over food, which could restrict dietary choices, interfere with cultural, ethnic, and religious traditions, and exacerbate socioeconomic inequalities" (31).

ENTRY IN THE LIST OF WORKS CITED

Resnik, David. "Trans Fat Bans and Human Freedom." *American Journal of Bioethics*, vol. 10, no. 3, Mar. 2010, pp. 27-32.

NOTE: This basic MLA format varies for different types of sources. For a detailed discussion and other models, see 33.

30c Enclosing borrowed language in quotation marks

To indicate that you are using a source's exact phrases or sentences, you must enclose them in quotation marks unless they have been set off from the text by indenting (see p. 121). To omit the quotation marks is to claim—falsely—that the language is your own. Such an omission is plagiarism even if you have cited the source.

ORIGINAL SOURCE

Although these policies may have a positive impact on human health, they open the door to excessive government control over food, which could restrict dietary choices, interfere with cultural, ethnic, and religious traditions, and exacerbate socioeconomic inequalities.

—David Resnik, "Trans Fat Bans and Human Freedom," p. 31

PLAGIARISM

Bioethicist David Resnik points out that policies to ban trans fats may protect human health, but they open the door to excessive government control over food, which might limit available food options and interfere with cultural, ethnic, and religious traditions (31).

BORROWED LANGUAGE IN QUOTATION MARKS

Bioethicist David Resnik points out that policies to ban trans fats may protect human health, but "they open the door to excessive government control over food," which might limit available food options and "interfere with cultural, ethnic, and religious traditions" (31).

30d Putting summaries and paraphrases in your own words

A summary condenses information from a source; a paraphrase conveys the information using roughly the same number of words as the original source. When you summarize or paraphrase, you must name the source and restate the source's meaning in your own words. Half-copying the author's sentences by using the author's phrases in your own sentences without quotation marks or by plugging synonyms into the author's sentence structure is a form of plagiarism.

The below paraphrase is plagiarized—even though the source is cited—because too much of its language is borrowed from the original. The highlighted strings of words have been copied exactly (without quotation marks). In addition, the writer has echoed the sentence structure of the source, merely substituting some synonyms (*interfere with* for *constitute paternalistic intervention into* and *decrease the feeling of* for *enfeeble the notion of*).

ORIGINAL SOURCE

[A]ntiobesity laws encounter strong opposition from some quarters on the grounds that they constitute paternalistic intervention into lifestyle choices and enfeeble the notion of personal responsibility. Such arguments echo those made in the early days of tobacco regulation.

— Michelle M. Mello et al., "Obesity—the New Frontier of Public Health Law," p. 2602

PLAGIARISM: UNACCEPTABLE BORROWING

Health policy experts Mello and others argue that antiobesity laws encounter strong opposition from some people because they interfere with lifestyle choices and decrease the feeling of personal responsibility. These arguments mirror those made in the early days of tobacco regulation (2602).

HOW TO Be a responsible research writer

Using good citation habits is the best way to demonstrate that you are a responsible researcher. Keeping the following tips in mind will help you avoid plagiarizing sources.

1 Cite your sources as you write drafts. Don't wait until your final draft is complete to include in-text citations.

2 Check quotations, summaries, and paraphrases against the source to make sure you're using the source accurately and fairly.

3 Place quotation marks around direct quotations, both in your notes and in your drafts.

4 Use your own language and sentence structure for summaries and paraphrases. Compare your writing against the original passage to protect against unintentional plagiarism.

5 Provide a full citation for each source in your list of works cited. (See pp. 176–77 for sample works cited lists.)

To avoid plagiarizing an author's language, resist the temptation to look at the source while you are summarizing or paraphrasing. After you've restated the author's ideas in your own words, return to the source and check that you haven't used the author's language or sentence structure or misrepresented the author's ideas.

ACCEPTABLE PARAPHRASE

As health policy experts Mello and others point out, opposition to food and beverage regulation is similar to the opposition to early tobacco legislation: the public views the issue as one of personal responsibility rather than one requiring government intervention (2602).

31 Integrating sources

Quotations, summaries, paraphrases, and facts will help you develop your argument, but they cannot speak for you. You can use several strategies to integrate information from sources into your paper while maintaining your own voice.

31a Summarizing and paraphrasing effectively

Summarizing When you summarize a source, you express another writer's ideas in your own words, condensing the author's key points and using fewer words than the author.

WHEN TO SUMMARIZE

- When a passage is lengthy and you want to condense a chapter to a short paragraph or a paragraph to a single sentence
- When you want to state the source's main ideas simply and briefly in your own words
- When you want to compare arguments or ideas from various sources
- When you want to provide readers with an understanding of the source's argument before you respond to it or launch your own argument

Paraphrasing When you paraphrase, you express an author's ideas in your own words, using approximately the same number of words and details as in the source.

WHEN TO PARAPHRASE

- When the ideas and information are important but the author's exact words are not needed for accuracy or emphasis
- When you want to restate the source's ideas in your own words
- When you need to simplify and explain a technical or complicated source
- When you need to reorder a source's ideas

31b Using quotations effectively

When you quote a source, you borrow some of the author's exact words and enclose them in quotation marks. Quotation marks show your readers that both the idea and the words belong to the author.

WHEN TO USE QUOTATIONS

- When language is especially vivid or expressive
- When exact wording is needed for technical accuracy
- When it is important to let the debaters of an issue explain their positions in their own words
- When the words of an authority lend weight to an argument
- When the language of a source is the topic of your discussion

Limiting your use of quotations Keep the emphasis on your own ideas. It is not always necessary to quote full sentences from a source. Often you can integrate words or phrases from a source into your own sentence structure.

Resnik acknowledges that his argument relies on "slippery slope" thinking, but he insists that "social and political pressures" regarding food regulations make his concerns valid (31).

Using the ellipsis mark   To condense a quoted passage, you can use the ellipsis mark (three periods, with spaces between) to indicate that you have omitted words. What remains must be grammatically complete.

In Mississippi, legislators passed "a ban on bans—a law that forbids . . . local restrictions on food or drink" (Conly A23).

The writer has omitted from the source the words *municipalities to place* before *local restrictions* to condense the quoted material.

If you want to omit one or more full sentences, use a period before the three ellipsis dots.

Legal scholars Gostin and Gostin argue that "individuals have limited willpower to defer immediate gratification for longer-term health benefits. . . . A person understands that high-fat foods or a sedentary lifestyle will cause adverse health effects, or that excessive spending or gambling will cause financial hardship, but it is not always easy to refrain" (217).

Ordinarily, do not use an ellipsis mark at the beginning or at the end of a quotation. Your readers will understand that the quoted material comes from a longer passage. The only exception occurs when you have dropped words at the end of the final quoted sentence. In such cases, put three ellipsis dots before the closing quotation mark and the parenthetical reference.

USING SOURCES RESPONSIBLY: Make sure that omissions and ellipsis marks do not distort the meaning of your source.

Using brackets   Brackets allow you to insert your own words into quoted material to clarify a confusing reference or to keep a sentence grammatical in your context.

Neergaard and Agiesta argue that "a new poll finds people are split on how much the government should do to help [find solutions to the national health crisis]—and most draw the line at attempts to force healthier eating."

To indicate an error in a quotation, such as a misspelling, insert [sic], including the brackets, right after the error.

Setting off long quotations   When you quote more than four typed lines of prose or more than three lines of poetry, set off the quotation by indenting it one-half inch from the left margin.

Long quotations should be introduced by an informative sentence, usually followed by a colon. Quotation marks are unnecessary because the indented format tells readers that the passage is taken word-for-word from the source.

> In response to critics who claim that laws aimed at stopping us from eating whatever we want are an assault on our freedom of choice, Conly offers a persuasive counterargument:
>
> [L]aws aren't designed for each one of us individually. Some of us can drive safely at 90 miles per hour, but we're bound by the same laws as the people who can't, because individual speeding laws aren't practical. Giving up a little liberty is something we agree to when we agree to live in a democratic society that is governed by laws. (A23)

At the end of an indented quotation, the parenthetical citation goes outside the final mark of punctuation.

31c Using signal phrases to integrate sources

Whenever you include a paraphrase, summary, or direct quotation of another writer's work in your paper, prepare your readers for it with introductory words called a *signal phrase*. A signal phrase usually names the author of the source and provides some context for the source material. (See the chart on p. 124 for a list of verbs commonly used in signal phrases.)

Marking boundaries   Readers need to move smoothly from your words to the words of a source. Avoid dropping a quotation into the text without warning. Provide a clear signal phrase, including at least the author's name, to indicate the boundary between your words and the source's words.

DROPPED QUOTATION

Laws designed to prevent chronic disease by promoting healthier food and beverage consumption also have potential

economic benefits. "[A] 1% reduction in the intake of saturated
fat across the population would prevent more than 30,000 cases
of coronary heart disease annually and would save more than a
billion dollars in health care costs" (Nestle 7).

QUOTATION WITH SIGNAL PHRASE

Laws designed to prevent chronic disease by promoting
healthier food and beverage consumption also have potential
economic benefits. Marion Nestle, New York University
professor of nutrition and public health, notes that "a 1%
reduction in the intake of saturated fat across the population
would prevent more than 30,000 cases of coronary heart
disease annually and would save more than a billion dollars in
health care costs" (7).

Establishing authority   The first time you mention a
source, include in the signal phrase the author's title,
credentials, or experience to help your readers recog-
nize the source's authority and your own credibility
as a responsible researcher who has located reliable
sources.

SOURCE WITH NO CREDENTIALS

Michael Pollan notes that "[t]he Centers for Disease Control
estimates that fully three quarters of US health care spending
goes to treat chronic diseases, most of which are preventable
and linked to diet: heart disease, stroke, type 2 diabetes, and
at least a third of all cancers."

SOURCE WITH CREDENTIALS

Journalist Michael Pollan, who has written extensively about
Americans' unhealthy eating habits, notes that "[t]he Centers
for Disease Control estimates that fully three quarters of US
health care spending goes to treat chronic diseases, most of
which are preventable and linked to diet: heart disease, stroke,
type 2 diabetes, and at least a third of all cancers."

Introducing summaries and paraphrases Introduce most summaries and paraphrases with a signal phrase that names the author and places the material in the context of your argument. Readers will then understand that everything between the signal phrase and the parenthetical citation summarizes or paraphrases the cited source.

Without the signal phrase (highlighted) in the following example, readers might think that only the quotation at the end is being cited, when in fact the whole paragraph is based on the source.

To improve public health, advocates such as Bowdoin College philosophy professor Sarah Conly contend that it is the government's duty to prevent people from making harmful choices, whenever feasible and whenever public benefits outweigh the costs. In response to critics who claim that laws aimed at stopping us from eating whatever we want are an assault on our freedom of choice, Conly asserts that "laws aren't designed for each one of us individually" (A23).

Sometimes a summary or a paraphrase does not require a signal phrase. When the context makes clear where the cited material begins, you may omit the signal phrase and include the author's last name in parentheses.

Integrating statistics and other facts When you cite a statistic or another specific fact, a signal phrase is often not necessary. Readers usually will understand that the citation refers to the statistic or fact (not the whole paragraph.)

Seventy-five percent of Americans are opposed to laws that restrict or put limitations on access to unhealthy foods (Neergaard and Agiesta).

Putting source material in context Readers should not have to guess why source material appears in your paper. A signal phrase can help you connect your own ideas with those of another writer by clarifying how the source will contribute to your paper.

Using signal phrases in MLA papers

To avoid monotony, try to vary both the language and the placement of your signal phrases.

Model signal phrases

According to Lorine Goodwin, a food historian, "..."

As journalist Michael Pollan has noted, "..."

The United States Department of Health and Human Services reports, "..."

As health policy experts Mello and others point out, "..."

"...," writes Bowdoin College philosophy professor Sarah Conly. "..."

Bioethicist David Resnik offers a persuasive argument: "..."

Verbs in signal phrases

Are you providing background, explaining a concept, supporting a claim, lending authority, or refuting a belief? Choose a verb that is appropriate for the way you are using the source.

acknowledges	contends	insists
adds	declares	notes
admits	denies	observes
agrees	describes	points out
argues	disputes	refutes
asserts	emphasizes	rejects
believes	endorses	reports
claims	grants	responds
compares	illustrates	suggests
confirms	implies	writes

NOTE: In MLA style, use the present tense or present perfect tense (*argues* or *has argued*) to introduce source material unless you include a date or other marker that specifies the time of the original author's writing.

If you use another writer's words, you must explain how they relate to your argument. Quotations don't speak for themselves; you must support them by creating a context for readers. Sandwich each quotation between sentences of your own: Introduce the quotation with a signal phrase, and follow it with interpretive comments that link the quotation to your paper's argument. (See also 31d.)

QUOTATION WITH EFFECTIVE CONTEXT (QUOTATION SANDWICH)

In response to critics who claim that laws aimed at stopping us from eating whatever we want are an assault on our freedom of choice, Conly offers a persuasive counterargument:

> [L]aws aren't designed for each one of us individually.
> Some of us can drive safely at 90 miles per hour, but we're
> bound by the same laws as the people who can't, because
> individual speeding laws aren't practical. Giving up a little
> liberty is something we agree to when we agree to live in
> a democratic society that is governed by laws. (A23)

As Conly suggests, we need to change our either/or thinking (either we have complete freedom of choice *or* we have government regulations and lose our freedom) and instead see health as a matter of public good, not individual liberty.

31d Synthesizing sources

When you synthesize multiple sources in a research paper, you create a conversation about your research topic. You show readers how the ideas of one source relate to those of another by connecting and analyzing the ideas in the context of your argument. Keep the emphasis on your own writing. The thread of your argument should be easy to identify and to understand, with or without your sources.

In the sample synthesis on pages 126–27, Sophie Harba uses her own analyses to shape the conversation among her sources. She does not simply string quotations together or allow sources to overwhelm her writing. In her final sentence, she delivers a key point of her own, supported by her sources.

SAMPLE SYNTHESIS

1   Why is the public largely resistant to laws   Student
that would limit unhealthy choices or penalize   writer
those choices with so-called fat taxes? Many
consumers and civil rights advocates find such
laws to be an unreasonable restriction on

2   individual freedom of choice. As health policy
experts Mello and others point out, opposition   Source 1
to food and beverage regulation is similar to the
opposition to early tobacco legislation: the public
views the issue as one of personal responsibility
rather than one requiring government intervention

3   (2602). In other words, if a person eats unhealthy   Student
food and becomes ill as a result, that is his or   writer
her choice. But those who favor legislation claim
that freedom of choice is a myth because of the
strong influence of food and beverage industry

4   marketing on consumers' dietary habits. According
to one nonprofit health advocacy group, food and   Source 2
beverage companies spend roughly two billion
dollars per year marketing directly to children.
As a result, kids see about four thousand ads per
year encouraging them to consume unhealthy
food and drinks ("Facts"). As was the case with   Student
antismoking laws passed in recent decades, taxes   writer
and legal restrictions on junk food sales could
help to counter the strong marketing messages
that promote unhealthy products.

The United States has a history of state and
local public health laws that have successfully
promoted a particular behavior by punishing an
undesirable behavior. The decline in tobacco use as
a result of antismoking taxes and laws is perhaps
the most obvious example. Another example is
legislation requiring the use of seat belts, which
have significantly reduced fatalities in car crashes.

5   One government agency reports that seat belt use   Source 3
saved an average of more than fourteen thousand
lives per year in the United States between 2000

and 2010 (United States, Dept. of Transportation,
Natl. Highway Traffic Safety Administration 231).

Perhaps seat belt laws have public support because   Student
the cost of wearing a seat belt is small, especially   writer
when compared with the benefit of saving fourteen
thousand lives per year.

1 Student writer Sophie Harba sets up her synthesis with a question.

2 A signal phrase indicates how the source contributes to Harba's argument and shows that the idea that follows is not her own.

3 Harba interprets a paraphrased source.

4 Harba uses a source to support her counterargument.

5 Harba uses a statistic to extend the argument and follows the source with a closing thought of her own.

32 Integrating literary quotations

When you are writing about literary works, the advice in section 31 about integrating quotations generally applies. This section provides guidance for situations that are unique to literary quotations. Parenthetical citations at the ends of examples are written in MLA style (see pp. 138–39 for specific guidelines on citing literary works).

32a Introducing quotations from literary works

When writing about a single work of literature, you do not need to include the author's name each time you quote from the work. Mention the author's name in the introduction to your paper; then refer, as appropriate, to the narrator of a story, the speaker of a poem, or the characters in a play. Do not confuse the author of the work with the narrator, speaker, or characters.

INAPPROPRIATE

Poet Andrew Marvell describes his fear of death like this: "But at my back I always hear / Time's wingèd chariot hurrying near" (21-22).

APPROPRIATE

Addressing his beloved in an attempt to win her sexual favors, the speaker of the poem argues that death gives them no time to waste: "But at my back I always hear / Time's wingèd chariot hurrying near" (21-22).

For examples of quoted dialogue from a short story, see page 175.

32b Avoiding shifts in tense

Because it is conventional to write about literature in the present tense (see p. 29) and because literary works often use other tenses, you will need to exercise some care when weaving quotations into your own text. A first-draft attempt may result in an awkward shift, as it did for one student who was writing about Nadine Gordimer's short story "Friday's Footprint."

TENSE SHIFT

When Rita sees Johnny's relaxed attitude, "she blushed, like a wave of illness" (159).

To avoid the distracting shift from present tense (*sees*) to past tense (*blushed*), the writer decided to paraphrase the reference to Rita's blushing and reduce the length of the quotation.

REVISED

When Rita sees Johnny's relaxed attitude, she is overcome with embarrassment, "like a wave of illness" (159).

The writer could have changed the quotation to the present tense, using brackets to indicate the change: *When Rita sees Johnny's relaxed attitude, "she blushe[s], like a wave of illness" (159).* (See also p. 120 for the use of brackets.)

32c Formatting and citing literary passages

MLA guidelines for formatting and citing quotations differ somewhat for short stories or novels, poems, and plays.

Short stories or novels If a quotation from a short story or a novel takes up four or fewer typed lines in your paper, put it in quotation marks and run it into the text of your essay. Include a page number in parentheses after the quotation.

The narrator of Eudora Welty's "Why I Live at the P.O.," known to us only as "Sister," makes many catty remarks about her enemies. For example, she calls Mr. Whitaker "this photographer with the pop-eyes" (46).

If a quotation from a short story or a novel is five typed lines or longer in your paper, set the quotation off from the text by indenting it one-half inch from the left margin; do not use quotation marks. (See also p. 121.) Put the page number in parentheses after the final mark of punctuation.

Sister's tale begins with "I," and she makes every event revolve around herself, even her sister's marriage:

> I was getting along fine with Mama, Papa-Daddy,
> and Uncle Rondo until my sister Stella-Rondo just
> separated from her husband and came back home again.
> Mr. Whitaker! Of course I went with Mr. Whitaker first,
> when he first appeared here in China Grove, taking "Pose
> Yourself" photos, and Stella-Rondo broke us up. (46)

Poems Enclose quotations of three or fewer lines of poetry in quotation marks within your text, and indicate line breaks with a slash with a space on each side. (Indicate a break between stanzas with a double slash.) Include line numbers in parentheses at the end of the quotation. For the first reference in the paper, use the word "lines." Thereafter, use just numbers.

The opening of Lewis Carroll's "The Aged Aged Man" strikes a conversational tone: "I'll tell thee everything I can; / There's little to relate" (lines 1-2).

When you quote four or more lines of poetry, set the quotation off from the text by indenting it one-half inch and omit the quotation marks. Put the line numbers in parentheses after the final mark of punctuation.

In the second stanza of his poem "London," William Blake argues that the city's inhabitants are bound to their plight by urban regulations and their inability to see beyond their own suffering:

> In every cry of every Man,
>
> In every Infants cry of fear,
>
> In every voice: in every ban,
>
> The mind-forg'd manacles I hear (lines 5-8)

Plays   If a quotation from a play takes up four or fewer typed lines in your paper and is spoken by only one character, put quotation marks around it and run it into the text of your paper. Whenever possible, include the act number, scene number, and line numbers in parentheses at the end of the quotation. Separate the numbers with periods and use arabic numerals unless your instructor prefers roman numerals.

Two attendants silently watch as the sleepwalking Lady Macbeth subconsciously struggles with her guilt: "Here's the smell of the blood still. All the perfumes of Arabia will not sweeten this little hand" (5.1.50-51).

33 MLA documentation style

In English and other humanities classes, you may be asked to use the MLA (Modern Language Association) system for documenting sources, which is set forth in the *MLA Handbook*, 8th edition (MLA, 2016).

MLA recommends in-text citations (33a) that refer readers to a list of works cited at the end of the paper (33b).

33a MLA in-text citations

MLA in-text citations are made with a combination of signal phrases and parenthetical references. A signal phrase introduces information taken from a source (a quotation, summary, paraphrase, or fact); usually the signal phrase includes the author's name. (See p. 124 about verbs in signal phrases.) The parenthetical reference comes after the cited material, often at the end of the sentence. It includes at least a page number (except for unpaginated sources). In the models in 33a, the elements of the in-text citation are highlighted in blue.

IN-TEXT CITATION

Resnik acknowledges that his argument relies on "slippery slope" thinking, but he insists that "social and political pressures" regarding food regulation make his concerns valid (31).

Readers can look up the author's last name in the alphabetized list of works cited, where they will learn the work's title and other publication information. If readers decide to consult the source, the page number will take them straight to the cited passage.

Directory to MLA in-text citation models

General guidelines for signal phrases and page numbers   Items 1–5 explain how the MLA system usually works for all sources—in print, on the Web, in other media, and with or without authors and page numbers. Items 6–27 give variations on the basic guidelines.

● **1. Author named in a signal phrase**   Ordinarily, introduce the material being cited with a signal phrase that includes the author's name.

According to Lorine Goodwin, a food historian, nineteenth-century reformers who sought to purify the food supply were called "fanatics" and "radicals" by critics who argued that consumers should be free to buy and eat what they want (77).

The signal phrase—*According to Lorine Goodwin*—names the author; the parenthetical citation gives the page number of the source in which the quoted words may be found. Notice that the period follows the parenthetical citation.

When a quotation ends with a question mark or an exclamation point, handle the citation like this:

Burgess asks a critical question: "How can we think differently about food labeling?" (51).

● **2. Author named in parentheses**   If you do not give the author's name in a signal phrase, put the last name in parentheses along with the page number (if the source has one). Use no punctuation between the name and the page number: (Moran 136).

According to a nationwide poll, 75% of Americans are opposed to laws that restrict or put limitations on access to unhealthy foods (Neergaard and Agiesta).

● **3. Author unknown**   If a source has no author, the works cited entry will begin with the title. In your in-text citation, either use the complete title in a signal phrase or use a shortened title in parentheses. Titles of books and other long works are italicized; titles of articles and other short works are put in quotation marks (see also p. 171).

As a result, kids see about four thousand ads per year encouraging them to eat unhealthy food and drinks ("Facts").

NOTE: If the author is a corporation or a government agency, see items 8 and 17 on pages 134 and 136.

● **4. Page number unknown** Do not include the page number if a work lacks page numbers, as is the case with many Web sources. Do not use page numbers from a printout from a Web site. (When the pages of a Web source are stable, as in PDF files, supply a page number in your in-text citation.)

Michael Pollan points out that "cheap food" actually has "significant costs—to the environment, to public health, to the public purse, even to the culture."

If a source has numbered paragraphs or sections, use "par." (or "pars.") or "sec." (or "secs.") in the parentheses: (Smith, par. 4). Do not use numbers if they are not in the source. A comma follows the author's name.

● **5. One-page source** It is a good idea to include the page number for a one-page source because without it readers may not know where your citation ends or, worse, may not realize that you have provided a citation at all.

Sarah Conly uses John Stuart Mill's "harm principle" to argue that citizens need their government to intervene to prevent them from taking harmful actions—such as driving too fast or buying unhealthy foods—out of ignorance of the harm they can do (A23). But government intervention may overstep in the case of food choices.

Variations on the general guidelines This section describes the MLA guidelines for handling a variety of situations not covered in items 1–5.

● **6. Two authors** Name the authors in a signal phrase, as in the following example, or include their last names in the parenthetical reference: (Gostin and Gostin 214).

As legal scholars Gostin and Gostin explain, "[I]nterventions that do not pose a truly significant burden on individual liberty" are justified if they "go a long way towards safeguarding the health and well-being of the populace" (214).

● **7. Three or more authors** In a parenthetical citation, give the first author's name followed by "et al." (Latin for "and others"). In a signal phrase, give the first author's name followed by "and others."

Only after results were reviewed by an independent panel did the researchers publish their findings (Blaine et al. 35).

Researchers Blaine and others note that clinical trial results were reviewed by an independent panel (35).

● **8. Organization as author**   When the author is a corporation or an organization, name that author either in the signal phrase or in the parentheses. For a government agency as author, see item 17 on page 136.

The American Diabetes Association estimates that the cost of diagnosed diabetes in the United States in 2012 was $245 billion.

In the list of works cited, the American Diabetes Association is treated as the author and alphabetized under *A*. When you give the organization name in the text, spell out the name; when you use it in parentheses, abbreviate common words in the name: "Assn.," "Dept.," "Natl.," "Soc.," and so on.

The cost of diagnosed diabetes in the United States in 2012 was estimated at $245 billion (Amer. Diabetes Assn.).

● **9. Authors with the same last name**   Include the author's first name in the signal phrase or first initial in parentheses.

One approach to the problem is to introduce nutrition literacy at the K-5 level in public schools (E. Chen 15).

● **10. Two or more works by the same author**   Mention the title of the work in the signal phrase or include a shortened version of the title in parentheses.

The American Diabetes Association tracks trends in diabetes across age groups. In 2012, more than 200,000 children and adolescents had diabetes ("Fast"). Because of an expected dramatic increase in diabetes in young people over the next forty years, the association encourages "strategies for implementing childhood obesity prevention programs and primary prevention programs for youth at risk of developing type 2 diabetes" ("Number").

Titles of articles and other short works are placed in quotation marks; titles of books and other long works are italicized. (See also p. 171.)

● **11. Two or more works in one citation**   List the authors (or titles) in alphabetical order and separate them with semicolons.

The prevalence of early-onset type 2 diabetes has been well documented (Finn 68; Sharma 2037; Whitaker 118).

It may be less distracting to use an information note for multiple citations (see 33c).

● **12. Repeated citations from the same source**   When you are writing about a single work, you may mention the author's name at the beginning of your paper and then include just the page numbers in your parenthetical citations. (See also 32a.)

    In Susan Glaspell's short story "A Jury of Her Peers," two women accompany their husbands and a county attorney to an isolated house where a farmer named John Wright has been choked to death. The chief suspect is Wright's wife, Minnie, who is in jail awaiting trial. The sheriff's wife, Mrs. Peters, has come along to gather some items for Minnie, and Mrs. Hale has joined her. Initially, Mrs. Hale sympathizes with Minnie and objects to the male investigators "snoopin' round and criticizin'" her kitchen (249). Mrs. Peters shows respect for the law, saying that the men are doing "no more than their duty" (249).

● **13. Encyclopedia or dictionary entry**   When an encyclopedia or a dictionary entry does not have an author, it will be alphabetized in the list of works cited under the word or entry that you consulted (see item 24 on p. 155). Either in your text or in parentheses, mention the word or entry and give the page number on which it appears.

The word *crocodile* has a complex etymology ("Crocodile" 139).

● **14. Multivolume work**   Indicate in parentheses the volume you are referring to, followed by a colon and the page number.

In his studies of gifted children, Terman describes a pattern of accelerated language acquisition (2: 279).

● **15. Entire work**   Use the author's name in a signal phrase or in parentheses. There is no need to use a page number.

Pollan explores the issues surrounding food production and consumption from a political angle.

● **16. Selection in an anthology or a collection**   Put the name of the author of the selection (not the editor of the anthology) in the signal phrase or the parentheses.

In "Love Is a Fallacy," the narrator's logical teachings disintegrate when Polly declares that she should date Petey because "[h]e's got a raccoon coat" (Shulman 391).

In the list of works cited, the work is alphabetized under *Shulman*, the author of the story, not under the name of the editor of the anthology. (See item 30 on p. 157.)

● **17. Government document**   When a government agency is the author, you will alphabetize it in the list of works cited under the name of the government, such as United States or Great Britain (see item 60 on p. 168). For this reason, you must name the government as well as the agency in your in-text citation.

One government agency reports that seat belt use saved an average of more than fourteen thousand lives per year in the United States between 2000 and 2010 (United States, Dept. of Transportation, Natl. Highway Traffic Safety Administration 231).

● **18. Historical document**   For a historical document, such as the Constitution of the United States or the Canadian Charter of Rights and Freedoms, provide the document title, neither italicized nor in quotation marks, along with relevant article and section numbers. In parenthetical citations, use common abbreviations such as "art." and "sec."

While the Constitution provides for the formation of new states (art. 4, sec. 3), it does not explicitly allow or prohibit the secession of states.

Cite other historical documents as you would any other work, by the first element in the works cited entry (see item 62 on p. 168).

● **19. Legal source**   For a legislative act (law) or court case, name the act or case either in a signal phrase or in parentheses. Italicize the names of cases but not the names of acts. (See also items 63 and 64 on p. 168.)

The Jones Act of 1917 granted US citizenship to Puerto Ricans.

In 1857, Chief Justice Roger B. Taney declared in *Dred Scott v. Sandford* that blacks, whether enslaved or free, could not be citizens of the United States.

● **20. Visual such as a table, a chart, or another graphic** To cite a visual that has a figure number in the source, use the abbreviation "fig." and the number in place of a page number in your parenthetical citation: (Manning, fig. 4). If you refer to the figure in your text, spell out the word "figure."

To cite a visual that does not have a figure number in a print source, use the visual's title or a description in your text and cite the author and page number as for any other source.

For a visual not in a print source, identify the visual in your text and then in parentheses use the first element in the works cited entry: the artist's or photographer's name or the title of the work. (See items 55–59 on pp. 166–67.)

Photographs such as *Woman Aircraft Worker* (Bransby) and *Women Welders* (Parks) demonstrate the US government's attempt to document the contributions of women during World War II.

● **21. Personal communication and social media** Cite personal letters, personal interviews, e-mail messages, and social media posts by the name listed in the works cited entry, as you would for any other source. Identify the type of source in your text if you feel it is necessary for clarity. (See items 23 and 65–69 in section 33b.)

● **22. Web source** Your in-text citation for a source from the Web should follow the same guidelines as for other sources. If the source lacks page numbers but has numbered paragraphs, sections, or divisions, use those numbers with the appropriate abbreviation in your parenthetical citation: "par.," "sec.," "ch.," "pt." Do not add such numbers if the source itself does not use them; simply give the author or title in your in-text citation.

Julian Hawthorne points out profound differences between his father and Ralph Waldo Emerson but concludes that "together they met the needs of nearly all that is worthy in human nature" (ch. 4).

● **23. Indirect source (source quoted in another source)**
When a writer's or a speaker's quoted words appear in a source written by someone else, begin the parenthetical citation with the abbreviation "qtd. in." (See also item 12 on p. 148.)

Peter Townson points out that social media in the Middle East are "kind of the preferred way for people to get news, because they know there's no self-censorship involved" (qtd. in Belmaker).

Literary works and sacred texts Literary works and sacred texts are usually available in a variety of editions. Your list of works cited will specify which edition you are using. When possible, give enough information—such as book parts, play divisions, or line numbers—so that readers can locate the cited passage in any edition of the work.

● **24. Literary work without parts or line numbers** Most short stories and many novels and plays do not have parts or line numbers. In such cases, simply cite the page number.

At the end of Kate Chopin's "The Story of an Hour," Mrs. Mallard drops dead upon learning that her husband is alive. In the final irony of the story, doctors report that she has died of a "joy that kills" (25).

● **25. Verse play or poem** For verse plays, give act, scene, and line numbers that can be located in any edition of the work. Use arabic numerals and separate the numbers with periods.

In Shakespeare's *King Lear*, Gloucester, blinded for suspected treason, learns a profound lesson from his tragic experience: "A man may see how this world goes / with no eyes" (4.2.148-49).

For a poem, cite the part, stanza, and line numbers, if it has them, separated with periods.

The Green Knight claims to approach King Arthur's court "because the praise of you, prince, is puffed so high, / And your manor and your men are considered so magnificent" (1.12.258-59).

For a poem that is not divided into numbered parts or stanzas, use line numbers. For a first reference, use the word "lines": (lines 5-8). Thereafter use just the numbers: (12-13). (See also 32c.)

● **26. Novel with numbered divisions** When a novel has numbered divisions, put the page number first, followed by a semicolon, and then the book, part, or chapter in which the passage may be found. Use abbreviations such as "bk.," "pt.," and "ch."

One of Kingsolver's narrators, teenager Rachel, complains that being forced to live in the Congo with her missionary family is "a sheer tapestry of justice" because her chances of finding a boyfriend are "dull and void" (117; bk. 2, ch. 10).

● **27. Sacred text** When citing a sacred text such as the Bible or the Qur'an, name the edition you are using in your works cited entry (see item 34 on p. 160). In your parenthetical citation, give the book, chapter, and verse (or their equivalent), separated with periods. Common abbreviations for books of the Bible are acceptable.

Consider the words of Solomon: "If your enemy is hungry, give him bread to eat; and if he is thirsty, give him water to drink" (*Oxford Annotated Bible*, Prov. 25.21).

The title of a sacred work is italicized when it refers to a specific edition of the work, as in the preceding example. If you refer to the book in a general sense in your text, neither italicize the title nor put it in quotation marks.

The Bible and the Qur'an provide allegories that help readers understand how to lead a moral life.

33b MLA list of works cited

The elements you will need for the works cited list will differ slightly for some sources, but the main principles apply to all sources: You should identify an author, a creator, or a producer whenever possible; give a title; and provide the date on which the source was produced. Some sources will require page numbers; some will require a publisher or sponsor; and some will require other identifying information.

▶ Directory to MLA works cited models, **page 140**
▶ General guidelines for the works cited list, **page 142**

Directory to MLA works cited models

General guidelines for the works cited list

In the list of works cited, include only sources that you have quoted, summarized, or paraphrased in your paper.

Organization of the list

The elements, or pieces of information, needed for a works cited entry are the following:

- The author (if a work has one)
- The title
- The title of the larger work in which the source is located, if any—a database, a journal, a website, and so on (MLA calls this a "container")
- As much of the following information as is available about the source and the container, listed in this order:

  Editor, translator, director, performer

  Version or edition

  Volume and issue numbers

  Publisher

  Date of publication

  Location of the source: page numbers, DOI, URL, and so on

Not all sources will require every element. See specific models in this section for more details.

Authors

- Arrange the works cited list alphabetically by authors' last names or by titles for works with no authors.
- For the first author, place the last name first, a comma, and the first name. Put a second author's name in normal order. For three or more authors, use "et al." after the first author's name.
- Spell out "editor," "translator," "edited by," and so on.

Titles

- In titles of works, capitalize all words except articles (*a, an, the*), prepositions, coordinating conjunctions, and the *to* in infinitives—unless the word is first or last in the title or subtitle.

- Use quotation marks for titles of articles and other short works. Use single quotation marks around a title of a short work or a quoted term that appears in an article title. Italicize a title or term normally italicized.

- Italicize titles of books and other long works. If the book title contains a title normally italicized, neither italicize the internal title nor place it in quotation marks. If the title within the title is normally put in quotation marks, retain the quotation marks and italicize the entire book title.

Publication information

- Do not give the place of publication for a book publisher.

- Use the complete version of publishers' names. Omit terms such as "Inc." and "Co."; retain terms such as "Books" and "Press." For university publishers, use "U" and "P" for "University" and "Press."

- For a book, take the name of the publisher from the title page (or from the copyright page if it is not on the title page). For a website, the publisher might be at the bottom of a page or on the "About" page.

- If the title of a website and the publisher are the same or similar, use the title of the site but omit the publisher.

Dates

- For a book, give the most recent year on the title page or the copyright page. For a web source, use the copyright date or the most recent update date. Use the complete date as listed in the source.

- Abbreviate all months except May, June, and July and give the date in inverted form: 13 Mar. 2016.

- If a web source has no date, give your date of access at the end of the entry: Accessed 24 Feb. 2016.

- If a book has been republished, give the original publication date after the title if the original date is relevant to your research.

Continued →

Page numbers

- For most articles and other short works, give page numbers when they are available in the source, preceded by "p." (or "pp." for more than one page).

- If an article does not appear on consecutive pages, give the number of the first page followed by a plus sign: 35+.

URLs and DOIs

- Give a permalink or a DOI (digital object identifier) if a source has one.

- If a source does not have a permalink or a DOI, include a URL (omitting the protocol, such as http://).

- If a database provides only a URL that is long and complicated and if your readers are not likely to be able to access it, your instructor may allow you to use the URL for the database home page (such as go.galegroup.com). Check with your instructor.

- For open databases and archives, such as Google Books, give the complete URL for the source.

- If a URL or a DOI must be divided across lines, break it before a period or a hyphen or before or after any other mark of punctuation. Do not add a hyphen.

General guidelines for listing authors The formatting of authors' names in items 1–12 applies to all sources—books, articles, websites—in print, on the web, or in other media. For more models of specific source types, see items 13–69.

● 1. Single author

author: last
name first   title (book)   publisher

Bowker, Gordon. *James Joyce: A New Biography*. Farrar, Straus

          year

and Giroux, 2012.

● 2. Two authors

first author: second author:
last name first   in normal order   title (book)

Gourevitch, Philip, and Errol Morris. *Standard Operating Procedure*.
          publisher   year

Penguin Books, 2008.

● **3. Three or more authors**   Name the first author followed by "et al." (Latin for "and others"). For in-text citations, see item 7 on page 133.

```
                    "et al."
    first author:   for all other
    last name first  authors            title (book)
```
Zumeta, William, et al. *Financing American Higher Education in*
```
                                    publisher          year
```
   the Era of Globalization. Harvard Education Press, 2012.

● **4. Organization or company as author**

```
    author: organization
    name, not abbreviated              title (book)
```
Human Rights Watch. *World Report of 2015: Events of 2014*.
```
            publisher        date
```
   Seven Stories Press, 2015.

Your in-text citation also should treat the organization as the author (see item 8 on p. 134).

● **5. No author listed**

a. Article or other short work

```
                                    newspaper title
                article title        (city in brackets)
```
"Policing Ohio's Online Courses." *Plain Dealer* [Cleveland],
```
        date        page(s)  label
```
   9 Oct. 2012, p. A5. Editorial.

b. Television program

```
                            title of
                            TV show
        episode title                        producer
```
"Fast Times at West Philly High." *Frontline*, produced by Debbie Morton,
```
network  date
```
   PBS, 2012.

NOTE: If an organization or a government is the author, see items 4 and 60.

● **6. Two or more works by the same author**   First alphabetize the works by title. Use the author's name for the first entry; for subsequent entries, use three hyphens and a period. The three hyphens must stand for exactly the same name as in the first entry.

García, Cristina. *Dreams of Significant Girls*. Simon and Schuster, 2011.

---. *The Lady Matador's Hotel*. Scribner, 2010.

● **7. Two or more works by the same group of authors** Alphabetize the works by title. Use the authors' names in the proper form for the first entry (see items 1–4). Begin subsequent entries with three hyphens and a period. The three hyphens must stand for the same names as in the first entry.

Agha, Hussein, and Robert Malley. "The Arab Counterrevolution."

The New York Review of Books, 29 Sept. 2011, www.nybooks
.com/articles/2011/09/29/arab-counterrevolution.

---. "This Is Not a Revolution." The New York Review of Books,

8 Nov. 2012, www.nybooks.com/articles/2012/11/08/

not-revolution.

● **8. Editor or translator** Begin with the editor's or translator's name. After the name(s), add "editor" (or "editors") or "translator" (or "translators").

first editor: second editor:
last name first   in normal order   title (book)

Horner, Avril, and Anne Rowe, editors. *Living on Paper: Letters from*

               publisher   year

    Iris Murdoch. Princeton UP, 2016.

● **9. Author with editor or translator** Begin with the name of the author. Place the editor's or translator's name after the title.

author: translator:
last name first   title (book)   in normal order

Ullmann, Regina. *The Country Road: Stories*. Translated by Kurt Beals,

         publisher   year

    New Directions Publishing, 2015.

● **10. Graphic narrative or other illustrated work** If a work has both an author and an illustrator, the order in your citation will depend on which of those persons you emphasize in your paper.

a. Author first

Gaiman, Neil. *The Sandman: Overture*. Illustrated by J. H.

    William III, DC Comics, 2015.

b. Illustrator first

Weaver, Dustin, illustrator. *The Tenth Circle*. By Jodi Picoult,

    Washington Square Press, 2006.

Answer the basic question
"Who is the author?"

PROBLEM: Sometimes when you need to cite a source, it's not clear who the author is. This is especially true for sources on the web or other nonprint sources, which may have been created by one person and uploaded by a different person or an organization. Whom do you cite as the author in such a case? How do you determine who *is* the author?

EXAMPLE: The video "Surfing the Web on the Job" (see below) was uploaded to YouTube by CBSNewsOnline. Is the person or organization who uploads the video the author of the video? Not necessarily.

Surfing the Web on The Job

 CBSNewsOnline · 42,491 videos

▶ Subscribe   85,736

Uploaded on Nov 12, 2009
As the Internet continues to emerge as a critical facet of everyday life, CBS News' Daniel Sieberg reports that companies are cracking down on employees' personal Web use.

STRATEGY: After you view or listen to the source a few times, ask yourself whether you can tell who is chiefly responsible for creating the content in the source. It might be an organization. It might be an identifiable individual. This video consists entirely of reporting by Daniel Sieberg, so in this case the author is Sieberg.

CITATION: To cite the source, you would use the basic MLA guidelines for a video found on the web (item 46).

```
author: last                                      website
  name first          title of video               title
┌──────────────┐ ┌─────────────────────────────┐ ┌───────┐
Sieberg, Daniel. "Surfing the Web on the Job." YouTube,

       upload information        update date
┌─────────────────────────────┐ ┌──────────────┐
uploaded by CBSNewsOnline, 12 Nov. 2009,

                     URL
┌─────────────────────────────────────────────┐
www.youtube.com/watch?v=1wLhNwY-enY.
```

● **11. Author using a pseudonym (pen name) or screen name** Begin with the author's name as it appears in the source (the pseudonym). Give the author's real name, if available, in parentheses.

Grammar Girl (Mignon Fogarty). "Lewis Carroll: He Loved to
      Play with Language." *QuickandDirtyTips.com*, 21 May
      2015, www.quickanddirtytips.com/education/grammar/
      lewis-carroll-he-loved-to-play-with-language.

Pauline. Comment on "Is This the End?" *The New York Times*,
      25 Nov. 2012, nyti.ms/1BRUvqQ.

● **12. Author quoted by another author (indirect source)**
If one of your sources uses a quotation from another source and you'd like to use the quotation, provide a works cited entry for the source in which you found the quotation. In your in-text citation, indicate that the quoted words appear in the source (see item 23 on p. 138).

Articles and other short works

▶ Citation at a glance: Article in an online journal,
   page 150

▶ Citation at a glance: Article from a database, **page 152**

● **13. Basic format for an article or other short work**

a. Print

author:
last name first   article title   journal title

Tilman, David. "Food and Health of a Full Earth." *Daedalus,*
        volume,
        issue   date   page(s)

      vol. 144, no. 4, Fall 2015, pp. 5-7.

b. Web

author:
last name first   title of short work

Nelson, Libby. "How Schools Will Be Different without No Child
        title of
        website   date   URL

    Left Behind." *Vox*, 11 Dec. 2015, www.vox.com/2015/12/11/

    9889350/every-student-succeeds-act-schools.

c. Database

author:
last name first · article title

Pytash, Kristine E. "Girls on the Fringe: The Writing Lives of Two

journal title

Adolescent Girls." *Reading and Writing Quarterly*,

volume,
issue   date   page(s)

vol. 32, no. 4, Oct.-Dec. 2016, pp. 299-316.

database title   DOI

Academic Search Premier, doi:10.1080/10573569.2014.936573.

● 14. Article in a journal

a. Print

author: last
name first   article title

Matchie, Thomas. "Law versus Love in *The Round House*."

journal title   volume, issue   date   page(s)

Midwest Quarterly, vol. 56, no. 4, Summer 2015, pp. 353-64.

b. Online journal

author:
last name first   article title

Cáceres, Sigfrido Burgos. "Towards Concert in Africa: Seeking Progress

journal title

and Power through Cohesion and Unity." *African Studies Quarterly*,

volume, issue   date   page(s)   URL

vol. 12, no. 4, Fall 2011, pp. 59-73, asq.africa.ufl.edu/files/

Caceres-Vol12Is4.pdf.

c. Database

author:
last name first   article title

Maier, Jessica. "A 'True Likeness': The Renaissance City Portrait."

journal title   volume, issue   date   page(s)

Renaissance Quarterly, vol. 65, no. 3, Fall 2012, pp. 711-52.

database
title   . DOI

JSTOR, doi:10.1086/668300.

Citation at a glance

Article in an online journal MLA

To cite an article in an online journal in MLA style, include the following elements.

1. Author(s) of article
2. Title and subtitle of article
3. Title of journal
4. Volume and issue numbers
5. Date of publication (including month or season, if any)
6. Page number(s) of article (if any)
7. DOI, permalink, or URL

FIRST PAGE OF ONLINE JOURNAL ARTICLE

WORKS CITED ENTRY FOR AN ARTICLE IN AN ONLINE JOURNAL

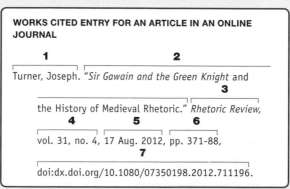

Turner, Joseph. "*Sir Gawain and the Green Knight* and the History of Medieval Rhetoric." *Rhetoric Review,* vol. 31, no. 4, 17 Aug. 2012, pp. 371-88, doi:dx.doi.org/10.1080/07350198.2012.711196.

For more on citing online articles in MLA style, see item 14.

● **15. Article in a magazine**

a. Print (monthly)

author:
last name first   article title   magazine title   date

Bryan, Christy. "Ivory Worship." *National Geographic*, Oct. 2012,

      page(s)

      pp. 28-61.

b. Print (weekly)

author: last
name first   article title   magazine
title   date   page(s)

Vick, Karl. "The Stateless Statesman." *Time*, 15 Oct. 2012, pp. 32-37.

c. Web

author:
last name first   article title   website
title

Leonard, Andrew. "The Surveillance State High School." *Salon*,

    date   URL

    27 Nov. 2012, www.salon.com/2012/11/27/the_surveillance

    _state_high_school.

● **16. Article in a newspaper** If the city of publication is not obvious from the title of the newspaper, include the city in brackets after the newspaper title (see item 5a).

a. Print

author:
last name first   article title

Sherry, Allison. "Volunteers' Personal Touch Turns High-Tech Data

    newspaper
title   date   page(s)

    into Votes." *The Denver Post*, 30 Oct. 2012, pp. 1A+.

b. Web

author:
last name first   article title

Crowell, Maddy. "How Computers Are Getting Better at Detecting Liars."

    website title   date

    The Christian Science Monitor, 12 Dec. 2015,

        URL

    www.csmonitor.com/Science/Science-Notebook/2015/1212/

    How-computers-are-getting-better-at-detecting-liars.

Citation at a glance

Article from a database MLA

To cite an article from a database in MLA style, include the following elements:

1. Author(s) of article
2. Title and subtitle of article
3. Title of journal, magazine, or newspaper
4. Volume and issue numbers (for journal)
5. Date of publication (including month or season, if any)
6. Page number(s) of article (if any)
7. Name of database
8. DOI or permalink, if available; otherwise, complete URL for article *or* shortened URL of database

DATABASE RECORD

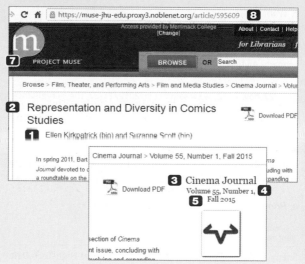

WORKS CITED ENTRY FOR AN ARTICLE FROM A DATABASE

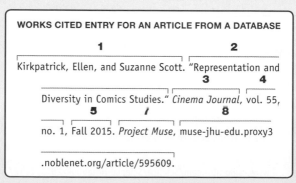

For more on citing articles from a database in MLA style, see items 13 and 14.

● **17. Abstract**

a. Abstract of an article

Bottomore, Stephen. "The Romance of the Cinematograph." *Film
    History*, vol. 24, no. 3, July 2012, pp. 341-44. Abstract.
    JSTOR, doi:10.2979/filmhistory.24.3.341.

b. Abstract of a dissertation

Moore, Courtney L. "Stress and Oppression: Identifying Possible
    Protective Factors for African American Men." Dissertation,
    Chicago School of Professional Psychology, 2016. Abstract.
    ProQuest Dissertations and Theses, search.proquest.com/
    docview/1707351557.

● **18. Editorial**

"City's Blight Fight Making Difference." *The Columbus Dispatch*, 17
    Nov. 2015, www.dispatch.com/content/stories/editorials/2015/
    11/17/1-citys-blight-fight-making-difference.html. Editorial.

● **19. Letter to the editor**   Use the label "Letter" at the
end of the entry (and before any database information). If the letter has no title, place the label directly
after the author's name.

Fahey, John A. "Recalling the Cuban Missile Crisis." *The
    Washington Post*, 28 Oct. 2012, p. A16. Letter. *LexisNexis
    Library Express*, www.lexisnexis.com/hottopics/
    lnpubliclibraryexpress.

● **20. Comment on an online article**   For use of a screen
name and a real name (if known), see item 11.

author:
screen name   article title

pablosharkman. Comment on "'We Are All Implicated': Wendell Berry

Laments a Disconnection from Community and the Land."
                        website title   date

The Chronicle of Higher Education, 23 Apr. 2012,
                        URL

chronicle.com/article/In-Jefferson-Lecture-Wendell/131648.

● **21. Paper or presentation at a conference**   See item
30; see also item 37 for proceedings of a conference. If
you viewed the presentation live, cite it as a lecture or
public address (see item 52).

● **21. Paper or presentation at a conference (*cont.*)**

first author: "et al."
last name first for others   presentation title

Zuckerman, Ethan, et al. "Big Data, Big Challenges, and Big
                                              conference title

Opportunities." Presentation at Wired for Change: The Power
                                        conference information

and the Pitfalls of Big Data, Ford Foundation, New York,
         date   URL

15 Oct. 2012, www.fordfoundation.org/library/multimedia/

wired-for-change-big-data-big-challenges-and-big-opportunities.

● **22. Review of a book, film, or another work**   For works
in print, provide a range of pages instead of a URL.

a. Book review

Della Subin, Anna. "It Has Burned My Heart." Review of *The
     Lives of Muhammad,* by Kecia Ali. *London Review of Books,*
     22 Oct. 2015, www.lrb.co.uk/v37/n20/anna-della-subin/
     it-has-burned-my-heart.

b. Film review

Lane, Anthony. "Human Bondage." Review of *Spectre,* directed
     by Sam Mendes. *The New Yorker,* 16 Nov. 2015, www
     .newyorker.com/magazine/2015/11/16/human-bondage.

c. Performance review

Stout, Gene. "The Ebullient Florence + the Machine Give
     KeyArena a Workout." Review of *How Big How Blue How
     Beautiful Odyssey. The Seattle Times,* 28 Oct. 2015, www
     .seattletimes.com/entertainment/music/the-ebullient
     -florence-the-machine-give-keyarena-a-workout.

● **23. Interview**

Weddington, Sarah. "Sarah Weddington: Still Arguing for *Roe.*"
     Interview by Michele Kort. *Ms.,* Winter 2013, pp. 32-35.

Putin, Vladimir. Interview by Charlie Rose. *Charlie Rose: The
     Week,* PBS, 19 June 2015.

Akufo, Dautey. Personal interview. 11 Apr. 2016.

● **24. Article in a dictionary or an encyclopedia (including a wiki)**

"Ball's in Your Court, The." *The American Heritage Dictionary of Idioms,* 2nd ed., Houghton Mifflin Harcourt, 2013, p. 29.

Durante, Amy M. "Finn Mac Cumhail." *Encyclopedia Mythica,* 17 Apr. 2011, www.pantheon.org/articles/f/finn_mac_cumhail.html.

● **25. Letter in a collection**

a. Print

Wharton, Edith. Letter to Henry James. 28 Feb. 1915. *Henry James and Edith Wharton: Letters, 1900-1915,* edited by Lyall H. Powers, Scribner, 1990, pp. 323-26.

b. Web

Oblinger, Maggie. Letter to Charlie Thomas. 31 Mar. 1895. *Prairie Settlement: Nebraska Photographs and Family Letters, 1862-1912,* Library of Congress / American Memory, memory.loc.gov/cgi-bin/query/r?ammem/ ps:@field(DOCID+l306)#l3060001.

Books and other long works

► Citation at a glance: Book, **page 156**

● **26. Basic format for a book**

a. Print book or e-book

author: last
name first   book title   publisher   year
Wolfe, Tom. *Back to Blood.* Little, Brown, 2012.

Beard, Mary. *SPQR: A History of Ancient Rome.* Nook ed., Liveright Publishing, 2015.

b. Web

Piketty, Thomas. *Capital in the Twenty-First Century.* Translated by Arthur Goldhammer, Harvard UP, 2014. *Google Books,* books.google.com/books?isbn=0674369556.

Citation at a glance
Book MLA

To cite a print book in MLA style, include the following elements:

1 Author(s)
2 Title and subtitle
3 Publisher
4 Year of publication (latest year)

TITLE PAGE

THE LADY AND THE PEACOCK

The Life of Aung San Suu Kyi

1 PETER POPHAM

3 THE EXPERIMENT
NEW YORK

THE EXPERIMENT
NEW YORK

FROM COPYRIGHT PAGE

THE LADY AND THE PEACOCK: *The Life of Aung San Suu Kyi*

Copyright © Peter Popham, 2011, 2012 **4**
Pages xii–xiv and 436 are a continuation of this copyright page.

WORKS CITED ENTRY FOR A PRINT BOOK

```
        1                          2
Popham, Peter. The Lady and the Peacock: The Life of
                              3              4
        Aung San Suu Kyi. The Experiment, 2012.
```

For more on citing books in MLA style, see items 26–37.

● **27. Parts of a book**

a. Foreword, introduction, preface, or afterword

author of foreword:
last name first   book part   book title

Bennett, Hal Zina. Foreword. *Shimmering Images: A Handy Little*
                        author of book:
                        in normal order   publisher

   Guide to Writing Memoir, by Lisa Dale Norton, St. Martin's Griffin,
        year   page(s)

   2008, pp. xiii-xvi.

Sullivan, John Jeremiah. "The Ill-Defined Plot." Introduction.

   The Best American Essays 2014, edited by Sullivan,

   Houghton Mifflin Harcourt, 2014, pp. xvii-xxvi.

b. Chapter in a book

Rizga, Kristina. "Mr. Hsu." *Mission High: One School, How*

   Experts Tried to Fail It, and the Students and Teachers Who

   Made It Triumph, Nation Books, 2015, pp. 89-114.

● **28. Book in a language other than English**   Capitalize
the original title according to the conventions of the
book's language.

Vargas Llosa, Mario. *El sueño del celta* [*The Dream of the Celt*].

   Alfaguara Ediciones, 2010.

● **29. Entire anthology or collection**

   editor: title of
last name first   anthology   publisher   year

Marcus, Ben, editor. *New American Stories.* Vintage Books, 2015.

● **30. One selection from an anthology or a collection**

   ▶ Citation at a glance: Selection from an anthology or a
     collection, **page 158**

   author of   title of   title of
   selection   selection   anthology

Sayrafiezadeh, Saïd. "Paranoia." *New American Stories,* edited by
       editor(s)
   of anthology   publisher   year   page(s)

   Ben Marcus, Vintage Books, 2015, pp. 3-29.

Citation at a glance
Selection from an anthology or a collection MLA

To cite a selection from an anthology in MLA style, include the following elements:

1 Author(s) of selection
2 Title and subtitle of selection
3 Title and subtitle of anthology
4 Editor(s) of anthology
5 Publisher
6 Date of publication
7 Page numbers of selection

TITLE PAGE OF ANTHOLOGY

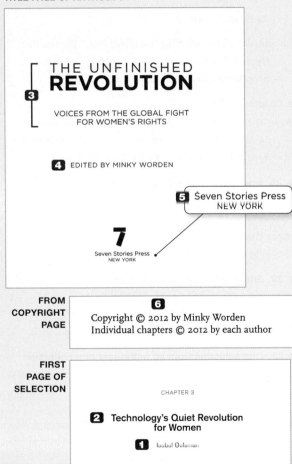

3 THE UNFINISHED **REVOLUTION**

VOICES FROM THE GLOBAL FIGHT FOR WOMEN'S RIGHTS

4 EDITED BY MINKY WORDEN

5 Seven Stories Press
NEW YORK

Seven Stories Press
NEW YORK

FROM COPYRIGHT PAGE

6
Copyright © 2012 by Minky Worden
Individual chapters © 2012 by each author

FIRST PAGE OF SELECTION

CHAPTER 3

2 Technology's Quiet Revolution for Women

1 Isobel Coleman

On the eve of Egypt's January 2011 revolution, I happened to be in Cairo, having dinner with Gamila Ismail, a longtime Egyptian

7
41   • 41

For more on citing selections from anthologies in MLA style,
see items 29–31.

● **31. Two or more selections from an anthology or a
collection** Provide an entry for the entire anthology
(see item 29) and a shortened entry for each selection.

   author of   title of   editor(s)
   selection   selection   of anthology page(s)

Eisenberg, Deborah. "Some Other, Better Otto." Marcus, pp. 94-136.

  editor: title of
last name first   anthology   publisher   year

Marcus, Ben, editor. *New American Stories.* Vintage Books, 2015,

             title of editor(s) of
 author of selection   selection anthology page(s)

Sayrafiezadeh, Saïd. "Paranoia." Marcus, pp. 3-29.

● **32. Edition other than the first** Give the name of the
translator or editor, if any, before the edition number (see
also item 9 for a book with an editor or a translator).

Eagleton, Terry. *Literary Theory: An Introduction.* 3rd ed., U of
    Minnesota P, 2008.

● **33. Multivolume work** See item 14 on page 135 for
an in-text citation of a multivolume work.

author: last   book   editor(s):
name first   title   in normal order   publisher

Stark, Freya. *Letters.* Edited by Lucy Moorehead, Compton Press,

    inclusive total
    dates   volumes

    1974-82. 8 vols.

● **34. Sacred text** Give the title of the edition (taken from the title page), italicized. Add the name of the version, if there is one, before the publisher.

The Oxford Annotated Bible with the Apocrypha. Edited by
    Herbert G. May and Bruce M. Metzger, Revised Standard
    Version, Oxford UP, 1965.

The Qur'an: Translation. Translated by Abdullah Yusuf Ali,
    Tahrike Tarsile Qur'an, 2001.

● **35. Pamphlet, brochure, or newsletter** Follow the basic format for a book (see item 26).

The Legendary Sleepy Hollow Cemetery. Friends of Sleepy Hollow
    Cemetery, 2008.

● **36. Dissertation**

Abbas, Megan Brankley. *Knowing Islam: The Entangled History
    of Western Academia and Modern Islamic Thought.* 2015.
    Princeton U, PhD dissertation. *DataSpace,* arks.princeton.edu/
    ark:/88435/dsp016682x6260.

● **37. Proceedings of a conference**

Sowards, Stacey K., et al., editors. *Across Borders and
    Environments: Communication and Environmental Justice in
    International Contexts.* Proceedings of Eleventh Biennial
    Conference on Communication and the Environment,
    25-28 June 2011, U of Texas at El Paso, International
    Environmental Communication Association, 2012.

Websites and parts of websites

● **38. An entire website**

a. Website with author or editor

author or editor: last name first	title of website	publisher

Railton, Stephen. *Mark Twain in His Times.* Stephen Railton /

                                    date   URL

    U of Virginia Library, 2012, twain.lib.virginia.edu.

Halsall, Paul, editor. *Internet Modern History Sourcebook.* Fordham U,
    4 Nov. 2011, legacy.fordham.edu/halsall/index.asp.

b. Website with organization as author

$$\overbrace{\text{Transparency International.}}^{\text{organization}} \overbrace{\textit{Transparency International: The Global}}^{\text{title of}}$$

$$\underbrace{\textit{Coalition against Corruption,}}_{\text{date}} \underbrace{2015,}_{} \underbrace{\text{www.transparency.org.}}_{\text{URL}}$$

c. Website with no author

The Newton Project. U of Sussex, 2016, www.newtonproject
    .sussex.ac.uk/prism.php?id=1.

d. Website with no title

Bae, Rebecca. Home page. Iowa State U, 2015, www.engl
    .iastate.edu/rebecca-bae-directory-page.

● **39. Work from a website** The titles of short works, such as articles or individual web pages, are placed in quotation marks. Titles of long works, such as books and reports, are italicized.

▶ Citation at a glance: Work from a website, **page 162**

$$\overbrace{\text{Gallagher, Sean.}}^{\substack{\text{author: last} \\ \text{name first}}} \overbrace{\text{"The Last Nomads of the Tibetan Plateau."}}^{\text{title of short work}}$$

$$\underbrace{\textit{Pulitzer Center on Crisis Reporting,}}_{\text{title of website}} \underbrace{25 \text{ Oct. } 2012,}_{\text{date}}$$

$$\underbrace{\text{pulitzercenter.org/reporting/china-glaciers-global}}_{\text{URL}}$$

-warming-climate-change-ecosystem-tibetan-plateau

-grasslands-nomads.

$$\overbrace{\text{Byndloss, D. Crystal, et al.}}^{\substack{\text{author: last} \\ \text{name first}}} \overbrace{\textit{In Search of a Match: A Guide for}}^{\substack{\text{title of} \\ \text{long work}}}$$

Helping Students Make Informed College Choices.

$$\underbrace{\textit{Ford Foundation,}}_{\substack{\text{title of} \\ \text{website}}} \underbrace{\text{Apr. } 2015,}_{\text{date}} \underbrace{\text{fordfoundcontent.blob.core}}_{\text{URL}}$$

.windows.net/media/2607/in_search_for_a_match.pdf.

NOTE: In an MLA paper or an MLA works cited list entry, "Web site" is spelled as two words, with a capital "W."

Citation at a glance

Work from a website MLA

To cite a work from a website in MLA style, include the following elements:

1 Author(s) of work (if any)
2 Title and subtitle
3 Title of website
4 Publisher of website (unless it is the same as the title of the site)
5 Update date
6 URL of page (or of home page of site)
7 Date of access (if no update date on site)

INTERNAL PAGE FROM A WEBSITE

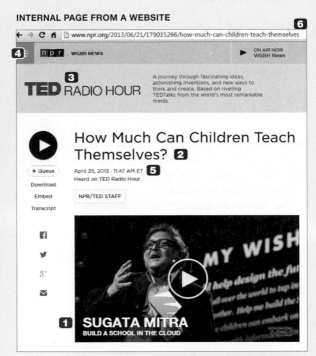

WORKS CITED ENTRY FOR A WORK FROM A WEBSITE

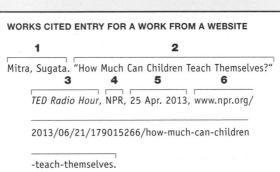

For more on citing sources from websites in MLA style, see item 39.

● **40. Entire blog**   Cite as an entire website (item 38).

Ng, Amy. *Pikaland*. Pikaland Media, 2015, www.pikaland.com.

● **41. Blog post or comment**   Cite a blog post or comment as a work from a website, with the title of the post in quotation marks (item 39). If the post or comment has no title, use the label "Blog post" or "Blog comment." (See item 11 on screen names.)

author: last
name first   title of blog post   title of
blog

Eakin, Emily. *"Cloud Atlas*'s Theory of Everything." *NYR Daily*,

  publisher date   URL

  NYREV, 2 Nov. 2012, www.nybooks.com/daily/2012/11/02/

  ken-wilber-cloud-atlas.

  author:
  screen name label   title of blog post

mitchellfreedman. Comment on *"Cloud Atlas*'s Theory of Everything."

   title of
   blog publisher date   URL

  NYR Daily, NYREV, 3 Nov. 2012, www.nybooks.com/daily/

  2012/11/02/ken-wilber-cloud-atlas.

● **42. Course materials**

  author:
last name first   article title

Jahn, Gary R. "The Image of the Railroad in *Anna Karenina*."

        course information

  Course materials, EN101, Fall 2016.

Audio, visual, and multimedia sources

● **43. Podcast**

  author:
last name first   podcast title   website title

Tanner, Laura. "Virtual Reality in 9/11 Fiction," *Literature Lab*,

       publisher   URL

  Department of English, Brandeis U, www.brandeis.edu/

  departments/english/literaturelab/tanner.html. Accessed

  date of access

  14 Feb. 2016.

● **43. Podcast (*cont.*)**

McDougall, Christopher. "How Did Endurance Help Early Humans
      Survive?" *TED Radio Hour*, NPR, 20 Nov. 2015, www.npr.org/
      2015/11/20/455904655/how-did-endurance-help-early
      -humans-survive.

● **44. Film** Generally, begin the entry with the title,
followed by the director and lead performers, as in the
first example. If your paper emphasizes one or more
people involved with the film, you may begin with
those names, as in the second example.

film title

Birdman or (The Unexpected Virtue of Ignorance). Directed by

director   major performers

      Alejandro González Iñárritu, performances by Michael Keaton,

      Emma Stone, Zach Galifianakis, Edward Norton, and Naomi Watts,

distributor   release date

      Fox Searchlight, 2014.

director,
last name first   film title

Scott, Ridley, director. *The Martian*. Performances by Matt Damon,

major performers

      Jessica Chastain, Kristen Wiig, and Kate Mara, Twentieth

distributor   release date

      Century Fox, 2015.

● **45. Supplementary material accompanying a film** Begin
with the title of the supplementary material and the names
of any contributors. Add information about the film, as
in item 44, and about the location of the supplementary
material.

"Sweeney's London." Produced by Eric Young. *Sweeney Todd:
      The Demon Barber of Fleet Street*, directed by Tim Burton,
      DreamWorks, 2007, disc 2.

● **46. Video or audio from the web** Cite as a work from
a website (item 39), with the title of the video or audio in
quotation marks.

Lewis, Paul. "Citizen Journalism." *YouTube*, 14 May 2011,

www.youtube.com/watch?v=9APO9_yNbcg.

Li, Fei-Fei. "How We're Teaching Computers to Understand

Pictures." *TED*, Mar. 2015, www.ted.com/talks/fei_fei_li_

how_we_re_teaching_computers_to_understand_pictures.

● **47. Video game** Begin with the developer or author (if any); the title; the version, if there is one; and the distributor and date of publication. If the game can be played on the web, add information as for a work from a website (item 39).

Firaxis Games. *Sid Meier's Civilization Revolution*. Take-Two

Interactive, 2008.

Edgeworld. Atom Entertainment, 1 May 2012, www.kabam.com/

games/edgeworld.

● **48. Computer software or app**

Words with Friends. Version 5.84, Zynga, 2013.

● **49. Television or radio episode or program**

a. Broadcast

title of episode | program title

"Federal Role in Support of Autism." *Washington Journal*,

narrator | network | broadcast date

narrated by Robb Harleston, C-SPAN, 1 Dec. 2012.

b. Web

title of episode | program title | narrator (or host or speaker) | episode

"The Cathedral." *Reply All*, narrated by Sruthi Pinnamaneni, episode 50,

publisher | date of posting | URL

Gimlet Media, 7 Jan. 2016, gimletmedia.com/episode/

50-the-cathedral.

● **50. Transcript**

"The Economics of Sleep, Part 1." *Freakonomics Radio*, narrated by
 Stephen J. Dubner, 9 July 2015, freakonomics.com/2015/07/09/
 the-economics-of-sleep-part-1-full-transcript. Transcript.

● **51. Performance**

The Draft. By Peter Snoad, directed by Diego Arciniegas,
 Hibernian Hall, Boston, 10 Sept. 2015.

Piano Concerto no. 3. By Ludwig van Beethoven, conducted by
 Andris Nelsons, performances by Paul Lewis and Boston
 Symphony Orchestra, Symphony Hall, Boston, 9 Oct. 2015.

● **52. Lecture or public address**

a. Live

Smith, Anna Deavere. "On the Road: A Search for American Character."
 National Endowment for the Humanities, John F. Kennedy Center
 for the Performing Arts, Washington, 6 Apr. 2015. Address.

b. Web

Khosla, Raj. "Precision Agriculture and Global Food Security."
 US Department of State. Diplomacy in Action, 26 Mar. 2013,
 www.state.gov/e/stas/series/212172.htm. Address.

● **53. Musical score**

Beethoven, Ludwig van. Symphony no. 5 in C Minor, op. 67. 1807.
 Center for Computer Assisted Research in the Humanities,
 Stanford U, 2000, scores.ccarh.org/beethoven/sym/
 beethoven-sym5-1.pdf.

● **54. Sound recording**

Bizet, Georges. *Carmen*. Performances by Jennifer Larmore, Thomas
 Moser, Angela Gheorghiu, Samuel Ramey, and Bavarian State
 Orchestra and Chorus, conducted by Giuseppe Sinopoli,
 Warner, 1996.

Blige, Mary J. "Don't Mind." *Life II: The Journey Continues
 (Act 1)*. Geffen, 2011.

● **55. Artwork, photograph, or other visual art** Begin
with the artist and the title of the work, italicized. If you
viewed the original, give the date of composition followed by a comma and the location. If you viewed the
work online, give the date of composition followed by a

period and the website title, publisher (if any), and URL. If you viewed the work reproduced in a book, cite as a work in an anthology or a collection (item 30), giving the date of composition after the title. If the medium of composition is not apparent or is important to your work, you may include it at the end (as in the third example).

Bradford, Mark. *Let's Walk to the Middle of the Ocean*. 2015, Museum of Modern Art, New York.

Hura, Sohrab. *Old Man Lighting a Fire*. 2015. *Magnum Photos*, www.magnumphotos.com/C.aspx?VP3=SearchResult&ALID =2K1HRG681B_Q.

Lindsey, Lindsay Jones. *Fibonacci Spiral*. 2012, University of Alabama, Tuscaloosa. Public sculpture.

● **56. Visual such as a table, a chart, or another graphic**

"Brazilian Waxing and Waning: The Economy." *The Economist*, 1 Dec. 2015, www.economist.com/blogs/graphicdetail/ 2015/12/economic-backgrounder. Graph.

"Number of Measles Cases by Year since 2010." *Centers for Disease Control and Prevention*, 2 Jan. 2016, www.cdc.gov/measles/ cases-outbreaks.html. Table.

● **57. Cartoon**

Zyglis, Adam. "City of Light." *Buffalo News*, 8 Nov. 2015, adamzyglis.buffalonews.com/2015/11/08/city-of-light. Cartoon.

● **58. Advertisement**

AT&T. *National Geographic*, Dec. 2015, p. 14. Advertisement.

Toyota. *The Root*. Slate Group, 28 Nov. 2015, www.theroot.com. Advertisement.

● **59. Map**

"Map of Sudan." *Global Citizen*, Citizens for Global Solutions, 2011, globalsolutions.org/blog/bashir#.VthzNMfi_FI.

"Vote on Secession, 1861." *Perry-Castañeda Library Map Collection*, U of Texas at Austin, 1976, www.lib.utexas.edu/ maps/atlas_texas/texas_vote_secession_1861.jpg.

Government and legal documents

● **60. Government document** Give the name of the government followed by the name of the department and the agency, if any.

```
government         department         agency (or agencies)
┌──────────┐ ┌──────────────────────┐ ┌─────────────────
United States, Department of Agriculture, Food and Nutrition
```

```
                                           title of work
                                        ┌──────────────────
Service, Child Nutrition Programs. Eligibility Manual for
```

```
School Meals: Determining and Verifying Eligibility. National
      website title          date              URL
┌──────────────────────┐ ┌──────────┐ ┌────────────────────
School Lunch Program, July 2015, www.fns.usda.gov/sites/
```

```
default/files/cn/SP40_CACFP18_SFSP20-2015a1.pdf.
```

Canada, Minister of Aboriginal Affairs and Northern Development.
  2015-16 Report on Plans and Priorities. Minister of Public
  Works and Government Services Canada, 2015.

● **61. Testimony before a legislative body**

Russel, Daniel R. "Burma's Challenge: Democracy, Human Rights,
  Peace, and the Plight of the Rohingya." Testimony before
  the US House Foreign Affairs Committee, Subcommittee
  on East Asian and Pacific Affairs. *US Department of State:
  Diplomacy in Action*, 21 Oct. 2015, www.state.gov/p/eap/
  rls/rm/2015/10/248420.htm.

● **62. Historical document** The titles of most historical documents, such as the US Constitution and the Canadian Charter of Rights and Freedoms, are neither italicized nor put in quotation marks.

Constitution of the United States. 1787. *The Charters of Freedom*,
  US National Archives and Records Administration, www
  .archives.gov/exhibits/charters.

● **63. Legislative act (law)** Begin with the name of the act, followed by its Public Law number; its Statutes at Large volume and page numbers; and its date of enactment.

Electronic Freedom of Information Act Amendments of 1996. Pub.
  L. 104-231. 110 Stat. 3048. 2 Oct. 1996.

● **64. Court case** Name the first plaintiff and the first defendant. Then give the volume, name, and page number of the law report; the court name; the year of the decision; and publication information. Do not italicize the name of the case. (In the text of the paper, the name of the case is italicized; see item 19 on p. 136.)

Utah v. Evans. 536 US 452. Supreme Court of the US. 2002. *Legal Information Institute*, Cornell U Law School, www.law .cornell.edu/supremecourt/text/536/452.

Personal communication and social media

● 65. Personal letter

Primak, Shoshana. Letter to the author. 6 May 2012.

● 66. Email message

Thornbrugh, Caitlin. "Coates Lecture." Received by Rita Anderson, 20 Oct. 2015.

● 67. Text message

Naqvi, Sahin. Message to the author. 18 Nov. 2015.

● 68. Online discussion list post

Robin, Griffith. "Write for the Reading Teacher." *Developing Digital Literacies*, NCTE, 23 Oct. 2015, ncte.connectedcommunity .org/communities/community-home/digestviewer/viewthread ?GroupId=1693&MID=24520&tab=digestviewer&CommunityKey =628d2ad6-8277-4042-a376-2b370ddceabf.

● 69. Social media post
Begin with the writer's screen name, followed by the real name in parentheses, if both are given. For a tweet, use the entire post as a title, in quotation marks. For other media, give a title if the post has one. If it does not, use the label "Post" in place of a title. Give the date of the post, the time (if the post specifies one), and the URL.

Curiosity Rover. "Can you see me waving? How to spot #Mars in the night sky: https://youtu.be/hv8hVvJlcJQ." *Twitter*, 5 Nov. 2015, 11:00 a.m., twitter.com/marscuriosity/ status/672859022911889408.

natgeo (National Geographic). Post. *Instagram*, 22 July 2016, instagram.com/p/BIKyGHtDD4W/?taken-by=natgeo.

33c MLA information notes (optional)

Researchers who use the MLA system of parenthetical documentation may also use information notes for one of two purposes:

1. to provide additional material that is important but might interrupt the flow of the paper
2. to refer to several sources that support a single point or to provide comments on sources

Information notes may be either footnotes or endnotes. Footnotes appear at the foot of the page; endnotes appear on a separate page at the end of the paper, before the list of works cited. For either style, the notes are numbered consecutively throughout the paper. The text of the paper contains a raised arabic numeral that corresponds to the number of the note.

TEXT

In the past several years, employees have filed a number of lawsuits against employers because of online monitoring practices.[1]

NOTE

1. For a discussion of federal law applicable to electronic surveillance in the workplace, see Kesan 293.

34 MLA manuscript format; sample pages

The following guidelines are consistent with advice given in the *MLA Handbook,* 8th edition (MLA, 2016), and with typical requirements for student papers. For pages from sample MLA papers, see pages 174–77.

34a MLA manuscript format

Formatting the paper   Papers written in MLA style should be formatted as follows.

Font   If your instructor does not require a specific font, choose one that is standard and easy to read (such as Times New Roman).

Title and identification   MLA does not require a title page. On the first page of your paper, place your name, your instructor's name, the course title, and the date on separate lines against the left margin. Then center your title. (See pp. 174 and 175 for sample first pages.)

If your instructor requires a title page, ask for formatting guidelines. A format similar to the one on page 227 may be acceptable.

Page numbers (running head)   Put the page number preceded by your last name in the upper right corner of each page, one-half inch below the top edge. Use arabic numerals (1, 2, 3, and so on).

Margins, line spacing, and paragraph indents   Leave margins of one inch on all sides of the page. Left-align the text.

Double-space throughout the paper. Do not add extra space above or below the title of the paper or between paragraphs.

Indent the first line of each paragraph one-half inch from the left margin.

Capitalization, italics, and quotation marks   In titles of works, capitalize all words except articles (*a*, *an*, *the*), prepositions (*to*, *from*, *between*, and so on), coordinating conjunctions (*and*, *but*, *or*, *nor*, *for*, *so*, *yet*), and the *to* in infinitives—unless the word is first or last in the title or subtitle.

In the text of an MLA paper, when a complete sentence follows a colon, lowercase the first word following the colon unless the sentence is a quotation or a well-known expression or principle.

Italicize the titles of books, journals, magazines, and other long works, such as websites. Use quotation marks around the titles of articles, short stories, poems, and other short works.

Long quotations   When a quotation is longer than four typed lines of prose or three lines of poetry, set it off from the text by indenting the entire quotation one-half inch from the left margin. Double-space the indented quotation and do not add extra space above or below it.

Do not use quotation marks when a quotation has been set off from the text by indenting. See page 175 for an example.

URLs If you need to break a URL at the end of a line in the text of a paper, break it before a period or hyphen or before or after any other mark of punctuation. Do not add a hyphen. If you will post your project online or submit it electronically and you want your readers to click on your URLs, do not insert any line breaks.

Headings MLA neither encourages nor discourages the use of headings and provides no guidelines for their use. If you would like to insert headings in a long essay or research paper, check first with your instructor.

Visuals MLA classifies visuals as tables and figures (figures include graphs, charts, maps, photographs, and drawings). Label each table with an arabic numeral ("Table 1," "Table 2," and so on) and provide a clear title that identifies the subject. Capitalize as you would the title of a short work (see 22c), but do not use italics or quotation marks. Place the table number and title on separate lines above the table, flush with the left margin.

For a table that you have borrowed or adapted, give the source below the table in a note like the following:

Source: Boris Groysberg and Michael Slind, "Leadership Is a Conversation," *Harvard Business Review*, June 2012, p. 83.

For each figure, place the figure number (using the abbreviation "Fig.") and a caption below the figure, flush left. Capitalize the caption as you would a sentence; include source information following the caption. (When referring to the figure in your paper, use the abbreviation "fig." in parenthetical citations; otherwise spell out the word.)

Place visuals in the text, as close as possible to the sentences that relate to them, unless your instructor prefers that visuals appear in an appendix.

Preparing the list of works cited Begin the list on a new page at the end of the paper. Center the title "Works Cited" about one inch from the top of the page. Double-space throughout. See pages 176 and 177 for sample lists of works cited.

Alphabetizing the list Alphabetize by the last names of the authors (or editors); if a work has no author or editor, alphabetize by the first word of the title other than *A*, *An*, or *The*.

If your list includes two or more works by the same author, see items 6 and 7 on pages 145–46.

Indenting   Do not indent the first line of each works cited entry, but indent any additional lines one-half inch.

URLs and DOIs   If a URL or a DOI in a works cited entry must be divided across lines, break it before a period or a hyphen or before or after any other mark of punctuation. Do not add a hyphen. If you will post your project online or submit it electronically and you want your readers to click on your URLs, do not insert any line breaks.

34b Sample pages from MLA papers

Following are excerpts from two MLA papers: a research paper written for a composition course and an analysis of a short story written for a literature class.

Sample MLA page: Research paper

Sophie Harba

Professor Baros-Moon

Engl 1101

30 April 2013

1   What's for Dinner? Personal Choices vs. Public Health

       Should the government enact laws to regulate healthy eating

2 choices? Many Americans would answer an emphatic "No," arguing

that what and how much we eat should be left to individual choice

3 rather than unreasonable laws. Others might argue that it would

be unreasonable for the government not to enact legislation,

given the rise of chronic diseases that result from harmful diets.

In this debate, both the definition of reasonable regulations and

the role of government to legislate food choices are at stake. In

4 the name of public health and safety, state governments have the

responsibility to shape health policies and to regulate healthy

eating choices, especially since doing so offers a potentially large

social benefit for a relatively small cost.

       Debates surrounding the government's role in regulating

5 food have a long history in the United States. According to Lorine

Goodwin, a food historian, nineteenth-century reformers who sought

6 to purify the food supply were called "fanatics" and "radicals" by

critics who argued that consumers should be free to buy and eat what

7 they want (77). Thanks to regulations, though, such as the 1906

federal Pure Food and Drug Act, food, beverages, and medicine are

largely free from toxins. In addition, to prevent contamination and

the spread of disease, meat and dairy products are now inspected by

government agents to ensure that they meet health requirements.

8 Such regulations can be considered reasonable because they protect

us from harm with little, if any, noticeable consumer cost.

---

1 Title, centered. **2** Opening research question engages readers. **3** Writer highlights the research conversation. **4** Thesis answers the research question and presents Harba's main point. **5** Signal phrase names the author. **6** Historical background provides context for debate. **7** Parenthetical citation includes a page number. **8** Harba explains her use of a key term, *reasonable*.

(Annotations indicate MLA-style formatting and effective writing.)

Sample MLA page: Literary analysis

Dan Larson

Professor Duncan

English 102

19 April 2013

The Transformation of Mrs. Peters:

An Analysis of "A Jury of Her Peers"   **1**

In Susan Glaspell's 1917 short story "A Jury of Her Peers," two women accompany their husbands and a county attorney to an isolated house where a farmer named John Wright has been choked to death. The chief suspect is Wright's wife, Minnie, who is in jail awaiting trial. The sheriff's wife, Mrs. Peters, has come along to gather some items for Minnie, and Mrs. Hale has joined her. Initially, Mrs. Hale sympathizes with Minnie and objects to the male investigators "snoopin' round and criticizin'" her kitchen (249). But Mrs. Peters shows respect for the law, saying that the   **2** men are doing "no more than their duty" (249). By the end of the story, however, Mrs. Peters has joined Mrs. Hale in lying to the men and committing a crime—hiding key evidence. What causes this   **3** dramatic change?

One critic, Leonard Mustazza, argues that Mrs. Hale recruits Mrs. Peters "as a fellow 'juror' in the case, moving the sheriff's wife ... towards identification with the accused wom[a]n" (494). However, Mrs. Peters also reaches insights on her own. Her   **4** observations in the kitchen lead her to understand Minnie's plight:

> The sheriff's wife had looked from the stove to the sink—to
> the pail of water which had been carried in from outside. . . .   **5**
> That look of seeing into things, of seeing through a thing
> to something else, was in the eyes of the sheriff's wife now.
> (251-52)

---

1 Title, centered. **2** Quotation from literary work followed by page number. **3** Writer's research question. **4** Debatable thesis. **5** Long quotation indented ½"; page numbers in parentheses after final period.

(Annotations indicate MLA-style formatting and effective writing.)

Sample MLA list of works cited

[1] Works Cited

Conly, Sarah. "Three Cheers for the Nanny State." *The New York Times*, 25 Mar. 2013, p. A23.

"The Facts on Junk Food Marketing and Kids." *Prevention Institute*, www.preventioninstitute.org/focus-areas/supporting-healthy -food-a-activity/supporting-healthy-food-and-activity -environments-advocacy/get-involved-were-not-buying-it/ 735-were-not-buying-it-the-facts-on-junk-food-marketing

[2] -and-kids.html. Accessed 21 Apr. 2013.

[3] Goodwin, Lorine Swainston. *The Pure Food, Drink, and Drug Crusaders, 1879-1914*. McFarland, 2006.

[4] Gostin, L. O., and K. G. Gostin. "A Broader Liberty: J. S. Mill, Paternalism, and the Public's Health." *Public Health*, vol. 123, no. 3, 2009, pp. 214-21, doi:10.1016/j.puhe.2008.12.024.

Mello, Michelle M., et al. "Obesity—the New Frontier of Public Health Law." *New England Journal of Medicine*, vol. 354, no. 24, 2006, pp. 2001-10, www.nejm.org/doi/pdf/10.1056/NEJMhpr060227.

[5] Neergaard, Lauran, and Jennifer Agiesta. "Obesity's a Crisis but We Want Our Junk Food, Poll Shows." *Huffington Post*, 4 Jan. 2013, www.huffingtonpost.com/2013/01/04/obesity-junk

[6] -food-government-intervention-poll_n_2410376.html.

Nestle, Marion. *Food Politics: How the Food Industry Influences Nutrition and Health*. U of California P, 2013.

[7] Pollan, Michael. "The Food Movement, Rising." *The New York Review of Books*, 10 June 2010, www.nybooks.com/articles/2010/ 06/10/food-movement-rising.

Resnik, David. "Trans Fat Bans and Human Freedom." *American Journal of Bioethics*, vol. 10, no. 3, Mar. 2010, pp. 27-32.

[8] United States, Department of Agriculture and Department of Health and Human Services. *Dietary Guidelines for Americans, 2010*, health.gov/dietaryguidelines/dga2010/dietaryguidelines2010 .pdf.

---

[1] Heading, centered. **[2]** Access date for online source with no update date. **[3]** Authors' names inverted; works alphabetized by last names. **[4]** First line of entry at left margin; extra lines indented ½". **[5]** Short work from website. **[6]** Double-spacing throughout. **[7]** Article from online periodical. **[8]** Government agency as author.

Sample MLA list of works cited

Larson 7

Works Cited

Ben-Zvi, Linda. "'Murder, She Wrote': The Genesis of Susan **1**
Glaspell's *Trifles*." *Susan Glaspell: Essays on Her Theater
and Fiction*, edited by Ben-Zvi, U of Michigan P, 1995,
pp. 19-48. Originally published in *Theatre Journal*, vol.
44, no. 2, May 1992, pp. 141-62.

Glaspell, Susan. "A Jury of Her Peers." *Literature and Its Writers:
An Introduction to Fiction, Poetry, and Drama*, edited by Ann
Charters and Samuel Charters, 6th ed., Bedford/St. Martin's,
2013, pp. 243-58.

Hedges, Elaine. "Small Things Reconsidered: 'A Jury of Her Peers.'" **2**
Susan Glaspell: Essays on Her Theater and Fiction, edited by
Linda Ben-Zvi, U of Michigan P, 1995, pp. 49-69.

Mustazza, Leonard. "Generic Translation and Thematic Shift in **3**
Susan Glaspell's *Trifles* and 'A Jury of Her Peers.'" *Studies in
Short Fiction*, vol. 26, no. 4, 1989, pp. 489-96.

1 List alphabetized by last names. **2** Article reprinted in
anthology. **3** Article in journal.

APA
Papers

Instructors in the social sciences and other disciplines may ask you to document your sources with the American Psychological Association (APA) system of in-text citations and references described in section 38. When writing an APA-style paper that draws on sources, you face three main challenges: (1) supporting a thesis, (2) citing your sources and avoiding plagiarism, and (3) integrating source material effectively.

35   Supporting a thesis

Most research assignments ask you to form a thesis, or main idea, and to support that thesis with well-organized evidence. A thesis, which usually appears at the end of the introduction, is a one-sentence (or occasionally a two-sentence) statement of your central idea. In a paper reviewing the literature on a topic, the thesis analyzes conclusions drawn by a variety of researchers.

35a   Forming a working thesis

Once you have read a variety of sources, considered your issue from different perspectives, and chosen an entry point in a research conversation, you are ready to form a working thesis. A working thesis expresses your informed, reasoned answer to your research question — a question about which people might disagree. Notice how each of the working thesis statements that follow takes a position on a debatable issue.

RESEARCH QUESTION

Can educational technology improve student learning and solve the problem of teacher shortages?

WORKING THESIS

Educational technology can help solve teacher shortages by shifting the focus from teachers to students.

RESEARCH QUESTION

Is medication the most effective treatment for the escalating problem of childhood obesity?

WORKING THESIS

Understanding the limitations of medical treatments for children highlights the complexity of the childhood obesity problem in the United States and underscores the need for physicians, advocacy groups, and policymakers to search for other solutions.

RESEARCH QUESTION

Why are boys diagnosed with ADHD more often than girls?

WORKING THESIS

Recent studies have suggested that ADHD is diagnosed more often in boys than in girls because of personality differences between boys and girls as well as gender bias in referring adults, but an overlooked cause is that ADHD often coexists with other behavior disorders that exaggerate or mask gender differences.

For help with testing your working thesis, see the guidelines on page 110.

35b Organizing your ideas

APA encourages the use of headings to help readers follow the organization of a paper. For an original research report, the major headings often follow a standard model: "Method," "Results," "Discussion." For a literature review, headings will vary, depending on the topic. For an example of headings in an APA paper, see page 233.

35c Using sources to inform and support your argument

The source materials you have gathered will help you develop and support your argument. Sources can play several different roles:

Providing background information or context You can describe a study or offer a statistic to help readers grasp the significance of your topic or understand generalizations about it.

Explaining terms or concepts Explain words, phrases, or ideas that might be unfamiliar to your readers. Quoting or paraphrasing a source can help you define terms and concepts clearly and concisely.

Supporting your claims Back up your assertions with facts, examples, and other evidence from your research.

Lending authority to your argument Expert opinion can give weight to your argument. But don't rely on experts to make your argument for you. Construct your argument in your own words and cite authorities in the field to support your position.

Anticipating and countering objections Do not ignore sources that seem to contradict your position or that offer arguments different from your own. Instead, use them to give voice to opposing points of view and to state potential objections to your argument before you counter them.

35d Getting feedback

Once you have developed a thesis, identified useful sources, and begun drafting your paper, seek out a classmate or a writing center consultant to provide feedback on your work in progress. Feedback gives you perspective on what's working and what's not working in your draft and keeps the expectations of your readers in mind.

To help your reviewer respond with useful comments, provide a copy of the assignment and, if possible, copies of any sources you used to write your draft. You might also share your purpose for writing, why your topic matters to you, and what you hope to accomplish in your draft. To encourage relevant, focused feedback, tell your reviewer about any specific questions or concerns you have. For some guiding questions you and your reader can use to review your writing, see the guidelines in 29d.

36 Avoiding plagiarism

In a research paper, you draw on the work of other researchers and writers, and you must document their contributions by citing your sources. When you acknowledge your sources, you avoid plagiarism, a serious academic offense.

Three different acts are considered plagiarism: (1) failing to cite quotations and borrowed ideas, (2) failing to enclose borrowed language in quotation marks, and (3) failing to put summaries and paraphrases in your own words.

36a Citing quotations and borrowed ideas

When you cite sources, you give credit to writers from whom you've borrowed words and ideas. You also let your readers know where your information comes from so that they can find and read the original sources. You must cite anything you borrow from a source, including direct quotations; statistics and other specific facts; visuals such as tables, graphs, and diagrams; and any ideas you present in a summary or a paraphrase.

The only exception is common knowledge— information your readers likely already know or could easily find in general sources. When you have seen certain information repeatedly in your reading, you don't need to cite it. However, when information has appeared in only a few sources, when it is highly specific (as with statistics), or when it is controversial, you should cite the source. If you're not sure whether you need to cite something, check with your instructor.

36b Understanding how the APA system works

APA recommends an author-date style of citation. Here, briefly, is how the author-date system usually works. See section 38 for a detailed discussion of variations.

1. The source is introduced by a signal phrase that includes the last name of the author followed by the date of publication in parentheses.
2. The material being cited is followed by a page number in parentheses (unless the source is unpaginated).
3. At the end of the paper, an alphabetized list of references gives publication information for the source.

IN-TEXT CITATION

Bell (2010) reported that students engaged in student-centered learning performed better on both project-based assessments and standardized tests (pp. 39-40).

ENTRY IN THE LIST OF REFERENCES

Bell, S. (2010). Project-based learning for the 21st century: Skills for the future. *The Clearing House, 83*(2), 39-43.

NOTE: This basic APA format varies for different types of sources. For a detailed discussion and other models, see 38.

36c Enclosing borrowed language in quotation marks

To indicate that you are using a source's exact phrases or sentences, you must enclose them in quotation marks. To omit the quotation marks is to claim— falsely—that the language is your own. Such an omission is plagiarism even if you have cited the source.

ORIGINAL SOURCE

Student-centered learning, or student centeredness, is a model which puts the student in the center of the learning process.

—Z. Çubukçu, "Teachers' Evaluation
of Student-Centered Learning
Environments" (2012), p. 50

PLAGIARISM

According to Çubukçu (2012), student-centered learning is a model which puts the student in the center of the learning process (p. 50).

BORROWED LANGUAGE IN QUOTATION MARKS

According to Çubukçu (2012), "student-centered learning . . . is a model which puts the student in the center of the learning process" (p. 50).

NOTE: Quotation marks are not used when quoted sentences are set off from the text by indenting (see p. 187).

36d Putting summaries and paraphrases in your own words

A summary condenses information from a source; a paraphrase conveys the information using roughly the same number of words as the original source. When you summarize or paraphrase, you must name the source and restate the source's meaning in your own words. Half-copying the author's sentences by using the author's phrases in your own sentences without quotation marks or by plugging synonyms into the author's sentence structure is a form of plagiarism. The following paraphrases are plagiarized—even though the source is cited—because their language or sentence structure is too close to that of the source.

ORIGINAL SOURCE

Student-centered teaching focuses on the student. Decision-making, organization and content are determined for most by taking individual students' needs and interests into consideration. Student-centered teaching provides opportunities to develop students' skills of transferring knowledge to other situations, triggering retention, and adapting a high motivation for learning.

—Z. Çubukçu, "Teachers' Evaluation of Student-Centered Learning Environments" (2012), p. 52

PLAGIARISM: UNACCEPTABLE BORROWING OF PHRASES

According to Çubukçu (2012), student-centered teaching takes into account the needs and interests of each student, making it possible to foster students' skills of transferring knowledge to new situations and triggering retention (p. 52).

PLAGIARISM: UNACCEPTABLE BORROWING OF STRUCTURE

According to Çubukçu (2012), this new model of teaching centers on the student. The material and flow of the course are chosen by considering the students' individual requirements. Student-centered teaching gives a chance for students to develop useful, transferable skills, ensuring they'll remember material and stay motivated (p. 52).

To avoid plagiarizing an author's language, don't look at the source while you are summarizing or paraphrasing. After you've restated the author's ideas in your own words, return to the source and check that you haven't used the author's language or sentence structure or misrepresented the author's ideas.

ACCEPTABLE PARAPHRASE

Çubukçu's (2012) research documents the numerous benefits of student-centered teaching in putting the student at the center of teaching and learning. When students are given the option of deciding what they learn and how they learn, they are motivated to apply their learning to new settings and to retain the content of their learning (p. 52).

See the box on page 117 for simple guidelines for being a responsible research writer.

37 Integrating sources

Quotations, summaries, paraphrases, and facts will help you develop your argument, but they cannot speak for you. You can use several strategies to integrate information from sources into your paper while maintaining your own voice.

37a Summarizing and paraphrasing effectively

When you summarize or paraphrase, you express an author's ideas in your own words. A summary should condense the author's key points and use fewer words than the original. You might summarize to compare arguments or ideas from various sources or to provide readers with an overview of a source before you discuss it.

A paraphrase should use approximately the same number of words and details as in the source. You might paraphrase to help readers understand complex ideas or data from a source.

Even though you're using your own words to summarize or paraphrase, the original ideas are the author's intellectual property, so you must include a citation. (For more advice, see 31a.)

37b Using quotations effectively

When you quote a source, you borrow some of the author's exact words and enclose them in quotation marks. Quotation marks show your readers that both the idea and the words belong to the author. You might quote a source when exact wording is needed for accuracy or when the original language is especially effective. Using the words of an authority can also lend weight to your argument.

Limiting your use of quotations   Keep the emphasis on your own words and ideas. It is not always necessary to quote full sentences from a source. Often you can integrate words or phrases from a source into your own sentence structure.

Citing federal data, *The New York Times* reported a 30% drop in "people entering teacher preparation programs" between 2010 and 2014 (Rich, 2015).

Using the ellipsis mark   To condense a quoted passage, you can use the ellipsis mark (three periods, with spaces between) to indicate that you have omitted words. What remains must be grammatically complete.

Demski (2012) noted that "personalized learning . . . acknowledges and accommodates the range of abilities, prior experiences, needs, and interests of each student" (p. 33).

The writer has omitted the phrase *a student-centered teaching and learning model that* from the source.

If you want to omit one or more full sentences, use a period before the three ellipsis dots.

According to Demski (2012), "In any personalized learning model, the student—not the teacher—is the central figure. . . . Personalized learning may finally allow individualization and differentiation to actually happen in the classroom" (p. 34).

Ordinarily, do not use an ellipsis mark at the beginning or at the end of a quotation. Readers will understand that you have taken the quoted material from a longer passage. The only exception occurs when you have dropped words at the end of the final quoted sentence. In such cases, put three ellipsis dots before the closing quotation mark and the parenthetical reference.

USING SOURCES RESPONSIBLY: Make sure that omissions and ellipsis marks do not distort the meaning of your source.

Using brackets   Brackets allow you to insert your own words into quoted material to clarify a confusing reference or to keep a sentence grammatical in the context of your writing.

Demski's (2012) research confirms that "implement[ing] a true personalized learning model on a national level" is difficult for a number of reasons (p. 36).

To indicate an error in a quotation, such as a misspelling, insert [*sic*], italicized and with brackets around it, right after the error.

Setting off long quotations When you quote forty or more words from a source, set off the quotation by indenting it one-half inch from the left margin.

Long quotations should be introduced by an informative sentence, usually followed by a colon. Quotation marks are unnecessary because the indented format tells readers that the passage is taken word-for-word from the source.

According to Svokos (2015), College and Education Fellow for *The Huffington Post*, some educational technology resources entertain students while supporting student-centered learning:

> GlassLab, a nonprofit that was launched with grants from the Bill & Melinda Gates and MacArthur Foundations, creates educational games that are now being used in more than 6,000 classrooms across the country. Some of the company's games are education versions of existing ones—for example, its first release was SimCity EDU—while others are originals. Teachers get real-time updates on students' progress as well as suggestions on what topics students need to spend more time on.

For a source with page numbers (unlike the example, which is a web source), the parenthetical citation with a page number goes outside the final mark of punctuation. (When a quotation is run into your text, the opposite is true. See the sample citations on p. 186.)

37c Using signal phrases to integrate sources

Whenever you include a paraphrase, summary, or direct quotation of another writer's work in your paper, prepare readers for it with a *signal phrase*. A signal phrase usually names the author of the source, gives the publication year in parentheses, and often provides some context. It is generally acceptable in APA style to call authors by their last name only, even on first mention. If your paper refers to two authors with the same last name, use their initials as well.

When you write a signal phrase, choose a verb that is appropriate for the way you are using the source. Are you providing background, explaining a concept, supporting a claim, lending authority, or refuting a belief? See the chart on page 190 for a list of verbs commonly used in signal phrases.

Marking boundaries   Readers need to move smoothly from your words to the words of a source. Avoid dropping a quotation into your text without warning. Instead, provide a clear signal phrase, including at least the author's name and the year of publication. A signal phrase marks the boundaries between the source material and your own words and can help readers understand why you're including the source.

DROPPED QUOTATION

Many educators have been intrigued by the concept of blended learning but have been unsure how to define it. "Blended learning is a formal education program in which a student learns at least in part through online delivery of content and instruction with some element of student control over time, place, and pace" (Horn & Staker, 2011, p. 4).

QUOTATION WITH SIGNAL PHRASE

Many educators have been intrigued by the concept of blended learning but have been unsure how to define it. As Horn and Staker (2011) have argued, "Blended learning is a formal education program in which a student learns at least in part through online delivery of content and instruction with some element of student control over time, place, and pace" (p. 4).

Introducing summaries and paraphrases   Introduce most summaries and paraphrases with a signal phrase that names the author and places the material in the context of your argument. Readers will then understand that everything between the signal phrase and the parenthetical citation summarizes or paraphrases the cited source.

Without the signal phrase (highlighted) in the following example, readers might think that only the last sentence is being cited, when in fact the whole paragraph is based on the source.

Watson (2008) reported that for American postsecondary students, technology is integral to their academic lives. Nearly three-quarters own their own laptops, and 83% have used a course management system for an online component of a class. Watson pointed out that online and blended learning models are even more widespread outside of the United States (p. 15).

There are times, however, when a summary or a paraphrase does not require a signal phrase naming the author. When the context makes clear where the cited material begins, you may omit the signal phrase and include the author's name and the year in parentheses.

Integrating statistics and other facts   When you cite a statistic or another specific fact, a signal phrase is often not necessary. In most cases, readers will understand that the citation refers to the statistic or fact (not the whole paragraph).

Of polled high school students, 43% said that they lacked confidence in their technological proficiency going into college and careers (Moeller & Reitzes, 2011)

There is nothing wrong, however, with using a signal phrase to introduce a statistic or another fact.

Using signal phrases in APA papers

To avoid monotony, try to vary both the language and the placement of your signal phrases.

Model signal phrases

In the words of Mitra (2013), "..."

As Bell (2010) has noted, "..."

Donitsa-Schmidt and Zuzovsky (2014), educational researchers, pointed out that "..."

"...," claimed Çubukçu (2012).

"...," explained Demski (2012), "..."

Horn and Staker (2011) have offered a compelling argument for this view: "..."

Moeller and Reitzes (2011) answered objections with the following analysis: "..."

Continued →

Verbs in signal phrases

Are you providing background, explaining a concept, supporting a claim, lending authority, or refuting a belief? Choose a verb that is appropriate for the way you are using the source.

admitted	contended	reasoned
agreed	declared	refuted
argued	denied	rejected
asserted	emphasized	reported
believed	insisted	responded
claimed	noted	suggested
compared	observed	thought
confirmed	pointed out	wrote

NOTE: In APA style, use the past tense or present perfect tense to introduce quotations and other source material: *Davis (2015) noted* or *Davis (2015) has noted.* Use the present tense only to discuss the application or effect of your own results (*the data suggest*) or knowledge that has been clearly established (*researchers agree*).

Putting source material in context   Provide context for any source material that appears in your paper. A signal phrase can help you connect your own ideas with those of another writer by clarifying how the source will contribute to your paper. It's a good idea to embed a quotation between sentences of your own, introducing it with a signal phrase and following it with interpretive comments that link the quotation to your paper's argument.

QUOTATION WITH EFFECTIVE CONTEXT

According to the International Society for Technology in Education (2016), "Student-centered learning moves students from passive receivers of information to active participants in their own discovery process." The results of student-centered learning have been positive, not only for academic achievement but also for student self-esteem, because students actively participate in the process of learning.

NOTE: When you bring other sources into a conversation about your research topic, you are synthesizing sources. For more on synthesis, see 31d.

38 APA documentation style

In most social science classes, you will be asked to use the APA system for documenting sources, which is set forth in the *Publication Manual of the American Psychological Association*, 6th ed. (Washington, DC: APA, 2010).

38a APA in-text citations

APA's in-text citations provide the author's last name and the year of publication, usually before the cited material, and a page number in parentheses directly after the cited material. In the following models, the elements of the in-text citation are highlighted.

NOTE: APA style requires the use of the past tense or the present perfect tense in signal phrases introducing cited material: *Smith (2012) reported, Smith (2012) has argued*. (See also p. 190.)

Directory to APA in-text citation models

● **1. Basic format for a quotation**   Ordinarily, introduce the quotation with a signal phrase that includes the author's last name followed by the year of publication in parentheses. Put the page number (preceded by "p.") in parentheses after the quotation. For sources from the web without page numbers, see item 12a on page 195.

Çubukçu (2012) argued that for a student-centered approach to work, students must maintain "ownership for their goals and activities" (p. 64).

If the author is not named in the signal phrase, place the author's name, the year, and the page number in parentheses after the quotation: (Çubukçu, 2012, p. 64). (See items 6 and 12 for citing sources that lack authors; item 12 also explains how to handle sources without dates or page numbers.)

NOTE: Do not include a month in an in-text citation, even if the entry in the reference list includes the month.

● **2. Basic format for a summary or a paraphrase**   As for a quotation (see item 1), include the author's last name and the year either in a signal phrase introducing the material or in parentheses following it. Use a page number, if one is available, following the cited material. For sources from the web without page numbers, see item 12a on page 195.

Watson (2008) offered a case study of the Cincinnati Public Schools Virtual High School, in which students were able to engage in highly individualized instruction according to their own needs, strengths, and learning styles, using 10 teachers as support (p. 7).

The Cincinnati Public Schools Virtual High School brought students together to engage in highly individualized instruction according to their own needs, strengths, and learning styles, using 10 teachers as support (Watson, 2008, p. 7).

● **3. Work with two authors**   Name both authors in the signal phrase or in parentheses each time you cite the work. In the parentheses, use "&" between the authors' names; in the signal phrase, use "and."

According to Donitsa-Schmidt and Zuzovsky (2014), "demographic growth in the school population" can lead to teacher shortages (p. 426).

In the United States, most public school systems are struggling with teacher shortages, which are projected to worsen as the number of applicants to education schools decreases (Donitsa-Schmidt & Zuzovsky, 2014, p. 420).

● **4. Work with three to five authors**   Identify all authors in the signal phrase or in parentheses the first time you cite the source.

In 2013, Harper, Findlen, Ibori, and Wenz studied teachers' perceptions of project-based learning (PBL) before and after participating in a PBL pilot program.

In subsequent citations, use the first author's name followed by "et al." in either the signal phrase or the parentheses.

Surprisingly, Harper et al. (2013) advised school administrators "not to jump into project-based pedagogy without training and feedback."

● **5. Work with six or more authors**   Use the first author's name followed by "et al." in the signal phrase or in parentheses.

Hermann et al. (2012) tracked 42 students over a three-year period to look closely at the performance of students in the laptop program (p. 49).

● **6. Work with unknown author**   If the author is unknown, mention the work's title in the signal phrase or give the first word or two of the title in the parentheses. Titles of short works such as articles are put in quotation marks; titles of long works such as books and reports are italicized.

Collaboration increases significantly among students who own or have regular access to a laptop ("Tech Seeds," 2015).

NOTE: In the rare case when "Anonymous" is specified as the author, treat it as if it were a real name: (Anonymous, 2011). In the list of references, also use the name Anonymous as author.

● **7. Organization as author**   Name the organization in the signal phrase or in the parentheses the first time you cite the source.

According to the International Society for Technology in Education (2016), "Student-centered learning moves students from passive receivers of information to active participants in their own discovery process."

If the organization has a familiar abbreviation, you may include it in brackets the first time you cite the source and use the abbreviation alone in later citations.

FIRST CITATION   (Texas Higher Education Coordinating Board [THECB], 2012)

LATER CITATIONS   (THECB, 2012)

● **8. Authors with the same last name**   If your reference list includes two or more authors with the same last name, use initials with the last names in your in-text citations.

Research by E. Smith (1989) revealed that . . .

One 2012 study contradicted . . . (R. Smith, p. 234).

● **9. Two or more works by the same author in the same year**   In the reference list, you will use lowercase letters ("a," "b," and so on) with the year to order the entries. (See item 8 on p. 203.) Use those same letters with the year in the in-text citation.

Research by Durgin (2013b) has yielded new findings about the role of smartphones in the classroom.

● **10. Two or more works in the same parentheses**   Put the works in the same order that they appear in the reference list, separated with semicolons.

Researchers have indicated that studies of educational technology initiatives reveal the high cost of change (Nazer, 2015; Serrao et al., 2014).

● **11. Multiple citations to the same work in one paragraph**   If you give the author's name in the text of your paper (not in parentheses) and you mention that source again in the text of the same paragraph, give only the author's name, not the date, in the later citation. If any subsequent reference in the same paragraph is in parentheses, include both the author and the date in the parentheses.

Principal Jean Patrice said, "You have to be able to reach
students where they are instead of making them come to you.
If you don't, you'll lose them" (personal communication, April
10, 2006). Patrice expressed her desire to see all students get
something out of their educational experience. This feeling is
common among members of Waverly's faculty. With such a positive
view of student potential, it is no wonder that 97% of Waverly High
School graduates go on to a four-year university (Patrice, 2006).

● **12. Web source** Cite sources from the web as you
would cite any other source, giving the author and the
year when they are available.

Atkinson (2011) found that children who spent at least four
hours a day engaged in online activities in an academic
environment were less likely to want to play video games or
watch TV after school.

Usually a page number is not available; occasionally a
web source will lack an author or a date (see 12a, 12b,
and 12c).

a. No page numbers When a web source lacks stable
numbered pages, you may include paragraph numbers
or headings to help readers locate the passage being
cited.
    If the source has numbered paragraphs, use the para-
graph number preceded by the abbreviation "para." (or
"paras." for more than one paragraph): (Hall, 2012, para.
5). If the source has no numbered paragraphs but contains
headings, cite the appropriate heading in parentheses.

Crush and Jayasingh (2015) pointed out that several other
school districts in low-income areas had "jump-started their
distance learning initiatives with available grant funds"
("Funding Change," para. 6).

b. Unknown author If no author is named in the source,
mention the title of the source in a signal phrase or
give the first word or two of the title in parentheses (see
also item 6). (If an organization serves as the author,
see item 7.)

A student's IEP may, in fact, recommend the use of mobile
technology ("Considerations," 2012).

● **12. Web source (*cont.*)**

c. Unknown date   When the source does not give a date, use the abbreviation "n.d." (for "no date").

Administrators believe 1-to-1 programs boost learner engagement (Magnus, n.d.).

● **13. An entire website**   If you are citing an entire website, not an internal page or a section, give the URL in the text of your paper but do not include it in the reference list.

The Berkeley Center for Teaching and Learning website (https://teaching.berkeley.edu/) shares ideas for using mobile technology in the classroom.

● **14. Multivolume work**   If you have used more than one volume from a multivolume work, add the volume number in parentheses with the page number.

Banford (2013) has demonstrated steady increases in performance since the program began a decade ago (Vol. 2, p. 135).

● **15. Personal communication**   Interviews that you conduct, memos, letters, email messages, social media posts, and similar communications that would be difficult for your readers to retrieve should be cited in the text only, not in the reference list. (Use the first initial with the last name in parentheses.)

One of Yim's colleagues, who has studied the effect of social media on children's academic progress, has contended that the benefits of this technology for children under 12 years old are few (F. Johnson, personal communication, October 20, 2013).

● **16. Course materials**   Cite lecture notes from your instructor or your own class notes as personal communication (see item 15). If your instructor's material contains publication information, cite as you would the appropriate source. See also item 62 on page 221.

● **17. Part of a source (chapter, figure)**   To cite a specific part of a source, such as a whole chapter or a figure or table, identify the element in parentheses. Don't abbreviate terms such as "Figure," "Chapter," and "Section";

"page" is abbreviated "p." (or "pp." for more than one page).

The data support the finding that peer relationships are difficult to replicate in a completely online environment (Hanniman, 2010, Figure 8-3, p. 345).

● **18. Indirect source (source quoted in another source)** When a writer's or a speaker's quoted words appear in a source written by someone else, begin the parenthetical citation with the words "as cited in." In the following example, Demski is the author of the source in the reference list; that source contains a quotation by Cator.

Karen Cator, director of the U.S. Department of Education's Office of Educational Technology, calls technology "the essence" of a personalized learning environment (as cited in Demski, 2012, p. 34).

● **19. Sacred or classical text** Identify the text, the version or edition you used, and the relevant part (chapter, verse, line). It is not necessary to include the source in the reference list.

Peace activists have long cited the biblical prophet's vision of a world without war: "And they shall beat their swords into plowshares, and their spears into pruning hooks; nation shall not lift up sword against nation, neither shall they learn war any more" (Isaiah 2:4 Revised Standard Version).

38b APA list of references

The information you will need for the reference list at the end of your paper will differ slightly for some sources, but the main principles apply to all sources: You should identify an author, a creator, or a producer whenever possible; give a title; and provide the date on which the source was produced. Some sources will require page numbers; some will require a publisher; and some will require retrieval information.

▶ Directory to APA reference list models, **page 198**
▶ General guidelines for the reference list, **page 200**

Directory to APA reference list models

General guidelines for the reference list

In the list of references, include only sources that you have quoted, summarized, or paraphrased in your paper.

Authors and dates

- Alphabetize entries by authors' last names; if a work has no author, alphabetize it by its title.

- For all authors' names, put the last name first, followed by a comma; use initials for the first and middle names.

- With two or more authors, use an ampersand (&) before the last author's name. Separate the names with commas. Include names for the first seven authors; if there are eight or more authors, give the first six authors, three ellipsis dots, and the last author.

- If the author is a company or an organization, give the name in normal order.

- Put the date of publication in parentheses immediately after the first element of the citation.

- For books, give the year of publication. For magazines, newspapers, and newsletters, give the year and month or the year, month, and day. For web sources, give the date of posting, if available. Use the season if a publication gives only a season, not a month.

Titles

- Italicize the titles and subtitles of books, journals, and other long works. If a book title contains another book title or an article title, do not italicize the internal title and do not put quotation marks around it.

- Use no italics or quotation marks for the titles of articles. If an article title contains another article title or a term usually placed in quotation marks, use quotation marks around the internal title or the term.

- For books and articles, capitalize only the first word of the title and subtitle and all proper nouns.

- For the titles of journals, magazines, and newspapers, capitalize all words of four letters or more (and all nouns, pronouns, verbs, adjectives, and adverbs of any length).

Place of publication and publisher

- Take the information about a book from its title page and copyright page. If more than one place of publication is listed, use only the first.
- Give the city and state for all US cities. Use postal abbreviations for all states.
- Give the city and country for all non-US cities; include the province for Canadian cities. Do not abbreviate the country and province.
- Do not give a state if the publisher's name includes it (Ann Arbor: University of Michigan Press, for example).
- In publishers' names, omit terms such as "Company" (or "Co.") and "Inc." but keep "Books" and "Press." Omit first names or initials (Norton, not W. W. Norton).
- If the publisher is the same as the author, use the word "Author" in the publisher position.

Volume, issue, and page numbers

- For a journal or a magazine, give only the volume number if the publication is paginated continuously through each volume; give the volume and issue numbers if each issue begins on page 1.
- Italicize the volume number and put the issue number, not italicized, in parentheses.
- When an article appears on consecutive pages, provide the range of pages. When an article does not appear on consecutive pages, give all page numbers: A1, A17.
- For daily and weekly newspapers, use "p." or "pp." before page numbers (if any). For journals and magazines, do not use "p." or "pp."

URLs, DOIs, and other retrieval information

- For articles and books from the web, use the DOI (digital object identifier) if the source has one, and do not give a URL. If a source does not have a DOI, give the URL.
- Use a retrieval date for a web source only if the content is likely to change. Most of the examples in 38b do not show a retrieval date because the content of the sources is stable. If you are unsure about whether to use a date, include it or consult your instructor.

General guidelines for listing authors   The formatting of authors' names in items 1–11 applies to all sources in print and on the web—books, articles, websites, and so on. For more models of specific source types, see items 12–65.

● **1. Single author**

author: last   year
name + initial(s)   (book)   title (book)

Rosenberg, T. (2011). *Join the club: How peer pressure can*

place of
publication   publisher

transform the world. New York, NY: Norton.

● **2. Two to seven authors**   List up to seven authors by last names followed by initials. Use an ampersand (&) before the name of the last author. (See items 3–5 on pp. 192–93 for in-text citations.)

all authors: year
last name + initial(s)   (journal)   title (article)

Kim, E. H., Hollon, S. D., & Olatunji, B. O. (2016). Clinical errors

journal
title   volume   page(s)

in cognitive-behavior therapy. *Psychotherapy, 53,* 325-330.

DOI

doi:dx.doi.org/10.1037/pst0000074

● **3. Eight or more authors**   List the first six authors followed by three ellipsis dots and the last author's name.

Tøttrup, A. P., Klaassen, R. H. G., Kristensen, M. W.,
    Strandberg, R., Vardanis, Y., Lindström, Å., . . . Thorup,
    K. (2012). Drought in Africa caused delayed arrival of
    European songbirds. *Science, 338,* 1307. doi:10.1126
    /science.1227548

● **4. Organization as author**

author:
organization name   year   title (book)

American Psychiatric Association. (2013). *Diagnostic and statistical manual*

organization
place   as author
edition   of publication   and publisher

of mental disorders (5th ed.). Washington, DC: Author.

● **5. Unknown author**

title (article) — year + month + day (weekly publication) — journal title

The rise of the sharing economy. (2013, March 9). *The Economist,*

volume, issue — page(s)

406(8826), 14.

● **6. Author using a pseudonym (pen name) or screen name** Use the author's real name, if known, and give the pseudonym or screen name in brackets exactly as it appears in the source. If only the screen name is known, begin with that name and do not use brackets. (See also items 44 and 65 on citing screen names in social media.)

screen name — year + month + day (daily publication) — title of original article

littlebigman. (2012, December 13). Re: Who's watching? Privacy

label

concerns persist as smart meters roll out [Comment].

title of publication

National Geographic Daily News. Retrieved from http://news

URL for web publication

.nationalgeographic.com/

● **7. Two or more works by the same author** Use the author's name for all entries. List the entries by year, the earliest first.

Heinrich, B. (2009). *Summer world: A season of bounty*. New

York, NY: Ecco.

Heinrich, B. (2012). *Life everlasting: The animal way of death*.

New York, NY: Houghton Mifflin Harcourt.

● **8. Two or more works by the same author in the same year** List the works alphabetically by title. In the parentheses, following the year add "a," "b," and so on. Use these same letters when giving the year in the in-text citation. (See also pp. 225–26 and item 9 on p. 194.)

Bower, B. (2012a, December 15). Families in flux. *Science News,*

182(12), 16.

Bower, B. (2012b, November 3). Human-Neandertal mating gets

a new date. *Science News, 182*(9), 8.

● **9. Editor** Use the abbreviation "Ed." for one editor, "Eds." for more than one editor.

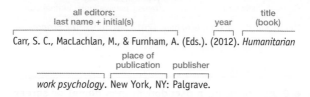

all editors:
last name + initial(s)   year   title (book)

Carr, S. C., MacLachlan, M., & Furnham, A. (Eds.). (2012). *Humanitarian*

place of
publication   publisher

work psychology. New York, NY: Palgrave.

● **10. Author and editor** Begin with the name of the author, followed by the name of the editor and the abbreviation "Ed." in parentheses. For a book with an author and two or more editors, use the abbreviation "Ed." after each editor's name: Gray, W., & Jones, P. (Ed.), & Smith, A. (Ed.).

author   editor   year   title (book)

James, W., & Pelikan, J. (Ed.). (2009). *The varieties of religious*

place of
publication   publisher

experience. New York, NY: Library of America. (Original

original
publication information

work published 1902)

● **11. Translator** Begin with the name of the author and the date. After the title, in parentheses place the name of the translator and the abbreviation "Trans." (for "Translator"). Add the original date of publication at the end of the entry.

author   year   title (book)   translator

Scheffer, P. (2011). *Immigrant nations* (L. Waters, Trans.).

place of
publication   publisher   original
publication information

Cambridge, England: Polity Press. (Original work published

2007)

Articles and other short works

► Citation at a glance: Online article in a journal or magazine, **page 207**

► Citation at a glance: Article from a database, **page 208**

● **12. Article in a journal**   If an article from the web or a database has no DOI, include the URL for the journal's home page.

a. Print

    all authors: last name + initial(s)   year

Bippus, A. M., Dunbar, N. E., & Liu, S.-J. (2012). Humorous

                    article title

responses to interpersonal complaints: Effects of humor

                         journal title   volume

style and nonverbal expression. *The Journal of Psychology, 146,*

   page(s)

437-453.

b. Web

    all authors:
    last name + initial(s)   year   article title

Vargas, N., & Schafer, M. H. (2013). Diversity in action:

Interpersonal networks and the distribution of advice.

                  volume,
     journal title   issue page(s)   DOI

Social Science Research, 42(1), 46-58. doi:10.1016/j

.ssresearch.2012.08.013

  author   year   article title

Brenton, S. (2011). When the personal becomes political:

                         journal title
                    (no volume available)

Mitigating damage following scandals. *Current Research in*

                    URL for journal home page

Social Psychology. Retrieved from https://uiowa.edu/crisp

/crisp/

c. Database

  author   year   article title

Sohn, K. (2012). The social class origins of U.S. teachers, 1860-1920.

                   volume,
       journal title   issue page(s)   DOI

Journal of Social History, 45(4), 908-935. doi:10.1093/jsh/shr121

● **13. Article in a magazine** If an article from the web or a database has no DOI, include the URL for the magazine's home page.

a. Print

author — Comstock, J.

year + month (monthly magazine) — (2012, December).

article title — The underrated sense.

magazine title — *Psychology Today,*

volume, issue — 45(6),

page(s) — 46-47.

b. Web

author — Burns, J.

date of posting (when available) — (2012, December 3).

article title — The measure of all things.

magazine title — *The American Prospect.*

URL for home page — Retrieved from http://prospect.org/

c. Database

author — Tucker, A.

year + month (monthly magazine) — (2012, November).

article title — Primal instinct.

magazine title — *Smithsonian,*

volume, issue — 43(7),

page(s) — 54-63.

URL for magazine home page — Retrieved from http://www.smithsonianmag.com/

● **14. Article in a newspaper**

a. Print

author — Swarns, R. L.

year + month + day — (2012, December 9).

article title — A family, for a few days a year.

newspaper title — *The New York Times,*

page(s) — pp. 1, 20.

b. Web

author: last name + initial(s) — Villanueva-Whitman, E.

year + month + day — (2012, November 27).

article title — Working to stimulate memory function.

newspaper title — *Des Moines Register.*

URL for home page — Retrieved from http://www.desmoinesregister.com/

Citation at a glance
Online article in a journal or magazine APA

To cite an online article in a journal or magazine in APA style, include the following elements:

1. Author(s)
2. Year of publication for journal; complete date for magazine
3. Title and subtitle of article
4. Name of journal or magazine
5. Volume number; issue number, if required (see p. 201)
6. DOI if the article has one; otherwise, URL for journal or magazine home page

ONLINE ARTICLE

REFERENCE LIST ENTRY FOR AN ONLINE ARTICLE IN A JOURNAL OR MAGAZINE

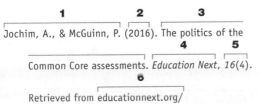

For more on citing articles in APA style, see items 12–14.

Citation at a glance

Article from a database APA

To cite an article from a database in APA style, include the following elements.

1 Author(s)
2 Year of publication for journal; complete date for magazine or newspaper
3 Title and subtitle of article
4 Name of periodical
5 Volume number; issue number, if required (see p. 201)
6 Page number(s)
7 DOI (digital object identifier)
8 URL for periodical's home page (if there is no DOI)

DATABASE RECORD

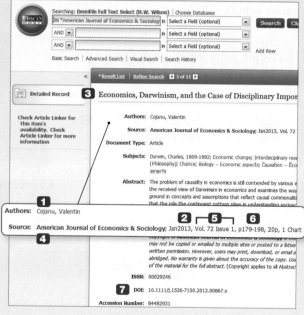

REFERENCE LIST ENTRY FOR AN ARTICLE FROM A DATABASE

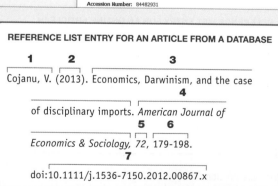

For more on citing articles from a database in APA style, see items 12 and 13.

● **15. Abstract**   Place the label "Abstract" in brackets after the article title.

a. Abstract of a journal article

Morales, J., Calvo, A., & Bialystok, E. (2013). Working memory
     development in monolingual and bilingual children
     [Abstract]. *Journal of Experimental Child Psychology, 114*,
     187-202. Retrieved from http://www.sciencedirect.com/

b. Abstract of a paper

Denham, B. (2012). Diffusing deviant behavior: A communication
     perspective on the construction of moral panics [Abstract].
     Paper presented at the AEJMC 2012 Conference, Chicago,
     IL. Retrieved from http://www.aejmc.org/home/2012/04
     /ctm-2012-abstracts/

● **16. Supplemental material**   Cite as you would an article, giving the author, date, and title of the supplemental material. Add the label "Supplemental material" in brackets following the title.

Reis, S., Grennfelt, P., Klimont, Z., Amann, M., ApSimon, H.,
     Hettelingh, J.-P., . . . Williams, M. (2012). From acid
     rain to climate change [Supplemental material]. *Science,
     338*(6111), 1153-1154. doi:10.1126/science.1226514

● **17. Letter to the editor**   If the letter has no title, use the bracketed label "Letter to the editor" as the title, as in the following example.

Lim, C. (2012, November-December). [Letter to the editor].
     Sierra. Retrieved from http://www.sierraclub.org/sierra/

● **18. Editorial or other unsigned article**

The business case for transit dollars [Editorial]. (2012,
     December 9). *Star Tribune*. Retrieved from http://www
     .startribune.com/

● **19. Newsletter article**

Scrivener, L. (n.d.). Why is the minimum wage issue important
     for food justice advocates? *Food Workers—Food Justice, 15*.
     Retrieved from http://www.thedatabank.com/dpg/199
     /pm.asp?nav=1&ID=41429

● **20. Review** In brackets, give the type of work reviewed, the title, and the author for a book or the year for a film. If the review has no author or title, use the material in brackets as the title.

Aviram, R. B. (2012). [Review of the book *What do I say? The therapist's guide to answering client questions*, by L. N. Edelstein & C. A. Waehler]. *Psychotherapy, 49*(4), 570-571. doi:10.1037/a0029815

Bradley, A., & Olufs, E. (2012). Family dynamics and school violence [Review of the motion picture *We need to talk about Kevin*, 2011]. *PsycCRITIQUES, 57*(49). doi:10.1037/a0030982

● **21. Published interview**

Githongo, J. (2012, November 20). A conversation with John Githongo [Interview by Baobab]. *The Economist*. Retrieved from http://www.economist.com/

● **22. Article in a reference work (encyclopedia, dictionary, wiki)**

a. Print

Konijn, E. A. (2008). Affects and media exposure. In W. Donsbach (Ed.), *The international encyclopedia of communication* (Vol. 1, pp. 123-129). Malden, MA: Blackwell.

b. Web

Ethnomethodology. (2006). In *STS wiki*. Retrieved December 15, 2012, from http://www.stswiki.org/index.php?title =Ethnomethodology

● **23. Comment on an online article** If the writer's real name and screen name are given, put the real name first, followed by the screen name in brackets.

Danboy125. (2012, November 9). Re: No flowers on the psych ward [Comment]. *The Atlantic*. Retrieved from http://www .theatlantic.com/

● **24. Testimony before a legislative body**

Carmona, R. H. (2004, March 2). *The growing epidemic of childhood obesity*. Testimony before the Subcommittee on Competition, Foreign Commerce, and Infrastructure of the U.S. Senate Committee on Commerce, Science, and Transportation. Retrieved from http://www.hhs.gov/asl/testify/t040302.html

● **25. Paper presented at a meeting or symposium (unpublished)**

Karimi, S., Key, G., & Tat, D. (2011, April 22). *Complex predicates in focus*. Paper presented at the West Coast Conference on Formal Linguistics, Tucson, AZ.

● **26. Poster session at a conference**

Lacara, N. (2011, April 24). *Predicate which appositives*. Poster session presented at the West Coast Conference on Formal Linguistics, Tucson, AZ.

Books and other long works

► Citation at a glance: Book, **page 212**

● **27. Basic format for a book**

a. Print

```
author(s):
last name
+ initial(s)     year              book title
┌─────────┐  ┌──────┐  ┌──────────────────────────────────┐
```
Child, B. J. (2012). *Holding our world together: Ojibwe women*
```
                            place of
                            publication   publisher
┌──────────────────────────────┐  ┌─────────┐ ┌──────┐
```
and the survival of community. New York, NY: Viking.

b. Web (or online library)   Give the URL for the home page of the website or the online library.

```
        author(s)              year       book title
┌──────────────────────────┐  ┌──────┐  ┌──────────────┐
```
Amponsah, N. A., & Falola, T. (2012). *Women's roles in sub-*
```
                                            URL
                            ┌──────────────────────────────┐
```
Saharan Africa. Retrieved from http://books.google.com/

c. E-book   Give the version in brackets after the title ("Kindle version," "Nook version," and so on). Include the DOI or, if a DOI is not available, the URL for the home page of the site from which you downloaded the book.

Wolf, D. A., & Folbre, N. (Eds.). (2012). *Universal coverage of long-term care in the United States* [Adobe Digital Editions version]. Retrieved from https://www.russellsage.org/

Citation at a glance
Book APA

To cite a print book in APA style, include the following elements.

1. Author(s)
2. Year of publication
3. Title and subtitle
4. Place of publication
5. Publisher

TITLE PAGE

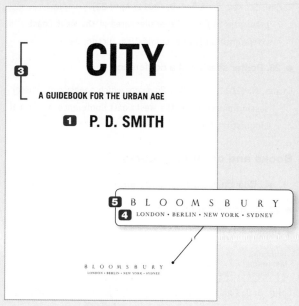

3 CITY
A GUIDEBOOK FOR THE URBAN AGE
1 P. D. SMITH

5 B L O O M S B U R Y
4 LONDON · BERLIN · NEW YORK · SYDNEY

BLOOMSBURY
LONDON · BERLIN · NEW YORK · SYDNEY

FROM COPYRIGHT PAGE

First published in Great Britain and the USA in 2012 **2**

Bloomsbury Publishing Plc, 50 Bedford Square, London WC1B 3DP
Bloomsbury USA, 175 Fifth Avenue, New York, NY 10010

Copyright © 2012 by P. D. Smith

REFERENCE LIST ENTRY FOR A PRINT BOOK

| 1 | 2 | 3 |

Smith, P. D. (2012). *City: A guidebook for the urban age.*
| 4 | 5 |
London, England: Bloomsbury.

For more on citing books in APA style, see items 27–34.

● **27. Basic format for a book (*cont.*)**

d. Database   Give the URL for the database.

Beasley, M. H. (2012). *Women of the Washington press: Politics,
    prejudice, and persistence*. Retrieved from http://muse.jhu.edu/

● **28. Edition other than the first**

Harvey, P. (2013). *An introduction to Buddhism: Teachings, history,
    and practices* (2nd ed.). Cambridge, England: Cambridge
    University Press.

● **29. Selection in an anthology or a collection**

a. Entire anthology

              editor(s)   year

Warren, A. E. A., Lerner, R. M., & Phelps, E. (Eds.). (2011).

                        title of anthology

Thriving and spirituality among youth: Research perspectives
                      place of
                  publication   publisher

and future possibilities. Hoboken, NJ: Wiley.

b. Selection in an anthology

author of
selection   year   title of selection

Lazar, S. W. (2012). Neural correlates of positive youth development.

                  editors of anthology

In A. E. A. Warren, R. M. Lerner, & E. Phelps (Eds.), *Thriving*

                title of anthology

and spirituality among youth: Research perspectives and future
          page numbers   place of
          of selection publication publisher

possibilities (pp. 77-90). Hoboken, NJ: Wiley.

● **30. Multivolume work**

a. All volumes

Khalakdina, M. (2008-2011). *Human development in the Indian context:
    A socio-cultural focus* (Vols. 1-2). New Delhi, India: Sage.

b. One volume, with title

Jensen, R. E. (Ed.). (2012). *Voices of the American West: Vol. 1.
    The Indian interviews of Eli S. Ricker, 1903-1919*. Lincoln:
    University of Nebraska Press.

● **31. Introduction, preface, foreword, or afterword**

Zachary, L. J. (2012). Foreword. In L. A. Daloz, *Mentor: Guiding the journey of adult learners* (pp. v-vii). San Francisco, CA: Jossey-Bass.

● **32. Dictionary or other reference work**

Leong, F. T. L. (Ed.). (2008). *Encyclopedia of counseling* (Vols. 1-4). Thousand Oaks, CA: Sage.

● **33. Republished book**

Mailer, N. (2008). *Miami and the siege of Chicago: An informal history of the Republican and Democratic conventions of 1968*. New York, NY: New York Review Books. (Original work published 1968)

● **34. Book in a language other than English**   Place the English translation, not italicized, in brackets.

Carminati, G. G., & Méndez, A. (2012). *Étapes de vie, étapes de soins* [Stages of life, stages of care]. Chêne-Bourg, Switzerland: Médecine & Hygiène.

● **35. Dissertation**

a. Published

Hymel, K. M. (2009). *Essays in urban economics* (Doctoral dissertation). Available from ProQuest Dissertations and Theses database. (AAT 3355930)

b. Unpublished

Mitchell, R. D. (2007). *The Wesleyan Quadrilateral: Relocating the conversation* (Unpublished doctoral dissertation). Claremont School of Theology, Claremont, CA.

● **36. Conference proceedings**

Yu, F.-Y., Hirashima, T., Supnithi, T., & Biswas, G. (2011). *Proceedings of the 19th International Conference on Computers in Education: ICCE 2011*. Retrieved from http://www.apsce.net:8080/icce2011/program/proceedings/

● **37. Government document**   If the document has a report number, place the number in parentheses after the title. If it does not have a number, place a period after the title.

U.S. Census Bureau, Bureau of Economic Analysis. (2012, December). *U.S. international trade in goods and services, October 2012* (Report No. CB12-232, BEA12-55, FT-900 [12-10]). Retrieved from http://www.census.gov/foreign-trade/Press-Release /2012pr/10/

● **38. Report from a private organization**   For a print source, if the publisher and the author are the same, see item 4 on page 202.

Ford Foundation. (2012, November). *Eastern Africa*. Retrieved from http://www.fordfoundation.org/pdfs/library/Eastern-Africa -brochure-2012.pdf

● **39. Legal source**   The title of a court case is italicized in an in-text citation but not in the reference list.

Sweatt v. Painter, 339 U.S. 629 (1950). Retrieved from Cornell University Law School, Legal Information Institute website: http://www.law.cornell.edu/supct/html/historics /USSC_CR_0339_0629_ZS.html

● **40. Sacred or classical text**   It is not necessary to list sacred works such as the Bible or the Qur'an or classical Greek and Roman works (such as the *Odyssey*) in your reference list. See item 19 on page 197 for how to cite these sources in the text of your paper.

Websites and parts of websites

▶ Citation at a glance: Section in a web document, **page 216**

● **41. Entire website**   Do not include an entire website in the reference list. Give the URL in parentheses in the text of your paper. (See item 13 on p. 196.)

● **42. Document from a website**   If the publisher is known and is not named as the author, include the publisher in your retrieval statement. (See models on p. 217.)

Citation at a glance
Section in a web document APA

To cite a section in a web document in APA style, include the following elements.

1   Author(s)
2   Date of publication or most recent update ("n.d." if there is no date)
3   Title of section
4   Title of document
5   URL of section

WEB DOCUMENT CONTENTS PAGE

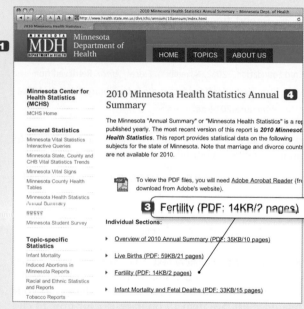

1

Minnesota Department of Health

HOME   TOPICS   ABOUT US

Minnesota Center for Health Statistics (MCHS)
MCHS Home

General Statistics
Minnesota Vital Statistics Interactive Queries
Minnesota State, County and CHB Vital Statistics Trends
Minnesota Vital Signs
Minnesota County Health Tables
Minnesota Health Statistics Annual Summary
Minnesota Student Survey

Topic-specific Statistics
Infant Mortality
Induced Abortions in Minnesota Reports
Racial and Ethnic Statistics and Reports
Tobacco Reports

4 2010 Minnesota Health Statistics Annual Summary

The Minnesota "Annual Summary" or "Minnesota Health Statistics" is a re[port] published yearly. The most recent version of this report is *2010 Minnesot[a] Health Statistics*. This report provides statistical data on the following subjects for the state of Minnesota. Note that marriage and divorce counts are not available for 2010.

To view the PDF files, you will need Adobe Acrobat Reader (fre[e] download from Adobe's website).

3 Fertility (PDF: 14KB/2 pages)

Individual Sections:

▸ Overview of 2010 Annual Summary (PDF: 35KB/10 pages)
▸ Live Births (PDF: 59KB/21 pages)
▸ Fertility (PDF: 14KB/2 pages)
▸ Infant Mortality and Fetal Deaths (PDF: 33KB/15 pages)

ON-SCREEN VIEW OF DOCUMENT

Fertility Table 1
Total Reported Pregnancies by Outcome and Rate
Minnesota Residents, 1981 - 2010

Year	Total Reported Pregnancies*	Live Births	Induced Abortions	Fetal Deaths	Female Population Ages 15-44	Pregnancy Rate**
1981	84,934	68,652	15,821	461	967,087	87.8
1982	84,500	68,512	15,559	429	977,905	86.4
1983	80,530	65,559	14,514	457	981,287	82.1
1984	82,736	66,715	15,556	465	985,608	83.9
1985	83,853	67,412	16,002	439	994,249	84.3
1986	81,882	65,766	15,716	400	997,501	82.1
1987	81,318	65,168	15,746	404	1,004,801	80.9
1988	83,335	66,745	16,124	466	1,020,209	81.7

5 http://www.health.state.mn.us/divs/chs/annsum/10annsum/Fertility2010.pdf

For more on citing documents from websites in APA style, see
items 42 and 43.

● **42. Document from a website** *(cont.)*

Wagner, D. A., Murphy, K. M., & De Korne, H. (2012, December).
    Learning first: A research agenda for improving learning in
    low-income countries. Retrieved from Brookings Institution
    website: http://www.brookings.edu/research/papers
    /2012/12/learning-first-wagner-murphy-de-korne

Centers for Disease Control and Prevention. (2012, December
    10). *Concussion in winter sports*. Retrieved from http://
    www.cdc.gov/Features/HockeyConcussions/index.html

● **43. Section in a web document**   Cite as a chapter in
a book or a selection in an anthology (see item 29b).

Chang, W.-Y., & Milan, L. M. (2012, October). Relationship
    between degree field and emigration. In *International*
    mobility and employment characteristics among recent
    recipients of U.S. doctorates. Retrieved from National
    Science Foundation website: http://www.nsf.gov
    /statistics/infbrief/nsf13300

● **44. Blog post**   If the writer's real name and screen
name are given, put the real name first, followed by
the screen name in brackets.

Kerssen, T. (2012, October 5). Hunger is political: Food
    Sovereignty Prize honors social movements [Blog post].
    Retrieved from http://www.foodfirst.org/en/node/4020

● **45. Blog comment**

Studebakerhawk_14611. (2012, December 5). Re: A people's history
of MOOCs [Blog comment]. Retrieved from http://www
.insidehighered.com/blogs/library-babel-fish/people's-history
-moocs

Audio, visual, and multimedia sources

● **46. Podcast**

Schulz, K. (2011, March). *Kathryn Schulz: On being wrong* [Video
podcast]. Retrieved from TED on http://itunes.apple.com/

Taylor, A., & Parfitt, G. (2011, January 13). *Physical activity
and mental health: What's the evidence?* [Audio podcast].
Retrieved from Open University on http://itunes.apple.com/

● **47. Video or audio on the web**

Kurzen, B. (2012, April 5). *Going beyond Muslim-Christian conflict
in Nigeria* [Video file]. Retrieved from http://www.youtube
.com/watch?v=JD8MIJOA050

Bever, T., Piattelli-Palmarini, M., Hammond, M., Barss, A., & Bergesen,
A. (2012, February 2). *A basic introduction to Chomsky's
linguistics* [Audio file]. Retrieved from University of Arizona,
College of Social & Behavioral Sciences, Department of
Linguistics website: http://linguistics.arizona.edu/node/711

● **48. Transcript of an audio or a video file**

Malone, T. W. (2012, November 21). *Collective intelligence*
[Transcript of video file]. Retrieved from http://edge.org
/conversation/collective-intelligence

● **49. Film (DVD, BD, or other format)** In brackets following the title, add a description of the medium: "Motion
picture," "Video file," "DVD," "BD," and so on. For a
motion picture or a DVD or BD, add the location where
the film was made and the studio. If you retrieved the
film from the web or used a streaming service, give
the URL for the home page.

Affleck, B. (Director). (2012). *Argo* [Motion picture]. Burbank,
CA: Warner Bros.

Ross, G. (Director and Writer), & Collins, S. (Writer). (2012). *The hunger games* [Video file]. Retrieved from http://netflix.com/

● **50. Television or radio program**

a. Series

Hager, M. (Executive producer), & Schieffer, B. (Moderator). (2012). *Face the nation* [Television series]. Washington, DC: CBS News.

b. Episode on the web

Morton, D. (Producer). (2012). Fast times at West Philly High [Television series episode]. In M. Hager (Executive producer), *Frontline*. Retrieved from http://www.wgbh.org/

● **51. Music recording**

Chibalonza, A. Jubilee. (2012). On *African voices* [CD]. Merenberg, Germany: ZYX Music.

African voices [CD]. (2012). Merenberg, Germany: ZYX Music.

● **52. Lecture, speech, or address**

Verghese, A. (2012, December 6). *Colonialism and patterns of ethnic conflict in contemporary India*. Address at the Freeman Spogli Institute, Stanford University, Stanford, CA.

● **53. Data set or graphic representation of data (graph, chart, table)** If the item is numbered in the source, indicate the number in parentheses after the title. If the graphic appears within a larger document, do not italicize the title of the graphic.

U.S. Department of Agriculture, Economic Research Service. (2011). *Daily intake of nutrients by food source: 2005-08* [Data set]. Retrieved from http://www.ers.usda.gov/data -products/food-consumption-and-nutrient-intakes.aspx

Gallup. (2012, December 5). *In U.S., more cite obesity as most urgent health problem* [Graphs]. Retrieved from http:// www.gallup.com/poll/159083/cite-obesity-urgent-health -problem.aspx

● **54. Mobile application software (app)** Begin with the developer of the app, if known (as in the second example on p. 220).

● **54. Mobile application software (app) (*cont.*)**

MindNode Touch 2.3 [Mobile application software]. (2012).
      Retrieved from http://itunes.apple.com/

Source Tree Solutions. (2012). mojoPortal [Mobile application
      software]. Retrieved from http://www.microsoft.com/web
      /gallery/

● **55. Video game**   If the game can be played on the
web or was downloaded from the web, give the URL
instead of publication information.

Firaxis Games. (2010). Sid Meier's civilization V [Video game].
      New York, NY: Take-Two Interactive. Xbox 360.

Atom Entertainment. (2012). Edgeworld [Video game]. Retrieved
      from http://www.addictinggames.com/

● **56. Map**

Ukraine [Map]. (2008). Retrieved from the University of Texas
      at Austin Perry-Castañeda Library Map Collection website:
      http://www.lib.utexas.edu/maps/cia08/ukraine_sm_2008.gif

Syrian uprising map [Map]. (2012, October). Retrieved from
      http://www.polgeonow.com/2012/10/syria-uprising-map
      -october-2012-7.html

● **57. Advertisement**

VMware [Advertisement]. (2012, September). *Harvard Business
      Review, 90*(9), 27.

● **58. Work of art or photograph**

Olson, A. (2011). *Short story* [Painting]. Museum of Contemporary
      Art, Chicago, IL.

Crowner, S. (2012). *Kurtyna fragments* [Painting]. Retrieved
      from http://www.walkerart.org/

Weber, J. (1992). *Toward freedom* [Outdoor mural]. Sherman Oaks, CA.

● **59. Brochure or fact sheet**

National Council of State Boards of Nursing. (2011). *A nurse's
      guide to professional boundaries* [Brochure]. Retrieved
      from https://www.ncsbn.org/

World Health Organization. (2012, September). *Road traffic injuries* (No. 358) [Fact sheet]. Retrieved from http://www.who.int/mediacentre/factsheets/fs358/en/index.html

● 60. Press release

Urban Institute. (2012, October 11). Two studies address health policy on campaign trail [Press release]. Retrieved from http://www.urban.org/publications/901537.html

● 61. Presentation slides

Boeninger, C. F. (2008, August). *Web 2.0 tools for reference and instructional services* [Presentation slides]. Retrieved from http://libraryvoice.com/archives/2008/08/04/opal-20-conference-presentation-slides

● **62. Lecture notes or other course materials** Cite materials that your instructor has posted on the web as you would a web document or a section in a web document (see item 42 or 43). Cite other material from your instructor as personal communication in the text of your paper (see items 15 and 16 on p. 196).

Blum, R. (2011). Neurodevelopment in the first decade of life [Lecture notes and audio file]. In R. Blum & L. M. Blum, *Child health and development*. Retrieved from http://ocw.jhsph.edu/index.cfm/go/viewCourse/course/childhealth/coursePage/lectureNotes/

Personal communication and social media

● **63. Email** Email messages, letters, and other personal communication are not included in the list of references. (See item 15 on p. 196 for citing these sources in the text of your paper.)

● **64. Online posting** If an online posting is not archived, cite it as a personal communication in the text of your paper and do not include it in the list of references. If the posting is archived, give the URL and the name of the discussion list if it is not part of the URL.

McKinney, J. (2006, December 19). Adult education-healthcare partnerships [Electronic mailing list message]. Retrieved from http://www.nifl.gov/pipermail/healthliteracy/2006/000524.html

● **65. Social media**   If the writer's real name and screen name are given, put the real name first, followed by the screen name in brackets. If only the screen name is known, begin with that name, not in brackets. Add the date of posting in parentheses (use "n.d." if the post has no date). For the title, include the entire post or a caption (up to forty words); use a description of the post if there is no title or caption. After the title, add an appropriate label in brackets such as "Tweet," "Facebook status update," or "Photograph." Include the URL for the post. Provide a retrieval date only if the content is undated. Cite personal media posts that are not accessible to all readers as personal communication in the text of your paper (see item 15 on p. 196).

National Science Foundation. (2015, December 8). Simulation shows key to building powerful magnetic fields 1.usa .gov/1TZUiJ6 #supernovas #supercomputers [Tweet]. Retrieved from https://twitter.com/NSF/status /674352440582545413/

U.S. Department of Education. (2015, December 10). We're watching President Obama sign the Every Student Succeeds Act [Facebook post]. Retrieved from http://www.facebook .com/ED.gov/

39 APA manuscript format; sample pages

The guidelines in this section are consistent with advice given in the *Publication Manual of the American Psychological Association*, 6th ed. (Washington, DC: APA, 2010), and with typical requirements for undergraduate papers.

39a APA manuscript format

Formatting the paper   The guidelines in this section describe APA's recommendations for formatting the text of your paper. For guidelines on preparing the reference list, see pages 225–26.

Font   If your instructor does not require a specific font, choose one that is standard and easy to read (such as Times New Roman).

Title page Begin at the top left, with the words "Running head," followed by a colon and the title of your paper (shortened to no more than fifty characters) in all capital letters. Put the page number 1 flush with the right margin.

About halfway down the page, on separate lines, center the full title of your paper, your name, and your school's name. At the bottom of the page, you may add the heading "Author Note," centered, followed by a brief paragraph that lists specific information about the course or department or provides acknowledgments or contact information. See pages 227 and 232 for sample title pages.

Page numbers and running head Number all pages with arabic numerals (1, 2, 3, and so on) in the upper right corner one-half inch from the top of the page. Flush with the left margin on the same line as the page number, type a running head consisting of the title of the paper (shortened to no more than fifty characters) in all capital letters. On the title page only, include the words "Running head" followed by a colon before the title. See pages 227–33.

Margins, line spacing, and paragraph indents Use margins of one inch on all sides of the page. Left-align the text.

Double-space throughout the paper. Indent the first line of each paragraph one-half inch.

Capitalization, italics, and quotation marks In headings and in titles of works in the text of the paper, capitalize all words of four letters or more (and all nouns, pronouns, verbs, adjectives, and adverbs of any length). (See "Headings" on p. 224 for an exception for third-level headings.) Capitalize the first word following a colon if the word begins a complete sentence.

Italicize the titles of books, journals, magazines, and other long works, such as websites. Use quotation marks around the titles of articles, short stories, and other short works.

NOTE: APA has different requirements for titles in the reference list. See page 226.

Long quotations When a quotation is forty or more words, set it off from the text by indenting it one-half inch from the left margin. Double-space the quotation.

Do not use quotation marks around it. (See p. 187 for more information and an example.)

Footnotes   To insert a footnote number in the text of your paper, place the number, raised above the line (superscript), immediately following any mark of punctuation except a dash. At the bottom of the page, begin the note with a one-half-inch indent and the superscript number corresponding to the number in the text. Insert an extra double-spaced line between the last line of text on the page and the footnote. Double-space the footnote.

Abstract and keywords   An abstract is a 150-to-250-word paragraph that provides readers with a quick overview of your essay. If your instructor requires one, include an abstract on a new page after the title page. Center the word "Abstract" (in regular font, not boldface) one inch from the top of the page. Double-space the abstract and do not indent the first line.

A list of keywords follows the abstract; the keywords help readers search for a published paper on the web or in a database. On the line following the abstract, begin with the word "Keywords" and a colon, italicized and indented one-half inch. Then list important words related to your paper. (See p. 228 for an example.) Check with your instructor for requirements in your course.

Headings   For most undergraduate papers, one level of heading is usually sufficient. (See pp. 233–34.)

First-level headings are centered and boldface. In research papers and laboratory reports, the major headings are "Method," "Results," and "Discussion." In other types of papers, the major headings should be informative and concise, conveying the structure of the paper. (The headings "Abstract" and "References" are not boldface.)

Second-level headings are flush left and boldface. Third-level headings are indented and boldface, followed by a period and the text on the same line.

First-Level Heading Centered

Second-Level Heading Flush Left

Third-level heading indented. Text immediately follows.

Visuals (tables and figures)   APA classifies visuals as tables and figures (figures include graphs, charts, drawings, and photographs).

Label each table with an arabic numeral (Table 1, Table 2, and so on) and provide a clear title. Place the label and the title on separate lines above the table, left-aligned and double-spaced. Type the table number in regular font; italicize the table title.

If you have used data from an outside source or have taken or adapted the table from a source, give the source information in a note below the table. Begin with the word "Note," italicized and followed by a period. If any data in the table require an explanatory footnote, use a superscript lowercase letter in the table and in a footnote following the source note. Double-space source notes and footnotes; do not indent the first line of each note. (See p. 230 for an example of a table.)

For each figure, place the figure number and a caption below the figure, left-aligned and double-spaced. Begin with the word "Figure" and an arabic numeral, both italicized, followed by a period. Place the caption, not italicized, on the same line. If you have taken or adapted the figure from an outside source, give the source information immediately following the caption. Use the term "From" or "Adapted from" before the source information.

Preparing the list of references   Begin your list of references on a new page at the end of the paper. Center the title "References" one inch from the top of the page. Double-space throughout. For a sample reference list, see page 231.

Indenting entries   Type the first line of each entry flush left and indent any additional lines one-half inch.

Alphabetizing the list   Alphabetize the reference list by the last names of the authors (or editors) or by the first word of an organization name (if the author is an organization). When a work has no author or editor, alphabetize by the first word of the title other than *A*, *An*, or *The*.

If your list includes two or more works by the same author, arrange the entries by year, the earliest first. If your list includes two or more works by the same author in the same year, arrange the works alphabetically by title. Add the letters "a," "b," and

so on within the parentheses after the year. For journal articles, use only the year and the letter: (2012a).
For articles in magazines and newspapers, use the
full date and the letter in the reference list: (2012a,
July 7); use only the year and the letter in the in-text
citation.

Authors' names Invert all authors' names and use initials for first and middle names. Separate the names
with commas. For two to seven authors, use an ampersand (&) before the last author's name. For eight or
more authors, give the first six authors, three ellipsis
dots, and the last author (see item 3 on p. 202).

Titles of books and articles In the reference list, italicize
the titles and subtitles of books. Do not italicize or use
quotation marks around the titles of articles. For both
books and articles, capitalize only the first word of the
title and subtitle (and all proper nouns). Capitalize names
of journals, magazines, and newspapers as you would
capitalize them normally (see 22c).

Abbreviations for page numbers Abbreviations for
"page" and "pages" ("p." and "pp.") are used before
page numbers of newspaper articles and selections in
anthologies (see item 14 on p. 206 and item 29 on p.
213). Do not use "p." or "pp." before page numbers of
articles in journals and magazines (see items 12 and 13
on pp. 205 and 206).

Breaking a URL or DOI When a URL or a DOI (digital
object identifier) must be divided, break it after a double slash or before any other mark of punctuation. Do
not insert a hyphen; do not add a period at the end. If
you will post your project online or submit it electronically and you want to include live URLs for readers to
click on, do not insert any line breaks.

39b Sample APA pages

On the following pages are excerpts from a research
paper written for an education class, a clinical practice
paper written for a nursing class, and a business proposal written for a business class.

Sample APA title page

Running head: TECHNOLOGY AND STUDENT-CENTERED LEARNING   1 **2**

1

Technology and the Shift From Teacher-Delivered

to Student-Centered Learning:

A Review of the Literature   **3**

April Bo Wang

Glen County Community College

Author Note

This paper was prepared for Education 107, taught by   **4**

Professor Gomez.

1 Short title, no more than 50 characters, in all capital
letters on all pages; words "Running head" on title page only.
2 Arabic page number on all pages. **3** Full title and writer's
name and affiliation, centered. **4** Author's note (optional)
for extra information.

(Annotations indicate APA-style formatting and effective writing.)

Sample APA abstract

1 TECHNOLOGY AND STUDENT-CENTERED LEARNING   2

2   Abstract

3 In recent decades, instructors and administrators have viewed
student-centered learning as a promising pedagogical practice that
offers both the hope of increasing academic performance and a
solution for teacher shortages. Differing from the traditional model
of instruction in which a teacher delivers content from the front
of a classroom, student-centered learning puts the students at the
center of teaching and learning. Students set their own learning
goals, select appropriate resources, and progress at their own pace.
Student-centered learning has produced both positive results and
increases in students' self-esteem. Given the recent proliferation
of technology in classrooms, school districts are poised for success
in making the shift to student-centered learning. The question for
district leaders, however, is how to effectively balance existing
teacher talent with educational technology.

4   *Keywords:* digital learning, student-centered learning,
personalized learning, education technology, transmissive, blended

1 Short title, no more than 50 characters, flush left; page
number flush right. **2** Abstract appears on separate page;
heading centered and not boldface. **3** Abstract is a 150-to-
250-word overview of paper. **4** Keywords (optional) help
readers search for a published paper on the web or in a
database.

Sample APA page

Technology and the Shift From Teacher-Delivered
to Student-Centered Learning: **1**
A Review of the Literature

In the United States, most public school systems are
struggling with teacher shortages, which are projected to worsen
as the number of applicants to education schools decreases
(Donitsa-Schmidt & Zuzovsky, 2014, p. 420). Citing federal data,
The New York Times reported a 30% drop in "people entering teacher
preparation programs" between 2010 and 2014 (Rich, 2015). Especially   **2**
in science and math fields, the teacher shortage is projected to
escalate in the next 10 years (Hutchison, 2012). In recent decades,
instructors and administrators have viewed the practice of student-
centered learning as one promising solution. Unlike traditional
teacher-delivered (also called "transmissive") instruction, student-
centered learning allows students to help direct their own education
by setting their own goals and selecting appropriate resources for
achieving those goals. Though student-centered learning might
once have been viewed as an experimental solution in understaffed
schools, it is gaining credibility as an effective pedagogical practice.
What is also gaining momentum is the idea that technology might
play a significant role in fostering student-centered learning. This
literature review will examine three key questions:

1. In what ways is student-centered learning effective?   **3**
2. Can educational technology help students drive their own
   learning?
3. How can public schools effectively combine teacher talent
   and educational technology?

In the face of mounting teacher shortages, public schools   **4**
should embrace educational technology that promotes student-
centered learning in order to help all students become engaged
and successful learners.

---

1 Full title, centered and not boldface. **2** Source provides
background information and context. **3** Questions provide
organization and are repeated as main headings. **4** Paper's
thesis.

Sample APA table

1 Table 1

2 *Comparison of Two Approaches to Teaching and Learning*

Teaching and learning period	Instructor-centered approach	Student-centered approach
Before class	• Instructor prepares lecture/instruction on new topic. • Students complete homework on previous topic.	• Students read and view new material, practice new concepts, and prepare questions ahead of class. • Instructor views student practice and questions and identifies learning opportunities.
During class	• Instructor delivers new material in a lecture or prepared discussion. • Students—unprepared—listen, watch, take notes, and try to follow along with the new material.	• Students lead discussions of the new material or practice applying the concepts or skills in an active environment. • Instructor answers student questions and provides immediate feedback.
After class	• Instructor grades homework and gives feedback about the previous lesson. • Students work independently to practice or apply the new concepts.	• Students apply concepts/skills to more complex tasks, some of their own choosing, individually and in groups. • Instructor posts additional resources to help students.

3 *Note.* Adapted from "The Flipped Class Demystified," n.d., retrieved from New York University website: https://www.nyu.edu/faculty/teaching -and-learning-resources/instructional-technology-support/instructional -design-assessment/flipped-classes/the-flipped-class-demystified.html.

1 Table compares and contrasts two key concepts. **2** Table number and title on separate lines; title italic. **3** Note gives sources of data used in table. Format of note differs from format of reference list.

Sample APA list of references

References   **1**

Bell, S. (2010). Project-based learning for the 21st century: Skills
    for the future. *The Clearing House, 83*(2), 39-43.

Çubukçu, Z. (2012). Teachers' evaluation of student-centered
    learning environments. *Education, 133*(1), 49-66.

Demski, J. (2012, January). This time it's personal. *THE Journal*   **2**
    (Technological Horizons in Education), 39(1), 32-36.

Donitsa-Schmidt, S., & Zuzovsky, R. (2014). Teacher supply and   **3**
    demand: The school level perspective. *American Journal of*
    Educational Research, 2(6), 420-429.

Friedlaender, D., Burns, D., Lewis-Charp, H., Cook-Harvey, C. M.,   **4**
    & Darling-Hammond, L. (2014). Student-centered schools:
    Closing the opportunity gap [Research brief]. Retrieved from
    Stanford Center for Opportunity Policy in Education website:
    https://edpolicy.stanford.edu/sites/default/files/scope-pub
    -student-centered-research-brief.pdf

Horn, M. B., & Staker, H. (2011). The rise of K-12 blended learning.   **5**
    Retrieved from Innosight Institute website: http://www
    .christenseninstitute.org/wp-content/uploads/2013/04/The
    -rise-of-K-12-blended-learning.pdf

Hutchison, L. F. (2012). Addressing the STEM teacher shortage in
    American schools: Ways to recruit and retain effective STEM
    teachers. *Action in Teacher Education, 34*(5/6), 541-550.

International Society for Technology in Education. (2016). *Student-*
    centered learning. Retrieved from http://www.iste.org
    /standards/essential-conditions/student-centered-learning

Mitra, S. (2013, February). *Build a school in the cloud* [Video file].
    Retrieved from https://www.ted.com/talks/sugata_mitra
    _build_a_school_in_the_cloud?language=en

1 List of references on new page; heading centered and not boldface. **2** List alphabetized by authors' last names (or by titles for works with no authors). **3** All authors' names inverted, with initials for first and middle name(s). **4** Work with up to seven authors: all authors listed, with ampersand (&) before last author's name. **5** First line of each entry left-aligned, subsequent lines indented ½". Double-spaced throughout.

Sample APA title page

1 Running head: ALL AND HTN IN ONE CLIENT   1

2

Acute Lymphoblastic Leukemia and Hypertension in One Client:

A Nursing Practice Paper

3

Julie Riss

George Mason University

4   Author Note

This paper was prepared for Nursing 451, taught by Professor Durham. The author wishes to thank the nursing staff of Milltown General Hospital for help in understanding client care and diagnosis.

---

1 Short title, no more than 50 characters, in all capital letters on all pages; words "Running head" on title page only. **2** Arabic page number on all pages. **3** Full title and writer's name and affiliation, centered. **4** Author's note (optional) for extra information.

(Annotations indicate APA-style formatting and effective writing.)

Sample APA page

Acute Lymphoblastic Leukemia and Hypertension in One Client: ❶

A Nursing Practice Paper

Historical and Physical Assessment   ❷

Physical History   ❸

E.B. is a 16-year-old white male 5'10" tall weighing 190
lb. He was admitted to the hospital on April 14, 2006, due to
decreased platelets and a need for a PRBC transfusion. He was
diagnosed in October 2005 with T-cell acute lymphoblastic   ❹
leukemia (ALL), after a 2-week period of decreased energy,
decreased oral intake, easy bruising, and petechia. The client had
experienced a 20-lb weight loss in the previous 6 months. At the
time of diagnosis, his CBC showed a WBC count of 32, an H & H
of 13/38, and a platelet count of 34,000. He began induction
chemotherapy on October 12, 2005, receiving vincristine,
6-mercaptopurine, doxorubicin, intrathecal methotrexate, and then
high-dose methotrexate per protocol. During his hospital stay he
required packed red cells and platelets on two different occasions.
He was diagnosed with hypertension (HTN) due to systolic blood
pressure readings consistently ranging between 130s and 150s
and was started on nifedipine. E.B. has a history of mild ADHD,
migraines, and deep vein thrombosis (DVT). He has tolerated the
induction and consolidation phases of chemotherapy well and is
now in the maintenance phase.

Psychosocial History   ❺

There is a possibility of a depressive episode a year
previously when he would not attend school. He got into serious
trouble and was sent to a shelter for 1 month. He currently lives
with his mother, father, and 14-year-old sister.

Family History

Paternal: prostate cancer and hypertension in grandfather

❶ Full title, centered and not boldface. ❷ First-level heading,
centered and boldface. ❸ Second-level heading, left-aligned
and boldface. ❹ Writer's summary of client's medical history.
❺ Headings guide readers and define sections.

Sample proposal (memo), APA style

❶ ❷   MEMORANDUM
To: Jay Crosson, Senior Vice President, Human Resources
From: Kelly Ratajczak, Intern, Purchasing Department
Subject: Proposal to Add a Wellness Program
Date: April 24, 2006

❸ Health care costs are rising. In the long run, implementing
a wellness program in our corporate culture will decrease the
company's health care costs.
❹

❺ Research indicates that nearly 70% of health care costs are from
common illnesses related to high blood pressure, overweight, lack
of exercise, high cholesterol, stress, poor nutrition, and other
preventable health issues (Hall, 2006). Health care costs are a
major expense for most businesses, and they do not reflect costs
due to the loss of productivity or absenteeism. A wellness program
would address most, if not all, of these health care issues and
related costs.

❻ **Benefits of Healthier Employees**

Not only would a wellness program substantially reduce costs
associated with employee health care, but our company would
prosper through many other benefits. Businesses that have
wellness programs show a lower cost in production, fewer sick
days, and healthier employees ("Workplace Health," 2006). Our
healthier employees will help to cut not only our production and
absenteeism costs but also potential costs such as higher turnover
because of low employee morale.

Implementing the Program

Implementing a good wellness program means making small
changes to the work environment, starting with a series of
information sessions.

❶ Formatting consistent with typical style for business memo.
❷ Title page counted in numbering, but no page number
appears. ❸ Clear point in first paragraph. ❹ Paragraphs
separated by extra line of space; first line of paragraph not
indented. ❺ Introduction provides background information.
❻ Headings, left-aligned and boldface, define sections.

Chicago
Papers

Most history instructors and some humanities instructors require you to document sources with footnotes or endnotes based on the *Chicago Manual of Style* system explained in section 43. When you write a *Chicago*-style paper using sources, you face three main challenges: (1) supporting a thesis, (2) citing your sources and avoiding plagiarism, and (3) integrating source material effectively.

40   Supporting a thesis

Most research assignments ask you to form a thesis, or main idea, and to support that thesis with well-organized evidence. A thesis is a one-sentence (or occasionally a two-sentence) statement of your central idea. Usually your thesis will appear at the end of the first paragraph (see the example on p. 273).

40a   Forming a working thesis

A working thesis expresses more than your opinion; it expresses your informed, reasoned answer to your research question—a question about which people might disagree. Here are some examples.

RESEARCH QUESTION

To what extent was Confederate Major General Nathan Bedford Forrest responsible for the massacre of Union troops at Fort Pillow?

WORKING THESIS

By encouraging racism among his troops, Nathan Bedford Forrest was directly responsible for the massacre of Union troops at Fort Pillow.

RESEARCH QUESTION

How did the 365-day combat tour affect soldiers' experiences of the Vietnam War?

WORKING THESIS

Letters and diaries written by combat soldiers in Vietnam reveal that when soldiers' tours of duty were shortened, their investment in the war shifted from fighting for victory to fighting for survival.

Each of these thesis statements expresses a view on a debatable issue—an issue about which intelligent, well-meaning people might disagree. The writer's job is to convince such readers that this view is worth taking seriously. For help with testing your working thesis, see the guidelines on page 110.

40b Organizing your ideas

The body of your paper will consist of evidence in support of your thesis. To get started, sketch an informal plan that organizes your evidence. The student who wrote about Fort Pillow used a simple list of questions to structure his ideas. These questions became headings that helped readers follow his line of argument.

What happened at Fort Pillow?

Did Forrest order the massacre?

Can Forrest be held responsible for the massacre?

40c Using sources to inform and support your argument

Sources can play several different roles as you develop your points.

Providing background information or context You can use facts and statistics to support generalizations about your topic or to establish its importance.

Explaining terms or concepts Explain words, phrases, or ideas important to your topic that might be unfamiliar to readers. Quoting or paraphrasing a source can help you define terms and concepts clearly and concisely.

Supporting your claims Back up your assertions with facts, examples, and other evidence from your research.

Lending authority to your argument Expert opinion can give weight to your argument. But don't rely on experts to make your argument for you. Construct your argument in your own words and cite authorities in the field to support your position.

Anticipating and countering objections Do not ignore sources that seem to contradict your position or that offer arguments different from your own. Instead, use them to

give voice to opposing points of view and to state potential objections to your argument before you counter them.

40d Getting feedback

Once you have developed a thesis, identified useful
sources, and begun drafting your paper, seek out a classmate or a writing center consultant to provide feedback
on your work in progress. Feedback gives you perspective on what's working and what's not working in your
draft and keeps the expectations of your readers in mind.

To help your reviewer respond with useful comments,
provide a copy of the assignment and, if possible, copies
of any sources you used to write your draft. You might
also share your purpose for writing, why your topic matters to you, and what you hope to accomplish in your
draft. To encourage relevant, focused feedback, tell your
reviewer about any specific questions or concerns you
have. For some guiding questions you and your reader
can use to review your writing, see the guidelines in 29d.

41 Avoiding plagiarism

In a research paper, you draw on the work of other writers, and you must document their contributions by citing your sources. When you acknowledge your sources,
you avoid plagiarism, a serious academic offense.

Three different acts are considered plagiarism:
(1) failing to cite quotations and borrowed ideas, (2) failing
to enclose borrowed language in quotation marks, and
(3) failing to put summaries and paraphrases in your
own words.

41a Citing quotations and borrowed ideas

When you cite sources, you give credit to writers from
whom you've borrowed words and ideas. You also let
your readers know where your information comes from
so that they can find and read the original sources. You
must cite anything you borrow from a source, including direct quotations; statistics and other specific facts;
visuals such as tables, graphs, and diagrams; and any
ideas you present in a summary or a paraphrase.

The only exception is common knowledge —
information your readers likely already know or could

easily find in general sources. When you have seen certain information repeatedly in your reading, you don't need to cite it. However, when information has appeared in only a few sources, when it is highly specific (as with statistics), or when it is controversial, you should cite the source. If you're not sure whether you need to cite something, check with your instructor.

41b Understanding how the *Chicago* system works

Chicago citations consist of superscript numbers in the text of the paper that refer readers to notes with corresponding numbers either at the foot of the page (footnotes) or at the end of the paper (endnotes).

TEXT

Governor John Andrew was not allowed to recruit black soldiers from out of state. "Ostensibly," writes Peter Burchard, "no recruiting was done outside Massachusetts, but it was an open secret that Andrew's agents were working far and wide."[1]

NOTE

   1. Peter Burchard, *One Gallant Rush: Robert Gould Shaw and His Brave Black Regiment* (New York: St. Martin's, 1965), 85.

For detailed advice on using *Chicago* notes, see 43a. When you use footnotes or endnotes, you will usually need to provide a bibliography as well (see 43b).

41c Enclosing borrowed language in quotation marks

To indicate that you are using a source's exact phrases or sentences, you must enclose them in quotation marks. To omit the quotation marks is to claim—falsely—that the language is your own. Such an omission is plagiarism even if you have cited the source.

ORIGINAL SOURCE

For many Southerners it was psychologically impossible to see a black man bearing arms as anything but an incipient slave uprising complete with arson, murder, pillage, and rapine.
       —Dudley Taylor Cornish, *The Sable Arm: Negro Troops in the Union Army, 1861–1865*, p. 158

PLAGIARISM

According to Civil War historian Dudley Taylor Cornish, for many Southerners it was psychologically impossible to see a black man bearing arms as anything but an incipient slave uprising complete with arson, murder, pillage, and rapine.[2]

BORROWED LANGUAGE IN QUOTATION MARKS

According to Civil War historian Dudley Taylor Cornish, "For many Southerners it was psychologically impossible to see a black man bearing arms as anything but an incipient slave uprising complete with arson, murder, pillage, and rapine."[2]

NOTE: Long quotations are set off from the text by indenting and do not need quotation marks (see pp. 243–44).

41d Putting summaries and paraphrases in your own words

A summary condenses information from a source; a paraphrase conveys the information using roughly the same number of words as the original source. When you summarize or paraphrase, you must name the source and restate the source's meaning in your own words. Half-copying the author's sentences by using the author's phrases in your own sentences without quotation marks or by plugging synonyms into the author's sentence structure is a form of plagiarism.

In the following example, the paraphrase is plagiarized — even though the source is cited — because too much of its language is borrowed from the original. The highlighted strings of words have been copied exactly (without quotation marks). In addition, the writer has closely followed the sentence structure of the original source, merely making a few substitutions (such as *Fifty percent* for *Half* and *angered and perhaps frightened* for *enraged and perhaps terrified*).

ORIGINAL SOURCE

Half of the force holding Fort Pillow were Negroes, former slaves now enrolled in the Union Army. Toward them Forrest's troops had the fierce, bitter animosity of men who had been educated to regard the colored race as inferior and who for the first time had encountered that race armed and fighting against

white men. The sight enraged and perhaps terrified
many of the Confederates and aroused in them the
ugly spirit of a lynching mob.
   —Albert Castel, "The Fort Pillow Massacre," pp. 46–47

PLAGIARISM: UNACCEPTABLE BORROWING

Albert Castel suggests that much of the brutality at Fort Pillow
can be traced to racial attitudes. Fifty percent of the troops
holding Fort Pillow were Negroes, former slaves who had joined
the Union Army. Toward them Forrest's soldiers displayed the
savage hatred of men who had been taught the inferiority of
blacks and who for the first time had confronted them armed
and fighting against white men. The vision angered and perhaps
frightened the Confederates and aroused in them the ugly spirit
of a lynching mob.[3]

   To avoid plagiarizing an author's language, don't
look at the source while you are summarizing or paraphrasing. After you've restated the author's ideas in
your own words, return to the source and check that
you haven't used the author's language or sentence
structure or misrepresented the author's ideas.

ACCEPTABLE PARAPHRASE

Albert Castel suggests that much of the brutality at Fort Pillow
can be traced to racial attitudes. Nearly half of the Union
troops were blacks, men whom the Confederates had been
raised to consider their inferiors. The shock and perhaps fear of
facing armed ex-slaves in battle for the first time may well have
unleashed the fury that led to the massacre.[3]

See the box on page 117 for simple guidelines for being
a responsible research writer.

42   **Integrating sources**

Quotations, summaries, paraphrases, and facts will help
you develop your argument, but they cannot speak for
you. You can use several strategies to integrate information from sources into your paper while maintaining
your own voice.

42a

42a Summarizing and paraphrasing effectively

When you summarize or paraphrase, you express an author's ideas in your own words. A summary should condense the author's key points and use fewer words than the original. You might summarize to compare arguments or ideas from various sources or to provide readers with an overview of a source before you discuss it.

A paraphrase should use approximately the same number of words and details as in the source. You might paraphrase to help readers understand complex ideas or data from a source.

Even though you're using your own words to summarize or paraphrase, the original ideas are the author's intellectual property, so you must include a citation. (For more advice, see 31a.)

42b Using quotations effectively

When you quote a source, you borrow some of the author's exact words and enclose them in quotation marks. Quotation marks show your readers that both the idea and the words belong to the author. You might quote a source when exact wording is needed for accuracy or when the original language is especially effective. Using the words of an authority can also lend weight to your argument.

Limiting your use of quotations   Keep the emphasis on your own words and ideas. It is not always necessary to quote full sentences from a source. Often you can integrate words or phrases from a source into your own sentence structure.

As Hurst has pointed out, until "an outcry erupted in the Northern press," even the Confederates did not deny that there had been a massacre at Fort Pillow.[4]

Union surgeon Dr. Charles Fitch testified that after he was in custody he "saw" Confederate soldiers "kill every negro that made his appearance dressed in Federal uniform."[5]

Using the ellipsis mark   To condense a quoted passage, you can use the ellipsis mark (three periods, with spaces between) to indicate that you have omitted words. What remains must be grammatically complete.

Union surgeon Fitch's testimony that all women and children had been evacuated from Fort Pillow before the attack conflicts with Forrest's report: "We captured . . . about 40 negro women and children."[6]

The writer has omitted several words not relevant to the issue at hand: *164 Federals, 75 negro troops, and.*

When you want to leave out one or more full sentences, use a period before the three ellipsis dots. For an example, see the long quotation on page 244.

You do not need an ellipsis mark at the beginning or at the end of a quotation. Readers will understand that you have taken the quoted material from a longer passage.

USING SOURCES RESPONSIBLY: Make sure that omissions and ellipsis marks do not distort the meaning of your source.

Using brackets   Brackets allow you to insert your own words into quoted material to clarify a confusing reference or to keep a sentence grammatical in the context of your writing.

According to Albert Castel, "It can be reasonably argued that he [Forrest] was justified in believing that the approaching steamships intended to aid the garrison [at Fort Pillow]."[7]

To indicate an error in a quotation, such as a misspelling, insert [*sic*], italicized and with brackets around it, right after the error.

Setting off long quotations   *Chicago* style allows you to set off a long quotation or run it into your text. For emphasis, you may want to set off a quotation of more than five typed lines; you should always set off quotations of ten lines or more. To set off a quotation, indent it one-half inch from the left margin.

Long quotations should be introduced by an informative sentence, usually ending in a colon. Quotation marks are unnecessary because the indented format tells readers that the passage is taken word-for-word from the source. (See the example on p. 244.)

42c

In a letter home, Confederate officer Achilles V. Clark recounted what happened at Fort Pillow:

> Words cannot describe the scene. The poor deluded negroes would run up to our men fall upon their knees and with uplifted hands scream for mercy but they were ordered to their feet and then shot down. The whitte [*sic*] men fared but little better. . . . I with several others tried to stop the butchery and at one time had partially succeeded, but Gen. Forrest ordered them shot down like dogs, and the carnage continued.[8]

42c Using signal phrases to integrate sources

Whenever you include a paraphrase, summary, or direct quotation of another writer's work in your paper, prepare readers for it with a *signal phrase*. A signal phrase usually names the author of the source, points out the author's credentials, and often provides some context for the source material. The first time you mention an author, use the full name: *Shelby Foote argues . . .* When you refer to the author again, you may use the last name only: *Foote raises an important question.*

When you write a signal phrase, choose a verb that is appropriate for the way you are using the source. Are you providing background, explaining a concept, supporting a claim, lending authority, or refuting a belief? See the chart on page 246 for a list of verbs commonly used in signal phrases.

Marking boundaries Avoid dropping a quotation into your text without warning. Provide a clear signal phrase, including at least the author's name, to indicate the boundary between your words and the source's words.

DROPPED QUOTATION

Unionists claimed that their troops had abandoned their arms and were in full retreat. "The Confederates, however, all agreed that the Union troops retreated to the river with arms in their hands."[9]

QUOTATION WITH SIGNAL PHRASE

Unionists claimed that their troops had abandoned their arms and were in full retreat. "The Confederates, however," writes historian Albert Castel, "all agreed that the Union troops retreated to the river with arms in their hands."[9]

Introducing summaries and paraphrases   Introduce most summaries and paraphrases with a signal phrase that mentions the author and places the material in context. Readers will then understand where the summary or paraphrase begins.

The signal phrase (highlighted) in the following example shows that the whole paragraph, not just the last sentence, is based on the source.

According to Jack Hurst, official Confederate policy was that black soldiers were to be treated as runaway slaves; in addition, the Confederate Congress decreed that white Union officers commanding black troops be killed. Confederate Lieutenant General Kirby Smith went one step further, declaring that he would kill all captured black troops. Smith's policy never met with strong opposition from the Richmond government.[10]

Integrating statistics and other facts   When you cite a statistic or another specific fact, a signal phrase is often not necessary. In most cases, readers will understand that the citation refers to the statistic or fact (not the whole paragraph).

Of 295 white troops garrisoned at Fort Pillow, 168 were taken prisoner. Black troops fared worse, with only 58 of 262 captured and most of the rest presumably killed or wounded.[11]

There is nothing wrong, however, with using a signal phrase to introduce a statistic or another specific fact.

Putting source material in context   Provide context for any source material that appears in your paper. A signal phrase can help you connect your own ideas with those of another writer by clarifying how the source will contribute to your paper. It's a good idea to embed a quotation between sentences of your own, introducing it with a signal phrase and following it with interpretive comments that link the quotation to your paper's argument.

QUOTATION WITH EFFECTIVE CONTEXT

In a respected biography of Nathan Bedford Forrest, Hurst suggests that the temperamental Forrest "may have ragingly

42c

Using signal phrases in *Chicago* papers

To avoid monotony, try to vary both the language and the placement of your signal phrases.

Model signal phrases

In the words of historian James M. McPherson, "..."[1]

As Dudley Taylor Cornish has argued, "..."[2]

In a letter to his wife, a Confederate soldier who witnessed the massacre wrote that "..."[3]

"...," claims Benjamin Quarles.[4]

"...," writes Albert Castel, "..."[5]

Shelby Foote offers an intriguing interpretation: "..."[6]

Verbs in signal phrases

Are you providing background, explaining a concept, supporting a claim, lending authority, or refuting a belief? Choose a verb that is appropriate for the way you are using the source.

admits	contends	reasons
agrees	declares	refutes
argues	denies	rejects
asserts	emphasizes	reports
believes	insists	responds
claims	notes	suggests
compares	observes	thinks
confirms	points out	writes

NOTE: In *Chicago* style, use the present tense or present perfect tense to introduce quotations or other material from nonfiction sources: *Foote points out* or *Foote has pointed out*. Use the past tense only if you include a date or another marker that specifies the time of the original author's writing.

---

ordered a massacre and even intended to carry it out—until he rode inside the fort and viewed the horrifying result" and ordered it stopped.[12] While this is an intriguing interpretation of events, even Hurst would probably admit that it is merely speculation.

NOTE: When you bring other sources into a conversation about your research topic, you are synthesizing sources. For more on synthesis, see 31d.

43 *Chicago* documentation style

In history and some other humanities courses, you may be asked to use the documentation system of *The Chicago Manual of Style*, 17th ed. (Chicago: University of Chicago Press, 2017). In *Chicago* style, superscript numbers (like this[1]) in the text of the paper refer readers to notes with corresponding numbers either at the foot of the page (footnotes) or at the end of the paper (endnotes). A bibliography is often required as well; it appears at the end of the paper and gives publication information for all the works cited in the notes.

TEXT

A Union soldier, Jacob Thompson, claimed to have seen Forrest order the killing, but when asked to describe the six-foot-two general, he called him "a little bit of a man."[12]

FOOTNOTE OR ENDNOTE

12. Brian Steel Wills, *A Battle from the Start: The Life of Nathan Bedford Forrest* (New York: HarperCollins, 1992), 187.

BIBLIOGRAPHY ENTRY

Wills, Brian Steel. *A Battle from the Start: The Life of Nathan Bedford Forrest*. New York: HarperCollins, 1992.

43a First and later notes for a source

The first time you cite a source, the note should include publication information for that work as well as the page number for the passage you are citing.

1. Peter Burchard, *One Gallant Rush: Robert Gould Shaw and His Brave Black Regiment* (New York: St. Martin's, 1965), 85.

For later references to a source you have already cited, you may simply give the author's last name, a short form of the title, and the page or pages cited. A short form of the title of a book or another long work is italicized; a short form of the title of an article or another short work is put in quotation marks.

4. Burchard, *One Gallant Rush*, 31.

When you have two notes in a row from the same source, you may give the author's last name and the page or pages cited.

5. Jack Hurst, *Nathan Bedford Forrest: A Biography* (New York: Knopf, 1993), 8.

6. Hurst, 174.

43b *Chicago*-style bibliography

A bibliography at the end of your paper lists the works you have cited in your notes; it may also include works you consulted but did not cite. See page 271 for formatting; see page 275 for a sample bibliography.

Directory to *Chicago*-style notes and bibliography entries

NOTE: If you include a bibliography, you may shorten all notes, including the first reference to a source (see p. 247). Check with your instructor, however, to see whether using an abbreviated note for a first reference to a source is acceptable.

43c Model notes and bibliography entries

The following models are consistent with guidelines in *The Chicago Manual of Style*, 17th ed. For each type of source, a model note appears first, followed by a model bibliography entry. The note shows the format you should use when citing a source for the first time. For subsequent citations of a source, use shortened notes.

Some sources from the web, typically periodical articles, use a permanent locator called a digital object identifier (DOI). Use the DOI, when it is available, in place of a URL. (For guidelines about breaking a URL or DOI across lines, see p. 270.)

General guidelines for listing authors

● **1. One author**

1. Salman Rushdie, *Joseph Anton: A Memoir* (New York: Random House, 2012), 135.

Rushdie, Salman. *Joseph Anton: A Memoir*. New York: Random House, 2012.

● **2. Two or three authors** Give all authors' names in both the note and the bibliography entry.

2. Bill O'Reilly and Martin Dugard, *Killing Lincoln: The Shocking Assassination That Changed America Forever* (New York: Holt, 2012), 33.

O'Reilly, Bill, and Martin Dugard. *Killing Lincoln: The Shocking Assassination That Changed America Forever*. New York: Holt, 2012.

● **3. Four or more authors** In the note, give the first author's name followed by "et al." (Latin for "and others"); in the bibliography entry, list all authors' names.

3. Lynn Hunt et al., *The Making of the West: Peoples and Cultures*, 5th ed. (Boston: Bedford/St. Martin's, 2015), 541.

Hunt, Lynn, Thomas R. Martin, Barbara H. Rosenwein, and Bonnie G. Smith. *The Making of the West: Peoples and Cultures*. 5th ed. Boston: Bedford/St. Martin's, 2015.

● **4. Organization as author**

4. Johnson Historical Society, *Images of America: Johnson* (Charleston, SC: Arcadia Publishing, 2011), 24.

Johnson Historical Society. *Images of America: Johnson*. Charleston, SC: Arcadia Publishing, 2011.

● **5. Unknown author**

5. *The Men's League Handbook on Women's Suffrage* (London, 1912), 23.

The Men's League Handbook on Women's Suffrage. London, 1912.

● **6. Multiple works by the same author**   In the bibliography, arrange the entries alphabetically by title. Use six hyphens in place of the author's name in the second and subsequent entries.

Winchester, Simon. *The Alice behind Wonderland*. New York: Oxford University Press, 2011.

------. *Atlantic: Great Sea Battles, Heroic Discoveries, Titanic Storms, and a Vast Ocean of a Million Stories*. New York: HarperCollins, 2010.

● **7. Editor**

7. Teresa Carpenter, ed., *New York Diaries: 1609-2009* (New York: Modern Library, 2012), 316.

Carpenter, Teresa, ed. *New York Diaries: 1609-2009*. New York: Modern Library, 2012.

● **8. Editor with author**

8. Susan Sontag, *As Consciousness Is Harnessed to Flesh: Journals and Notebooks, 1964-1980*, ed. David Rieff (New York: Farrar, Straus and Giroux, 2012), 265.

Sontag, Susan. *As Consciousness Is Harnessed to Flesh: Journals and Notebooks, 1964-1980*. Edited by David Rieff. New York: Farrar, Straus and Giroux, 2012.

● **9. Translator with author**

9. Richard Bidlack and Nikita Lomagin, *The Leningrad Blockade, 1941-1944: A New Documentary from the Soviet Archives*, trans. Marian Schwartz (New Haven: Yale University Press, 2012), 26.

Bidlack, Richard, and Nikita Lomagin. *The Leningrad Blockade, 1941-1944: A New Documentary from the Soviet Archives*. Translated by Marian Schwartz. New Haven: Yale University Press, 2012.

Books and other long works

▸ Citation at a glance: Book, **page 252**

● **10. Basic format for a book**

a. Print

10. Mary N. Woods, *Beyond the Architect's Eye: Photographs and the American Built Environment* (Philadelphia: University of Pennsylvania Press, 2009), 45.

(See p. 253 for the related bibliography entry.)

Citation at a glance

Book Chicago

To cite a print book in *Chicago* style, include the following elements.

1. Author(s)
2. Title and subtitle
3. City of publication
4. Publisher
5. Year of publication
6. Page number(s) cited (for notes)

TITLE PAGE

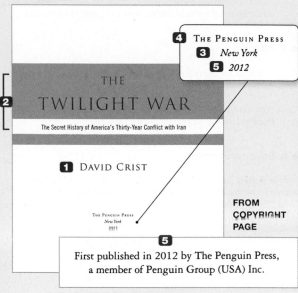

4 THE PENGUIN PRESS
3 *New York*
5 *2012*

THE
TWILIGHT WAR

The Secret History of America's Thirty-Year Conflict with Iran

1 DAVID CRIST

THE PENGUIN PRESS
New York
2012

FROM COPYRIGHT PAGE

5
First published in 2012 by The Penguin Press, a member of Penguin Group (USA) Inc.

The Penguin Press, New York, 2012.

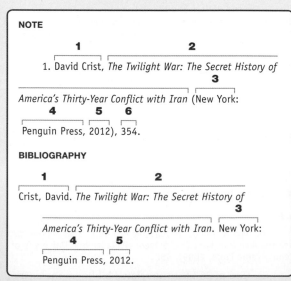

NOTE

    1   **2**

1. David Crist, *The Twilight War: The Secret History of*

                           3

America's Thirty-Year Conflict with Iran (New York:

4   **5**   **6**

Penguin Press, 2012), 354.

BIBLIOGRAPHY

  1   **2**

Crist, David. *The Twilight War: The Secret History of*

                           3

    America's Thirty-Year Conflict with Iran. New York:

    4   **5**

Penguin Press, 2012.

For more on citing books in *Chicago* style, see items 10–17.

● **10. Basic format for a book (_cont._)**

a. Print (cont.)

Woods, Mary N. _Beyond the Architect's Eye: Photographs and the American Built Environment_. Philadelphia: University of Pennsylvania Press, 2009.

b. E-book

10. Drew Gilpin Faust, _This Republic of Suffering: Death and the American Civil War_ (New York: Knopf, 2008), chap. 4, NOOK.

Faust, Drew Gilpin. _This Republic of Suffering: Death and the American Civil War_. New York: Knopf, 2008. NOOK.

c. Web (or online library)

10. Charles Hursthouse, _New Zealand, or Zealandia, the Britain of the South_ (1857; HathiTrust Digital Library, n.d.), 2:356, http://hdl.handle.net/2027/uc1.b304920.

Hursthouse, Charles. _New Zealand, or Zealandia, the Britain of the South_. 2 vols. 1857. HathiTrust Digital Library, n.d. http://hdl.handle.net/2027/uc1.b304920.

● **11. Edition other than the first**

11. Josephine Donovan, _Feminist Theory: The Intellectual Traditions_, 4th ed. (New York: Continuum, 2012), 86.

Donovan, Josephine. _Feminist Theory: The Intellectual Traditions_. 4th ed. New York: Continuum, 2012.

● **12. Volume in a multivolume work**

12. Robert A. Caro, _The Passage of Power_, vol. 4 of _The Years of Lyndon Johnson_ (New York: Knopf, 2012), 198.

Caro, Robert A. _The Passage of Power_. Vol. 4 of _The Years of Lyndon Johnson_. New York: Knopf, 2012.

If the volumes do not have individual titles, give the volume and page number in the note (for example, 2:356) and the total number of volumes in the bibliography entry (see item 10c).

● **13. Work in an anthology or a collection**

13. Janet Walsh, "Unequal in Africa: How Property Rights Can Empower Women," in _The Unfinished Revolution: Voices from the Global Fight for Women's Rights_, ed. Minky Worden (New York: Seven Stories Press, 2012), 161.

(See p. 254 for the related bibliography entry.)

● **13. Work in an anthology or a collection (cont.)**

Walsh, Janet. "Unequal in Africa: How Property Rights Can
    Empower Women." In *The Unfinished Revolution: Voices from
    the Global Fight for Women's Rights*, edited by Minky Worden,
    159-66. New York: Seven Stories Press, 2012.

● **14. Introduction, preface, foreword, or afterword**

14. Alice Walker, afterword to *The Indispensable Zinn: The
Essential Writings of the "People's Historian,"* by Howard Zinn,
ed. Timothy Patrick McCarthy (New York: Free Press, 2012), 373.

Walker, Alice. Afterword to *The Indispensable Zinn: The Essential
    Writings of the "People's Historian,"* by Howard Zinn, 371-76.
    Edited by Timothy Patrick McCarthy. New York: Free Press, 2012.

● **15. Republished book**

15. W. S. Blatchley, *A Nature Wooing at Ormond by the Sea*
(1902; repr., Stockbridge, MA: Hard Press, 2012), 26.

Blatchley, W. S. *A Nature Wooing at Ormond by the Sea*. 1902.
    Reprint, Stockbridge, MA: Hard Press, 2012.

● **16. Book with a title in its title**   Use quotation marks
around any title within an italicized title.

16. Claudia Durst Johnson, ed., *Race in Mark Twain's
"Adventures of Huckleberry Finn"* (Detroit: Greenhaven Press, 2009).

Johnson, Claudia Durst, ed. *Race in Mark Twain's "Adventures of
    Huckleberry Finn."* Detroit: Greenhaven Press, 2009.

● **17. Sacred text**   Sacred texts are usually not included
in the bibliography.

17. Matt. 20:4-9 (Revised Standard Version).

● **18. Government document**

18. United States Senate, Committee on Foreign Relations,
*Implications of the Kyoto Protocol on Climate Change: Hearing
before the Committee on Foreign Relations, United States Senate*,
105th Cong., 2nd sess. (Washington, DC: GPO, 1998).

United States Senate. Committee on Foreign Relations.
    *Implications of the Kyoto Protocol on Climate Change:
    Hearing before the Committee on Foreign Relations, United
    States Senate*, 105th Cong., 2nd sess. Washington, DC:
    GPO, 1998.

● **19. Unpublished dissertation**

19. Stephanie Lynn Budin, "The Origins of Aphrodite" (PhD diss., University of Pennsylvania, 2000), 301-?, ProQuest (AAT 9976404).

Budin, Stephanie Lynn. "The Origins of Aphrodite." PhD diss., University of Pennsylvania, 2000. ProQuest (AAT 9976404).

For a published dissertation, cite as a book.

● **20. Published proceedings of a conference**   Cite as a book, adding the location and dates of the conference after the title.

20. Stacey K. Sowards et al., eds., *Across Borders and Environments: Communication and Environmental Justice in International Contexts*, University of Texas at El Paso, June 25-28, 2011 (Cincinnati, OH: International Environmental Communication Association, 2012), 114.

Sowards, Stacey K., Kyle Alvarado, Diana Arrieta, and Jacob Barde, eds. *Across Borders and Environments: Communication and Environmental Justice in International Contexts*. University of Texas at El Paso, June 25-28, 2011. Cincinnati, OH: International Environmental Communication Association, 2012.

● **21. Source quoted in another source (a secondary source)**

21. Thomas Wentworth Higginson, *Margaret Fuller Ossoli* (Boston: Houghton Mifflin, 1890), 11, quoted in John Matteson, *The Lives of Margaret Fuller* (New York: Norton, 2012), 7.

Higginson, Thomas Wentworth. *Margaret Fuller Ossoli*. Boston: Houghton Mifflin, 1890, 11. Quoted in John Matteson, *The Lives of Margaret Fuller* (New York: Norton, 2012), 7.

Articles and other short works

▶   Citation at a glance: Article in an online journal, **page 256**
▶   Citation at a glance: Article from a database, **page 258**

● **22. Article in a journal**   If an article in a database or on the web shows only a beginning page, use a plus sign after the page number in the bibliography: 212+.

a. Print

22. Catherine Foisy, "Preparing the Quebec Church for Vatican II: Missionary Lessons from Asia, Africa, and Latin America, 1945-1962," *Historical Studies* 78 (2012): 8.

(See p. 257 for the related bibliography entry.)

Citation at a glance

Article in an online journal *Chicago*

To cite an article in an online journal in *Chicago* style, include the following elements:

1 Author(s)
2 Title and subtitle of article
3 Title of journal
4 Volume and issue numbers
5 Year of publication
6 Page number(s) cited (for notes); page range of article (for bibliography), if available
7 DOI, if article has one; otherwise, URL for article

ISSUE CONTENTS PAGE

ARTICLE HOME PAGE (top) AND FULL TEXT (bottom)

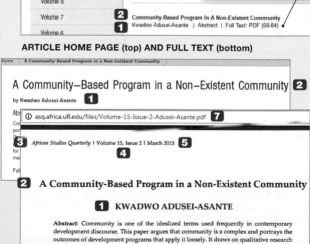

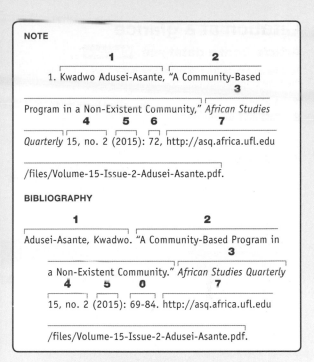

NOTE

1. Kwadwo Adusei-Asante, "A Community-Based Program in a Non-Existent Community," *African Studies Quarterly* 15, no. 2 (2015): 72, http://asq.africa.ufl.edu /files/Volume-15-Issue-2-Adusei-Asante.pdf.

BIBLIOGRAPHY

Adusei-Asante, Kwadwo. "A Community-Based Program in a Non-Existent Community." *African Studies Quarterly* 15, no. 2 (2015): 69-84. http://asq.africa.ufl.edu /files/Volume-15-Issue-2-Adusei-Asante.pdf.

For more on citing articles in *Chicago* style, see items 22–24.

● 22. Article in a journal (*cont.*)

a. Print (*cont.*)

Foisy, Catherine. "Preparing the Quebec Church for Vatican II: Missionary Lessons from Asia, Africa, and Latin America, 1945-1962." *Historical Studies* 78 (2012): 7-26.

b. Web   If no DOI is available, give the URL for the article.

22. Anne-Lise François, "Flower Fisting," *Postmodern Culture* 22, no. 1 (2011), https://doi.org/10.1353/pmc.2012.0004.

François, Anne-Lise. "Flower Fisting." *Postmodern Culture* 22, no. 1 (2011). https://doi.org/10.1353/pmc.2012.0004.

c. Database   Give one of the following pieces of information from the database listing, in this order of preference: a DOI for the article; or the name of the database; or a "stable" or "persistent" URL for the article. (The DOI consists of the prefix https://doi.org/ followed by the DOI identifier.)

22. Patrick Zuk, "Nikolay Myaskovsky and the Events of 1948," *Music and Letters* 93, no. 1 (2012): 61, Project Muse.

Zuk, Patrick. "Nikolay Myaskovsky and the Events of 1948." *Music and Letters* 93, no. 1 (2012): 61. Project Muse.

Citation at a glance

Article from a database ❲Chicago❳

To cite an article from a database in *Chicago* style, include the following elements:

1. Author(s)
2. Title and subtitle of article
3. Title of journal
4. Volume and issue numbers
5. Year of publication
6. Page number(s) cited (for notes); page range of article (for bibliography), if available
7. DOI; *or* database name; *or* "stable" or "persistent" URL for article

ISSUE CONTENTS PAGE

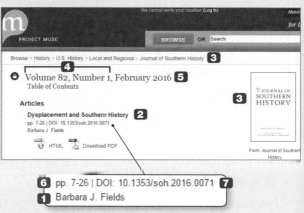

● **23. Article in a magazine** Give the month and year for a monthly publication; give the month, day, and year for a weekly publication. If an article in a database or on the web shows only a beginning page, use a plus sign after the page number in the bibliography: 212+.

a. Print

23. Alan Lightman, "Our Place in the Universe: Face to Face with the Infinite," *Harper's*, December 2012, 34.

Lightman, Alan. "Our Place in the Universe: Face to Face with the Infinite." *Harper's*, December 2012, 33–38.

b. Web If no DOI is available, include the URL for the article.

23. James Verini, "The Tunnels of Gaza," *National Geographic*, December 2012, http://ngm.nationalgeographic.com/2012/12/gaza-tunnels/verini-text.

ARTICLE FIRST PAGE

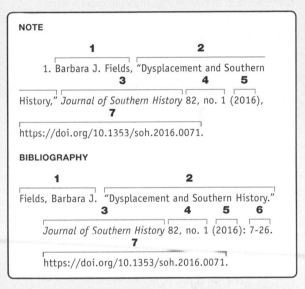

NOTE

1. Barbara J. Fields, "Dysplacement and Southern History," *Journal of Southern History* 82, no. 1 (2016), https://doi.org/10.1353/soh.2016.0071.

BIBLIOGRAPHY

Fields, Barbara J. "Dysplacement and Southern History." *Journal of Southern History* 82, no. 1 (2016): 7-26. https://doi.org/10.1353/soh.2016.0071.

For more on citing articles in *Chicago* style, see items 22–24.

Verini, James. "The Tunnels of Gaza." *National Geographic*, December 2012. http://ngm.nationalgeographic.com/2012/12/gaza-tunnels/verini-text.

c. Database   Give one of the following from the database listing, in this order of preference: a DOI for the article; or the name of the database; or a "stable" or "persistent" URL for the article.

23. Ron Rosenbaum, "The Last Renaissance Man," *Smithsonian*, November 2012, 40, OmniFile Full Text Select.

Rosenbaum, Ron. "The Last Renaissance Man." *Smithsonian*, November 2012, 39-44. OmniFile Full Text Select.

● **24. Article in a newspaper**   Page numbers are not necessary; a section letter or number, if available, is sufficient.

a. Print

24. Alissa J. Rubin, "A Pristine Afghan Prison Faces a
Murky Future," *New York Times*, December 18, 2012, sec. A.

Rubin, Alissa J. "A Pristine Afghan Prison Faces a Murky
    Future." *New York Times*, December 18, 2012, sec. A.

b. Web   Include the complete URL for the article.

24. David Brown, "New Burden of Disease Study Shows
World's People Living Longer but with More Disability," *Washington
Post*, December 13, 2012, https://www.washingtonpost.com
/national/health-science/burden-of-disease-study-shows-a-world
-living-longer-and-with-more-disability/2012/12/13/9d1e5278
-4320-11e2-8061-253bccfc7532_story.html.

Brown, David. "New Burden of Disease Study Shows World's
    People Living Longer but with More Disability."
    Washington Post, December 13, 2012. https://www
    .washingtonpost.com/national/health-science
    /burden-of-disease-study-shows-a-world-living-longer
    -and-with-more-disability/2012/12/13/9d1e5278-4320
    -11e2-8061-253bccfc7532_story.html.

c. Database   Give one of the following from the database listing, in this order of preference: a DOI for the
article; or the name of the database; or a "stable" or
"persistent" URL for the article.

24. "Safe in Sioux City at Last: Union Pacific Succeeds in
Securing Trackage from the St. Paul Road," *Omaha Daily Herald*,
May 16, 1889, America's Historical Newspapers.

"Safe in Sioux City at Last: Union Pacific Succeeds in Securing
    Trackage from the St. Paul Road." *Omaha Daily Herald*, May
    16, 1889. America's Historical Newspapers.

● **25. Unsigned newspaper article**

25. "Next President Better Be a Climate Change Believer,"
Chicago Sun-Times, June 24, 2016, https://chicago.suntimes
.com/opinion/editorial-next-president-better-be-a-climate
-change-believer/.

Chicago Sun-Times. "Next President Better Be a Climate Change
    Believer." June 24, 2016. https://chicago.suntimes.com
    /opinion/editorial-next-president-better-be-a-climate
    -change-believer/.

● **26. Article with a title in its title**   Use italics for titles
of long works such as books and for terms that are normally italicized. Use single quotation marks for titles of
short works and terms that would otherwise be placed
in double quotation marks.

26. Karen Garner, "Global Gender Policy in the 1990s: Incorporating the 'Vital Voices' of Women," *Journal of Women's History* 24, no. 4 (2012): 130.

Garner, Karen. "Global Gender Policy in the 1990s: Incorporating the 'Vital Voices' of Women." *Journal of Women's History* 24, no. 4 (2012): 121-48.

● **27. Review**

27. David Eggleton, review of *Stalking Nabokov*, by Brian Boyd, *New Zealand Listener*, December 13, 2012, http://www.listener.co.nz/culture/books/stalking-nabokov-by-brian-boyd-review/.

Eggleton, David. Review of *Stalking Nabokov*, by Brian Boyd. *New Zealand Listener*, December 13, 2012. http://www.listener.co.nz/culture/books/stalking-nabokov-by-brian-boyd-review/.

● **28. Letter to the editor**   Do not use the letter's title, even if the publication gives one.

28. Andy Bush, letter to the editor, *Economist*, December 15, 2012, http://www.economist.com/.

Bush, Andy. Letter to the editor. *Economist*, December 15, 2012. http://www.economist.com/.

● **29. Article in a reference work (encyclopedia, dictionary, wiki)**   Reference works such as encyclopedias do not require publication information and are usually not included in the bibliography. The abbreviation "s.v." is for the Latin *sub verbo* ("under the word").

29. *Encyclopaedia Britannica*, 15th ed. (2010), s.v. "Monroe Doctrine."

29. Wikipedia, s.v. "James Monroe," last modified December 19, 2012, http://en.wikipedia.org/wiki/James_Monroe.

29. Bryan A. Garner, *Garner's Modern American Usage*, 3rd ed. (Oxford: Oxford University Press, 2009), s.v. "brideprice."

Garner, Bryan A. *Garner's Modern American Usage*. 3rd ed. Oxford: Oxford University Press, 2009.

● **30. Letter in a published collection**   Use the day-month-year form for the date of the letter. If the letter writer's name is part of the book title, begin the note with only the last name but begin the bibliography entry with the full name. (See models on p. 263.)

▶ Citation at a glance: Letter in a published collection, **page 262**

Citation at a glance
Letter in a published collection `Chicago`

To cite a letter in a published collection in *Chicago* style, include the following elements:

1. Author of letter
2. Recipient of letter
3. Date of letter
4. Title of collection
5. Editor of collection
6. City of publication
7. Publisher
8. Year of publication
9. Page number(s) cited (for notes)

TITLE PAGE OF BOOK

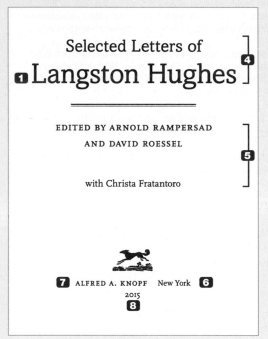

Selected Letters of
1 **Langston Hughes** **4**

EDITED BY ARNOLD RAMPERSAD
AND DAVID ROESSEL **5**

with Christa Fratantoro

7 ALFRED A. KNOPF   New York **6**
2015
8

FROM COPYRIGHT PAGE (top) AND LETTER (bottom)

8
Copyright © 2015 by The Estate of Langston Hughes
Additional material copyright © 2015 by Arnold Rampersad

All rights reserved. Published in the United States by Alfred A. Knopf, a division of Random House LLC, New York, and distributed in Canada by Random House of

9 344   SELECTED LETTERS OF LANGSTON HUGHES

2 TO RICHARD WRIGHT   [TLS]

August 11, 1957 **3**

Dear Dick:
Sometime ago, Knopf forwarded to me your request to use the last four lines of LET AMERICA BE AMERICA AGAIN in your book of four lectures.* I am

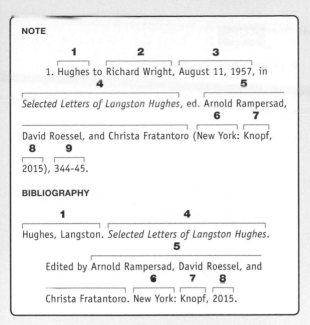

NOTE

1. Hughes to Richard Wright, August 11, 1957, in *Selected Letters of Langston Hughes*, ed. Arnold Rampersad, David Roessel, and Christa Fratantoro (New York: Knopf, 2015), 344-45.

BIBLIOGRAPHY

Hughes, Langston. *Selected Letters of Langston Hughes*. Edited by Arnold Rampersad, David Roessel, and Christa Fratantoro. New York: Knopf, 2015.

For another citation of a letter in *Chicago* style, see item 30.

For another citation of a letter in *Chicago* style, see item 30.

● **30. Letter in a published collection (*cont.*)**

30. Dickens to Thomas Beard, 1 June 1840, in *The Selected Letters of Charles Dickens*, ed. Jenny Hartley (New York: Oxford University Press, 2012), 65.

Dickens, Charles. *The Selected Letters of Charles Dickens*. Edited by Jenny Hartley. New York: Oxford University Press, 2012.

Web sources For most websites, include an author if a site has one, the title of the site, the sponsor, the date of publication or the modified (update) date, and the site's complete URL. Do not italicize a website title unless the site is an online book or periodical. Use quotation marks for the titles of sections or pages in a website. If a site does not have a date of publication or a modified date, give the date you accessed the site ("accessed January 3, 2016").

● **31. An entire website**

31. Chesapeake and Ohio Canal National Historical Park (website), National Park Service, last modified November 25, 2012, http://www.nps.gov/choh/index.htm.

National Park Service. Chesapeake and Ohio Canal National Historical Park (website). Last modified November 25, 2012. http://www.nps.gov/choh/index.htm.

● **32. Work from a website**

▶ Citation at a glance: Primary source from a website, **page 266**

32. Dan Archer, "Using Illustrated Reportage to Cover Human Trafficking in Nepal's Brick Kilns," Poynter, last modified December 18, 2012, https://www.poynter.org/news/using-illustrated -reportage-cover-human-trafficking-nepals-brick-kilns.

Archer, Dan. "Using Illustrated Reportage to Cover Human Trafficking in Nepal's Brick Kilns." Poynter, last modified December 18, 2012. https://www.poynter.org/news/using-illustrated -reportage-cover-human-trafficking-nepals-brick-kilns.

● **33. Blog post**   Italicize the name of the blog. Insert "blog" in parentheses after the name if the word *blog* is not part of the name. If the blog is part of a larger site, add the title of the site after the blog title (see item 34).

33. Gregory LeFever, "Skull Fraud 'Created' the Brontosaurus," *Ancient Tides* (blog), December 16, 2012, http://ancient-tides .blogspot.com/2012/12/skull-fraud-created-brontosaurus.html.

LeFever, Gregory. *Ancient Tides* (blog). http://ancient-tides .blogspot.com/

● **34. Comment on a blog post**

34. Didomyk, December 18, 2012, comment on B.C., "A New Spokesman," *Pomegranate: The Middle East* (blog), *Economist*, https://www.economist.com/blogs /pomegranate/2012/12/christians-middle-east.

Didomyk. December 18, 2012. Comment on B.C., "A New Spokesman." *Pomegranate: The Middle East* (blog). *Economist*. https://www.economist.com/blogs /pomegranate/2012/12/christians-middle-east.

Audio, visual, and multimedia sources

● **35. Podcast**

35. Peter Limb, "Economic and Cultural History of the Slave Trade in Western Africa," Episode 69, December 12, 2012, in *Africa Past and Present*, African Online Digital Library, podcast, MP3 audio, 25:32, http://afripod.aodl.org/2012/12/afripod-69/.

Limb, Peter. "Economic and Cultural History of the Slave Trade in Western Africa." Episode 69, December 12, 2012. *Africa Past and Present*. African Online Digital Library. Podcast, MP3 audio, 25:32. http://afripod.aodl.org/2012/12 /afripod-69/.

● **36. Online audio or video** If the source is a down-loadable file, identify the file format or medium before the URL.

36. Tom Brokaw, "Global Warming: What You Need to Know," Discovery Channel, January 23, 2012, http://www.youtube.com /watch?v=xcVwLrAavyA.

Brokaw, Tom. "Global Warming: What You Need to Know." Discovery Channel, January 23, 2012. http://www.youtube.com/watch ?v=xcVwLrAavyA.

● **37. Published or broadcast interview**

37. Jane Goodall, interview by Suza Scalora, *Origin*, n.d., http:// www.originmagazine.com/2012/12/07/dr-jane-goodall-interview -with-suza-scalora.

Goodall, Jane. Interview by Suza Scalora. *Origin*, n.d. http://www .originmagazine.com/2012/12/07/dr-jane-goodall-interview -with-suza-scalora.

37. Julian Castro and Joaquin Castro, interview by Charlie Rose, *Charlie Rose Show*, WGBH, Boston, December 17, 2012.

Castro, Julian, and Joaquin Castro. Interview by Charlie Rose. *Charlie Rose Show*. WGBH, Boston, December 17, 2012.

● **38. Film (DVD, BD, or other format)** Include both the date of original release and the date of release for the format being cited.

38. *Argo*, directed by Ben Affleck (2012; Burbank, CA: Warner Bros. Pictures, 2013), DVD.

Affleck, Ben, dir. *Argo*. 2012; Burbank, CA: Warner Bros. Pictures, 2013. DVD.

● **39. Sound recording**

39. Gustav Holst, *The Planets*, Royal Philharmonic Orchestra, conducted by André Previn, recorded April 14-15, 1986, Telarc 80133, compact disc.

Holst, Gustav. *The Planets*. Royal Philharmonic Orchestra. Recorded April 14-15, 1986. Conducted by André Previn. Telarc 80133, compact disc.

● **40. Musical score or composition**

40. Antonio Vivaldi, *L'Estro armonico*, op. 3, ed. Eleanor Selfridge-Field (Mineola, NY: Dover, 1999).

Vivaldi, Antonio. *L'Estro armonico*, op. 3. Edited by Eleanor Selfridge-Field. Mineola, NY: Dover, 1999.

Citation at a glance
Primary source from a website ‹Chicago›

To cite a primary source (or any other document) from a website in *Chicago* style, include as many of the following elements as are available:

1 Author(s)
2 Title of document
3 Title of site
4 Sponsor of site

5 Publication date or modified date; date of access (if no publication date)
6 URL of document page

WEBSITE HOME PAGE

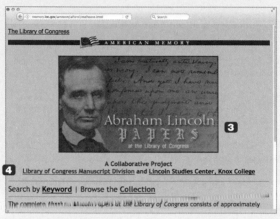

FIRST PAGE OF DOCUMENT

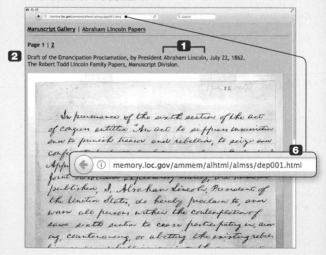

    1   **2**

  1. Abraham Lincoln, "Draft of the Emancipation
         3

Proclamation," Abraham Lincoln Papers at the Library of
         4

Congress, Library of Congress Manuscript Division and
          5

Lincoln Studies Center, Knox College, accessed February 4,
       6

2017, http://memory.loc.gov/ammem/alhtml/almss

/dep001.html.

   1   **2**

Lincoln, Abraham. "Draft of the Emancipation
       3

   Proclamation." Abraham Lincoln Papers at the Library
       4

   of Congress. Library of Congress Manuscript Division

   and Lincoln Studies Center, Knox College. Accessed
   5   **6**

   February 4, 2017. http://memory.loc.gov/ammem

   /alhtml/almss/dep001.html.

For more on citing documents from websites in *Chicago* style, see item 32.

● **41. Work of art**

    41. Aaron Siskind, *Untitled (The Most Crowded Block)*, 1939, gelatin silver print, Kemper Museum of Contemporary Art, Kansas City, MO.

Siskind, Aaron. *Untitled (The Most Crowded Block)*. 1939. Gelatin silver print. Kemper Museum of Contemporary Art, Kansas City, MO.

● **42. Performance**

    42. Jackie Sibblies Drury, *Social Creatures*, directed by Curt Columbus, Trinity Repertory Company, Providence, RI, March 15, 2013.

Drury, Jackie Sibblies. *Social Creatures*. Directed by Curt Columbus. Trinity Repertory Company, Providence, RI, March 15, 2013.

Personal communication and social media

● **43. Personal communication**   Personal communications are not included in the bibliography.

> 43. Sara Lehman, email message to author, August 13, 2012.

● **44. Online posting or email**   If an online posting has been archived, include a URL. Emails that are not part of an online discussion are treated as personal communication (see item 43). Online postings and emails are not included in the bibliography.

> 44. Bart Dale, reply to "Which country made best science/technology contribution?," Historum General History Forums, December 15, 2015, http://historum.com/general -history/46089-country-made-best-science-technology -contribution-16.html.

● **45. Social media post**

> 45. NASA (@nasa), "This galaxy is a whirl of color," Instagram photo, September 23, 2017, https://www.instagram .com/p/BZY8adnnZQJ/.

NASA. "This galaxy is a whirl of color." Instagram photo, September 23, 2017. https://www.instagram.com/p /BZY8adnnZQJ/.

44   *Chicago* manuscript format; sample pages

44a *Chicago* manuscript format

The following guidelines for formatting a *Chicago*-style paper and preparing its endnotes and bibliography are based on advice given in *The Chicago Manual of Style*, 17th ed. (Chicago: University of Chicago Press, 2017). For pages from a sample paper, see 44b.

Formatting the paper

Font   If your instructor does not require a specific font, choose one that is standard and easy to read (such as Times New Roman).

Title page   Include the full title of your paper, your name, the course title, the instructor's name, and the date. See page 272 for a sample title page.

Pagination   Using arabic numerals, number the pages in the upper right corner. Do not number the title page but count it in the manuscript numbering; that is, the first page of the text will be numbered 2. Depending on your instructor's preference, you may also use a short title or your last name before the page numbers to help identify pages.

Margins, line spacing, and paragraph indents   Leave margins of at least one inch at the top, bottom, and sides of the page. Double-space the body of the paper, including long quotations that have been set off from the text. (For line spacing in notes and the bibliography, see pp. 270 and 271.) Left-align the text.

Indent the first line of each paragraph one-half inch from the left margin.

Capitalization, italics, and quotation marks   In titles of works, capitalize all words except articles (*a, an, the*), prepositions (*at, from, between*, and so on), coordinating conjunctions (*and, but, or, nor, for, so, yet*), and *to* and *as*—unless the word is first or last in the title or subtitle. Follow these guidelines in your paper even if the title is styled differently in the source.

In your text, lowercase the first word following a colon even if the word begins a complete sentence. When the colon introduces a series of sentences or questions, capitalize the first word in all sentences in the series, including the first.

Italicize the titles of books and other long works. Use quotation marks around the titles of periodical articles, short stories, poems, and other short works.

Long quotations   You can choose to set off a long quotation of five to ten typed lines by indenting the entire quotation one-half inch from the left margin. (Always set off quotations of ten or more lines.) Double-space the quotation; do not use quotation marks and do not add extra space above or below it. (See also pp. 243–44.)

Visuals   *Chicago* classifies visuals as tables and figures (graphs, drawings, photographs, maps, and charts). Keep visuals as simple as possible.

Label each table with an arabic numeral (Table 1, Table 2, and so on) and provide a clear title that identifies the table's subject. The label and the title should appear on separate lines above the table, left-aligned.

For a table that you have borrowed or adapted, give its source in a note like this one, below the table:

Source: Edna Bonacich and Richard P. Appelbaum, *Behind the Label* (Berkeley: University of California Press, 2000), 145.

For each figure, place a label and a caption below the figure, left-aligned. The label and caption need not appear on separate lines. The word "Figure" may be abbreviated to "Fig."

In the text of your paper, discuss the most significant features of each visual. Place visuals as close as possible to the sentences that relate to them unless your instructor prefers that visuals appear in an appendix.

URLs and DOIs   When a URL or a DOI (digital object identifier) must break across lines, do not insert a hyphen or break at a hyphen. Instead, break after a colon or a double slash or before any other mark of punctuation. If you will post your project online or submit it electronically and you want to include live URLs for readers to click on, do not insert any line breaks.

Headings   *Chicago* does not provide guidelines for the use of headings in student papers. If you would like to insert headings in a long essay or research paper, check first with your instructor. See page 273 for typical placement and formatting of headings in a *Chicago*-style paper.

Preparing the endnotes   Begin the endnotes on a new page at the end of the paper. Center the title "Notes" about one inch from the top of the page, and number the pages consecutively with the rest of the paper. See page 274 for an example.

Indenting and numbering   Indent the first line of each note one-half inch from the left margin; do not indent additional lines in the note. Begin the note with the arabic numeral that corresponds to the number in the text. Put a period after the number.

Line spacing   Single-space each note and double-space between notes (unless your instructor prefers double-spacing throughout).

Preparing the bibliography Typically, the notes in *Chicago*-style papers are followed by a bibliography, an alphabetically arranged list of all the works cited or consulted. Begin the bibliography on a new page, and center the title "Bibliography" about one inch from the top of the page. Number bibliography pages consecutively with the rest of the paper. See page 275 for a sample bibliography.

Alphabetizing the list Alphabetize the bibliography by the last names of the authors (or editors); when a work has no author or editor, alphabetize it by the first word of the title other than *A*, *An*, or *The*.

If your list includes two or more works by the same author, arrange the entries alphabetically by title. Then use six hyphens instead of the author's name in all entries after the first. (See item 6 on p. 251.)

Indenting and line spacing Begin each entry at the left margin, and indent any additional lines one-half inch. Single-space each entry and double-space between entries (unless your instructor prefers double-spacing throughout).

44b Sample pages from a *Chicago* research paper

Following are pages from a research paper by Ned Bishop, a student in a history class. Bishop used *Chicago*-style endnotes, bibliography, and manuscript format.

Sample *Chicago* title page

1   The Massacre at Fort Pillow:
Holding Nathan Bedford Forrest Accountable

2   Ned Bishop

3   History 214
Professor Citro
March 22, 2012

1 Paper title, centered. **2** Writer's name. **3** Course title,
instructor's name, date.

(Annotations indicate *Chicago*-style formatting and effective
writing.)

Sample *Chicago* page

Although Northern newspapers of the time no doubt exaggerated some of the Confederate atrocities at Fort Pillow, most modern sources agree that a massacre of Union troops took place there on April 12, 1864. It seems clear that Union soldiers, particularly black soldiers, were killed after they had stopped fighting or had surrendered or were being held prisoner. Less clear is the role played by Major General Nathan Bedford Forrest in leading his troops. Although we will never know whether Forrest directly ordered the massacre, evidence suggests that he was responsible for it. **❶**

What happened at Fort Pillow? **❷**

Fort Pillow, Tennessee, which sat on a bluff overlooking the Mississippi River, had been held by the Union for two years. It was garrisoned by 580 men, 292 of them from United States Colored Heavy and Light Artillery regiments, 285 from the white Thirteenth Tennessee Cavalry. Nathan Bedford Forrest commanded about 1,500 troops.[1]

The Confederates attacked Fort Pillow on April 12, 1864, and had virtually surrounded the fort by the time Forrest arrived on the battlefield. At 3:30 p.m., Forrest demanded the surrender of the Union forces: "The conduct of the officers and men garrisoning Fort Pillow has been such as to entitle them to being treated as prisoners of war. . . . Should my demand be refused, I cannot be responsible for the fate of your command."[2] Union Major **❸** William Bradford, who had replaced Major Booth, killed earlier by sharpshooters, asked for an hour to consider the demand. Forrest, worried that vessels in the river were bringing in more Union troops, "shortened the time to twenty minutes."[3] Bradford refused to surrender, and Forrest quickly ordered the attack.

The Confederates charged to the fort, scaled the parapet, and fired on the forces within. Victory came quickly, with the Union

---

❶ Writer's thesis. **❷** Headings (centered) guide readers.
❸ Quotation cited with endnote.

Sample *Chicago* endnotes

Notes

1   1. John Cimprich and Robert C. Mainfort Jr., eds., "Fort Pillow Revisited: New Evidence about an Old Controversy," *Civil War History* 28, no. 4 (1982): 293-94.

2   2. Quoted in Brian Steel Wills, *A Battle from the Start: The Life of Nathan Bedford Forrest* (New York: HarperCollins, 1992), 182.

     3. Quoted in Wills, 183.

     4. Shelby Foote, *The Civil War, a Narrative: Red River to Appomattox* (New York: Vintage, 1986), 110.

     5. Nathan Bedford Forrest, "Report of Maj. Gen. Nathan B. Forrest, C. S. Army, Commanding Cavalry, of the Capture of Fort Pillow," Shotgun's Home of the American Civil War, accessed March 6, 2012, http://www.civilwarhome.com/forrest.htm.

3   6. Jack Hurst, *Nathan Bedford Forrest: A Biography* (New York: Knopf, 1993), 174.

     7 Foote, *Civil War,* 111.

4   8. Cimprich and Mainfort, "Fort Pillow," 295.

     9. Cimprich and Mainfort, 305.

     10. Cimprich and Mainfort, 299.

     11. Foote, *Civil War,* 110.

     12. Quoted in Wills, *Battle from the Start,* 187.

5   13. Albert Castel, "The Fort Pillow Massacre: A Fresh Examination of the Evidence," *Civil War History* 4, no. 1 (1958): 44-45.

     14. Cimprich and Mainfort, "Fort Pillow," 300.

---

1 First line of note indented ½". **2** Note number not raised, followed by period. **3** Authors' names not inverted. **4** Last names and shortened title refer to earlier note by same authors. **5** Notes single-spaced; double-spacing between notes.

Sample *Chicago* bibliography

Bibliography

Castel, Albert. "The Fort Pillow Massacre: A Fresh Examination of the Evidence." *Civil War History* 4, no. 1 (1958): 37-50.

Cimprich, John, and Robert C. Mainfort Jr., eds. "Fort Pillow Revisited: New Evidence about an Old Controversy." *Civil War History* 28, no. 4 (1982): 293-306.

Cornish, Dudley Taylor. *The Sable Arm: Black Troops in the Union Army, 1861-1865*. Lawrence: University Press of Kansas, 1987.

Foote, Shelby. *The Civil War, a Narrative: Red River to Appomattox*. New York: Vintage, 1986.

Forrest, Nathan Bedford. "Report of Maj. Gen. Nathan B. Forrest, C. S. Army, Commanding Cavalry, of the Capture of Fort Pillow." Shotgun's Home of the American Civil War. Accessed March 6, 2012. http://www.civilwarhome.com/forrest.htm.

Hurst, Jack. *Nathan Bedford Forrest: A Biography*. New York: Knopf, 1993.

McPherson, James M. *Battle Cry of Freedom: The Civil War Era*. New York: Oxford University Press, 1988.

Wills, Brian Steel. *A Battle from the Start: The Life of Nathan Bedford Forrest*. New York: HarperCollins, 1992.

1 Alphabetized by authors' last names. **2** First line of each entry at left margin; additional lines indented ½". **3** Entries single-spaced; double-spacing between entries.

CSE
Papers

45 CSE documentation style

In many science classes, you may be asked to use one of three systems of documentation recommended by the Council of Science Editors (CSE) in *Scientific Style and Format: The CSE Manual for Authors, Editors, and Publishers*, 8th ed. (Chicago: Council of Science Editors, 2014).

45a CSE documentation systems

The three CSE documentation systems specify the ways that sources are cited in the text of the paper and in the reference list at the end of the paper.

In the *citation-sequence system*, each source is given a superscript number the first time it appears in the paper. Any subsequent references to that source are marked with the same number. At the end of the paper, a list of references provides full publication information for each numbered source. Entries in the reference list are numbered in the order in which they are mentioned in the paper.

In the *citation-name system*, the list of references is created first, with entries alphabetized by authors' last names. The entries are numbered according to their alphabetical order, and the numbers are used in the text to cite the sources from the list.

In the *name-year system*, the author of the source is named in the text or in parentheses, and the date is given in parentheses. The reference list at the end of the paper is arranged alphabetically by authors' last names.

Sections 45b and 45c describe formatting of in-text citations and the reference list, respectively, in all three systems.

Directory to CSE in-text citation models

45b CSE in-text citations

In-text citations in all three CSE systems refer readers to the reference list at the end of the paper. The reference list is organized differently in the three systems (see 45c).

● 1. Basic format

Citation-sequence or citation-name

Scientists are beginning to question the validity of linking genes to a number of human traits and disorders.[1]

Name-year

Scientists are beginning to question the validity of linking genes to a number of human traits and disorders (Allen 2009).

● 2. Author named in the text

Citation-sequence or citation-name

Smith,[2] studying three species of tree frogs, identified variations in coloring over a small geographic area.

Name-year

Smith (2010), studying three species of tree frogs, identified variations in coloring over a small geographic area.

● 3. Specific part of source

Citation-sequence or citation-name

Our data differed markedly from Markam's study[3(Figs. 2,7)] on the same species in North Dakota.

Researchers observed an immune response in "19 of 20 people who ate a potato vaccine aimed at the Norwalk virus," according to Langridge.[4(p. 68)]

Name-year

Our data differed markedly from Markam's study (2010, Figs. 2, 7) on the same species in North Dakota.

Researchers observed an immune response in "19 of 20 people who ate a potato vaccine aimed at the Norwalk virus," according to Langridge (2009, p. 68).

● **4. Work by two authors**   See item 2 on page 282 for a work with multiple authors in the reference list.

Citation-sequence or citation-name

Follow item 1, 2, or 3 on page 278, depending on how you use the source in your paper. Use "and" between the two authors' names.

Name-year

Use "and" between the two authors' names in parentheses or in the text.

Self-organization plays a complex role in the evolution of biological systems (Johnson and Lam 2010).

Johnson and Lam (2010) explored the complex role of self-organization in evolution.

● **5. Work by three or more authors**   See item 2 on page 282 for a work with multiple authors in the reference list.

Citation-sequence or citation-name

Follow item 1, 2, or 3 on page 278, depending on how you use the source in your paper.

Name-year

Give the first author's name followed by "et al." in parentheses or in the text.

Orchid seed banking is a promising method of conservation to preserve species in situ (Seaton et al. 2010).

Seaton et al. (2010) provided a range of in situ techniques for orchid seed banking as a method of conservation of species.

● **6. Multiple works by one author**

Citation-sequence or citation-name

Gawande's work[4,5,6] deals not just with the practice of modern medicine but more broadly with the way we rely on human expertise in every aspect of society.

Name-year: works in different years

Gawande's work (2003, 2007, 2009) deals not just with the practice of modern medicine but more broadly with the way we rely on human expertise in every aspect of society.

● **6. Multiple works by one author (*cont.*)**

Name-year: works in the same year

The works are arranged in the reference list in chronological order (the earliest first). The letters "a," "b," and so on are added after the year, in both the reference list and the in-text citation. (See also the name-year model on p. 283.)

Scientists have investigated the role of follicle stimulating hormone (FSH) in the growth of cancer cells beyond the ovaries and testes (Seppa 2010a).

● **7. Organization as author**

Citation-sequence or citation-name

Follow item 1, 2, or 3 on page 278, depending on how you use the source in your paper.

Name-year

Developing standards for handling and processing biospecimens is essential to ensure the validity of cancer research and, ultimately, treatment (OBBR 2010).

The reference list entry gives the abbreviation for the organization's name, followed by the full name of the organization (Office of Biorepositories and Biospecimen Research); only the abbreviation is used in the in-text citation. (See item 3 on p. 282.)

Directory to CSE reference list models

45c CSE reference list

In the citation-sequence system, entries in the reference list are numbered in the order in which they appear in the text of the paper. In the citation-name system, entries in the reference list are put into alphabetical order and then numbered in that order. In the name-year system, entries are listed alphabetically in the reference list; they are not numbered. See 45b for examples of in-text citations using all three systems. See 46b for details about formatting the reference list.

Basic guidelines

● **1. Single author**

Citation-sequence or citation-name

1. Bliss M. The making of modern medicine: turning points in the treatment of disease. Chicago (IL): University of Chicago Press; 2011.

Name-year

Bliss M. 2011. The making of modern medicine: turning points in the treatment of disease. Chicago (IL): University of Chicago Press.

● **2. Two or more authors** For a source with two to ten authors, list all authors' names; for a source with more than ten authors, list the first ten authors followed by a comma and "et al." (for "and others").

Citation-sequence or citation-name

2. Seaton PT, Hong H, Perner H, Pritchard HW. Ex situ conservation of orchids in a warming world. Bot Rev. 2010;76(2):193-203.

Name-year

Seaton PT, Hong H, Perner H, Pritchard HW. 2010. Ex situ conservation of orchids in a warming world. Bot Rev. 76(2):193-203.

● **3. Organization as author**

Citation-sequence or citation-name

3. American Cancer Society. Cancer facts and figures for African Americans 2005-2006. Atlanta (GA): The Society; 2005.

Name-year

Give the abbreviation of the organization name in brackets at the beginning of the entry; alphabetize the entry by the first word of the full name. (For an in-text citation, see the name-year model in item 7 on p. 280.)

[ACS] American Cancer Society. 2005. Cancer facts and figures for African Americans 2005-2006. Atlanta (GA): The Society.

● **4. Two or more works by the same author**

Citation-sequence or citation-name

In the citation-sequence system, list the works in the order in which they appear in the paper. In the citation-name system, order the works alphabetically by title. (The following examples are presented in the citation-name system.)

4. Gawande A. Better: a surgeon's notes on performance. New York (NY): Metropolitan; 2007.
5. Gawande A. The checklist manifesto: how to get things right. New York (NY): Metropolitan; 2009.
6. Gawande A. Complications: a surgeon's notes on an imperfect science. New York (NY): Picador; 2003.

Name-year

List the works chronologically (the earliest first).

Gawande A. 2003. Complications: a surgeon's notes on an imperfect science. New York (NY): Picador.

Gawande A. 2007. Better: a surgeon's notes on performance. New York (NY): Metropolitan.

Gawande A. 2009. The checklist manifesto: how to get things right. New York (NY): Metropolitan.

● 5. Two or more works by the same author in the same year

Citation-sequence or citation-name

In the citation-sequence system, list the works in the order in which they appear in the paper. In the citation-name system, order the works alphabetically by title. (The following examples are presented in the citation-sequence system.)

5. Seppa N. Protein implicated in many cancers. Sci News. 2010 Oct 20 [accessed 2011 Jan 22]. http://www.sciencenews.org/view/generic/id/64426.

8. Seppa N. Anticancer protein might combat HIV. Sci News. 2010 Nov 20:9.

Name-year

List the works in chronological order (the earliest first), and add the letters "a," "b," and so on after the year. If the works have only a year but not exact dates, arrange the entries alphabetically by title.

Seppa N. 2010a Jul 31. Fish oil may fend off breast cancer: other supplements studied show no signs of protection. Sci News. 13.

Seppa N. 2010b Sep 25. Ovary removal boosts survival: procedure shown to benefit women with BRCA mutations. Sci News. 12.

Articles and other short works

Use the basic format for an article in print publications when citing articles or other short works in most other media. See also "Online sources" on page 286.

● **6. Article in a print journal**

Citation-sequence or citation-name

6. Wasserman EA, Blumberg MS. Designing minds: how should we explain the origins of novel behaviors? Am Sci. 2010;98(3):183-185.

Name-year

Wasserman EA, Blumberg MS. 2010. Designing minds: how should we explain the origins of novel behaviors? Am Sci. 98(3):183-185.

● **7. Article in a print magazine**

Citation-sequence or citation-name

7. Quammen D. Great migrations. Natl Geogr. 2010 Nov:31-51.

Name-year

Quammen D. 2010 Nov. Great migrations. Natl Geogr. 31-51.

● **8. Article in a print newspaper**

Citation-sequence or citation-name

8. Wald M. Scientists call for new sources of critical elements. New York Times (New York Ed.). 2011 Feb 19;Sect. B:5 (col. 1).

Name-year

Wald M. 2011 Feb 19. Scientists call for new sources of critical elements. New York Times (New York Ed.). Sect. B:5 (col. 1).

● **9. Selection or chapter in an edited book**

Citation-sequence or citation-name

9. Underwood AJ, Chapman MG. Intertidal ecosystems. In: Levin SA, editor. Encyclopedia of biodiversity. Vol. 3. San Diego (CA): Academic Press; 2000. p. 485-499.

Name-year

Underwood AJ, Chapman MG. 2000. Intertidal ecosystems. In: Levin SA, editor. Encyclopedia of biodiversity. Vol. 3. San Diego (CA): Academic Press; p. 485-499.

Books and other long works

Use the basic format for a print book when citing books and other long works in most other media. See also "Online sources" on page 286.

● 10. Print book

Citation-sequence or citation-name

10. Tobin M. Endangered: biodiversity on the brink. Golden (CO): Fulcrum; 2010.

Name-year

Tobin M. 2010. Endangered: biodiversity on the brink. Golden (CO): Fulcrum.

● 11. Book with an editor

Citation-sequence or citation-name

11. Kurimoto N, Fielding D, Musani A, editors. Endobronchial ultrasonography. New York (NY): Wiley-Blackwell; 2011.

Name-year

Kurimoto N, Fielding D, Musani A, editors. 2011. Endobronchial ultrasonography. New York (NY): Wiley-Blackwell.

● 12. Edition other than the first

Citation-sequence or citation-name

12. Mai J, Paxinos G, Assheuer J. Atlas of the human brain. 2nd ed. Burlington (MA): Elsevier; 2004.

Name-year

Mai J, Paxinos G, Assheuer J. 2004. Atlas of the human brain. 2nd ed. Burlington (MA): Elsevier.

● 13. Report from an organization or a government agency

Citation-sequence or citation-name

13. National Institute on Drug Abuse (US). Inhalant abuse. Bethesda (MD): National Institutes of Health (US); 2010 Jul. NIH Pub. No.: 10-3818. Available from: National Clearinghouse on Alcohol and Drug Information, Rockville, MD 20852.

● **13. Report from an organization or a government agency (cont.)**

13. National Institute on Drug Abuse (US). Inhalant abuse. Bethesda (MD): National Institutes of Health (US); [accessed 2011 Jan 23]. NIH Pub. No.: 10-3818. http://www.drugabuse .gov/ResearchReports/Inhalants/inhalants.html.

Name-year

[NIDA] National Institute on Drug Abuse (US). 2010 Jul. Inhalant abuse. Bethesda (MD): National Institutes of Health (US). NIH Pub. No.: 10-3818. Available from: National Clearinghouse on Alcohol and Drug Information, Rockville, MD 20852.

[NIDA] National Institute on Drug Abuse (US). 2010 Jul. Inhalant abuse. Bethesda (MD): National Institutes of Health (US); [accessed 2010 Jan 23]. NIH Pub. No.: 10-3818. http://www .drugabuse.gov/ResearchReports/Inhalants/inhalants.html.

● **14. Conference proceedings** Cite a paper or presentation from the conference proceedings as you would a selection in an edited book (see Item 9).

Citation-sequence or citation-name

14. Proceedings of the 2004 National Beaches Conference; 2004 Oct 13-15; San Diego, CA. Washington (DC): Environmental Protection Agency (US); 2005 Mar. Document No.: EPA-823-R-05-001.

Name-year

Proceedings of the 2004 National Beaches Conference. 2005 Mar. 2004 Oct 13-15; San Diego, CA. Washington (DC): Environmental Protection Agency (US). Document No.: EPA-823-R-05-001.

Online sources

● **15. Entire website**

Citation-sequence or citation-name

15. American Society of Gene and Cell Therapy. Milwaukee (WI): The Society; c2000-2011 [accessed 2011 Jan 16]. http:// www.asgt.org/.

Name-year

[ASGCT] American Society of Gene and Cell Therapy. c2000-2011.
     Milwaukee (WI): The Society; [accessed 2011 Jan 16].
     Available from: http://www.asgt.org/.

● **16. Short work from a website**   Begin with the author
of the short work, if there is one, and include the
date of the short work in brackets as an "updated" or
"modified" date. Include the title of the website and
publishing information for the website.

Citation-sequence or citation-name

16. Butler R. The year in review for rain forests. Mongabay.com.
     Menlo Park (CA): Mongabay; c2011 [updated 2011 Dec 28;
     accessed 2012 Jan 11]. http://news.mongabay.com/2011/
     1228-year_in_rainforests_2011.html.

Name-year

Butler R. c2011. The year in review for rain forests. Mongabay.com.
     Menlo Park (CA): Mongabay; [updated 2011 Dec 28; accessed
     2012 Jan 11]. http://news.mongabay.com/2011/1228
     -year_in_rainforests_2011.html.

● **17. Online book**

Citation-sequence or citation-name

17. Wilson DE, Reeder DM, editors. Mammal species of the world.
     Washington (DC): Smithsonian Institution; c2011 [accessed
     2012 Oct 14]. http://vertebrates.si.edu/msw/mswcfapp/msw/
     index.cfm.

Name-year

Wilson DE, Reeder DM, editors. c2011. Mammal species of the
     world. Washington (DC): Smithsonian Institution; [accessed
     2012 Oct 14]. http://vertebrates.si.edu/msw/mswcfapp/msw/
     index/cfm.

● **18. Article in an online journal or magazine**   Give whatever publication information is available as for a print
source. End with the URL and DOI (if any).

● **18. Article in an online journal or magazine (*cont.*)**

Citation-sequence or citation-name

18. Leslie M. The power of one. Science. 2011 [accessed 2011
    Feb 3];331(6013):24-26. http://www.sciencemag.org/
    content/331/6013/24.1.summary. doi:10.1126/science
    .331.6013.24-a.

18. Matson J. Twisted light could enable black hole detection.
    Sci Am. 2011 Feb 14 [accessed 2011 Feb 28]. http://www
    .scientificamerican.com/article.cfm?id=twisting-light-oam.

Name-year

Leslie M. 2011. The power of one. Science. [accessed 2011
    Feb 3];331(6013):24-26. http://www.sciencemag
    .org/content/331/6013/24.1.summary. doi:10.1126/
    science.331.6013.24-a.

Matson J. 2011 Feb 14. Twisted light could enable black hole
    detection. Sci Am. [accessed 2011 Feb 28]. http://www
    .scientificamerican.com/article.cfm?id=twisting-light-oam.

● **19. Article from a database**

Citation-sequence or citation-name

19. Logan CA. A review of ocean acidification and America's
    response. BioScience. 2010 [accessed 2011 Jun 17];60(10):
    819-828. General OneFile. http://find.galegroup.com.ezproxy
    .bpl.org/. Document No.: A241952492.

Name-year

Logan CA. 2010. A review of ocean acidification and America's
    response. BioScience. [accessed 2011 Jun 17];60(10):
    819-828. General OneFile. http://find.galegroup.com
    .ezproxy.bpl.org/. Document No.: A241952492.

● **20. Blog post**

Citation-sequence or citation-name

20. Salopek P. The river door [blog post]. Out of Eden walk:
    dispatches from the field from Paul Salopek. 2014 Apr 17
    [accessed 2014 May 19]. http://outofedenwalk
    .nationalgeographic.com/.

Name-year

Salopek P. 2014 Apr 17. The river door [blog post]. Out of Eden
  walk: dispatches from the field from Paul Salopek. [accessed
  2014 May 19]. http://outofedenwalk.nationalgeographic.com/.

● **21. Social media**

Citation-sequence or citation-name

21. National Science Foundation. Facebook [organization page].
  2013 Jan 21, 10:31 a.m. [accessed 2013 Jan 22]. https://
  www.facebook.com/US.NSF.

Name-year

National Science Foundation. 2013 Jan 21, 10:31 a.m. Facebook
  [organization page]. [accessed 2013 Jan 22]. https://
  www.facebook.com/US.NSF.

● **22. Email or other personal communication** CSE recommends not including personal communications such
as email and personal letters in the reference list. A parenthetical note in the text usually suffices: (2010 email
to me; unreferenced).

Audio, visual, and multimedia sources

● **23. CD, DVD, or Blu-ray Disc**

Citation-sequence or citation-name

23. NOVA: secrets beneath the ice [DVD]. Seifferlein B, editor;
  Hochman G, producer. Boston (MA): WGBH Educational
  Foundation; 2010. 1 DVD: 52 min.

Name-year

NOVA: secrets beneath the ice [DVD]. 2010. Seifferlein B,
  editor; Hochman G, producer. Boston (MA): WGBH Educational
  Foundation. 1 DVD: 52 min.

● **24. Online video**

Citation-sequence or citation-name

24. Life: creatures of the deep: nemertean worms and sea stars
  [video]. Gunton M, executive producer; Holmes M, series
  producer. 2010 Mar 21, 2:55 min. [accessed 2011 Feb 4].
  http://dsc.discovery.com/videos/life-the-series-videos/?bcid
  =73073289001.

● **24. Online video (*cont.*)**

Name-year

Life: creatures of the deep: nemertean worms and sea stars
    [video]. 2010 Mar 21, 2:55 min. Gunton M, executive
    producer; Holmes M, series producer. [accessed 2011 Feb 4].
    http://dsc.discovery.com/videos/life-the-series-videos
    /?bcid=73073289001.

● **25. Podcast**

Citation-sequence or citation-name

25. Mirsky S, host; Conrad N, interviewee. The spirit of
    innovation:from high school to the moon [podcast]. Sci Am.
    2011 Feb 17, 19:26 min. [accessed 2011 Feb 27]. http://www
    .scientificamerican.com/podcast/episode.cfm?id=from-high
    -school-innovation-to-the-11-02-17.

Name-year

Mirsky, S, host; Conrad N, interviewee. 2011 Feb 17, 19:26 min.
    The spirit of innovation: from high school to the moon
    [podcast]. Sci Am. [accessed 2011 Feb 27]. http://www
    .scientificamerican.com/podcast/episode.cfm?id=from
    -high-school-innovation-to-the-11-02-17.

46 CSE manuscript format

The guidelines in this section are adapted from advice
given in *Scientific Style and Format: The CSE Manual for
Authors, Editors, and Publishers*, 8th ed. (Chicago: Council
of Science Editors, 2014). When in doubt about the
formatting required in your course, check with your
instructor.

46a Formatting the paper

Font If your instructor does not require a specific font,
choose one that is standard and easy to read (such as
Times New Roman).

Title page Center all information on the title page:
the title of your paper, your name, the course name,
and the date.

Pagination The title page is counted as page 1, although a number does not appear. Number the first page of the text of the paper as page 2. Type a shortened form of the title followed by the page number in the top right corner of each page.

Margins, spacing, and indentation Leave margins of at least one inch on all sides of the page. Double-space throughout the paper. Indent the first line of each paragraph one-half inch. When a quotation is set off from the text, indent the entire quotation one-half inch from the left margin.

Abstract An abstract is a single paragraph at the beginning of the paper that summarizes the paper and might include your research methods, findings, and conclusions. Do not include citations in the abstract.

Headings CSE encourages the use of headings to help readers follow the organization of a paper. Common headings for papers reporting research are "Introduction," "Methods," "Results," and "Discussion."

Visuals A visual, such as a table, figure, or chart, should be placed as close as possible to the text that discusses it. In general, try to place visuals at the top of a page.

Appendixes Appendixes may be used for relevant information that is too long to include in the body of the paper. Label each appendix and give it a title (for example, "Appendix 1: Methodologies of Previous Researchers").

Acknowledgments An acknowledgments section is common in scientific writing because research is often conducted with help from others. Place the acknowledgments at the end of the paper, before the reference list.

46b Formatting the reference list

Basic format Begin on a new page. Center the title "References" and then list the works you have cited in the paper. Double-space throughout.

Organization of the list In the citation-sequence system, number the entries in the order in which they appear in the text.

In the citation-name system, first alphabetize all the entries by authors' last names (or by organization name or by title for works with no author, ignoring any initial *A*, *An*, or *The*); for two or more works by the same author, arrange the entries alphabetically by title.

In both systems, number the entries in the order in which they appear in the list. Left-align the first line of each entry, and indent subsequent lines one-quarter inch. In both systems, use the number from the reference list whenever you refer to the source in the text of the paper.

In the name-year system, alphabetize the entries by authors' last names (or by organization name or by title for works with no author, ignoring any initial *A*, *An*, or *The*). Place the year after the last author's name, followed by a period. For two or more works by the same author, arrange the entries by year, the earliest first. For two or more works by the same author in the same year, see item 5 on page 283. Left-align the first line of each entry, and indent any additional lines one-quarter inch.

Authors' names Give the last name first; use initials for first and middle names, with no periods after the initials and no space between them. Do not use a comma between the last name and the initials. For a work with up to ten authors, use all authors' names; for a work with eleven or more authors, list the first ten names followed by a comma and "et al." (for "and others").

Titles of books and articles Capitalize only the first word and all proper nouns in the title and subtitle of a book or an article. Do not underline or italicize titles of books; do not place titles of articles in quotation marks.

Titles of journals Abbreviate titles of journals that consist of more than one word. Omit the words *the* and *of* and apostrophes. Capitalize all the words or abbreviated words in the title; do not underline or italicize the title: Science, Sci Am, N Engl J Med, Womens Health.

Page ranges Do not abbreviate page ranges for articles in journals or periodicals or for chapters in edited works. When an article appears on discontinuous pages, list all pages or page ranges, separated by commas: 145-149, 162-174. For chapters in edited volumes, use the abbreviation "p." before the numbers (p. 63-90).

Breaking a URL or DOI When a URL or a DOI (digital object identifier) must be divided, break it before or after a double slash, a slash, or any other mark of punctuation. Do not insert a hyphen. If you will post your project online or submit it electronically and you want to include live URLs for readers to click on, do not insert any line breaks.

Glossaries

Glossary of usage

This glossary includes words commonly confused, words commonly misused, and words that are nonstandard. It also lists colloquialisms that may be appropriate in informal speech but are inappropriate in formal writing.

a, an   Use *an* before a vowel sound, *a* before a consonant sound: *an apple, a peach.* Problems sometimes arise with words beginning with *h* or *u*. If the *h* is silent, the word begins with a vowel sound, so use *an*: *an hour, an heir, an honest senator.* If the *h* is pronounced, the word begins with a consonant sound, so use *a*: *a hospital, a historian, a hotel.* Words such as *university* and *union* begin with a consonant sound, so use *a*: *a union.* Words such as *uncle* and *umbrella* begin with a vowel sound, so use *an*: *an underground well.* When an abbreviation or acronym begins with a vowel sound, use *an*: *an EKG, an MRI.*

accept, except   *Accept* is a verb meaning "to receive." *Except* is usually a preposition meaning "excluding." *I will accept all the packages except that one. Except* is also a verb meaning "to exclude." *Please except that item from the list.*

adapt, adopt   *Adapt* means "to adjust or become accustomed"; it is usually followed by *to. Adopt* means "to take as one's own." *Our family adopted a Vietnamese child, who quickly adapted to his new life.*

adverse, averse   *Adverse* means "unfavorable." *Averse* means "opposed" or "reluctant"; it is usually followed by *to. I am averse to your proposal because it could have an adverse impact on the economy.*

advice, advise   *Advice* is a noun, *advise* a verb. *We advise you to follow John's advice.*

affect, effect   *Affect* is usually a verb meaning "to influence." *Effect* is usually a noun meaning "result." *The drug did not affect the disease, and it had adverse side effects. Effect* can also be a verb meaning "to bring about." *Only the president can effect such a change.*

all ready, already   *All ready* means "completely prepared." *Already* means "previously." *Susan was all ready for the concert, but her friends had already left.*

all right   *All right*, written as two words, is correct. *Alright* is nonstandard.

all together, altogether   *All together* means "everyone gathered." *Altogether* means "entirely." *We were not altogether sure that we could bring the family all together for the reunion.*

allusion, illusion   An *allusion* is an indirect reference; an *illusion* is a misconception or false impression. *Did you* *catch my allusion to Shakespeare? Mirrors give the room an illusion of depth.*

a lot   *A lot* is two words. Do not write *alot.*

among, between   Ordinarily, use *among* with three or more entities, *between* with two. *The prize was divided among several contestants. You have a choice between carrots and beans.*

amoral, immoral   *Amoral* means "neither moral nor immoral"; it also means "not caring about moral judgments." *Immoral* means "morally wrong." *Many business courses are taught from an amoral perspective. Murder is immoral.*

amount, number   Use *amount* with quantities that cannot be counted; use *number* with those that can. *This recipe calls for a large amount of sugar. We have a large number of toads in our garden.*

an   See *a, an.*

and/or   Avoid *and/or* except in technical or legal documents.

anxious   *Anxious* means "worried" or "apprehensive." In formal writing, avoid using *anxious* to mean "eager." *We are eager* (not *anxious*) *to see your new house.*

anybody, anyone   See pages 21 and 31.

anyone, any one   *Anyone,* an indefinite pronoun, means "any person at all." *Any one* refers to a particular person or thing in a group. *Anyone in the class may choose any one of the books to read.*

anyways, anywheres   *Anyways* and *anywheres* are nonstandard for *anyway* and *anywhere.*

as   *As* is sometimes used to mean "because." But do not use it if there is any chance of ambiguity. *We canceled the picnic because* (not *as*) *it began raining. As here could mean "because" or "when."*

as, like   See *like, as.*

averse   See *adverse, averse.*

awhile, a while   *Awhile* is an adverb; it can modify a verb, but it cannot be the object of a preposition such as *for.* The two-word form *a while* is a noun preceded by an article and therefore can be the object of a preposition. *Stay awhile. Stay for a while.*

back up, backup   *Back up* is a verb phrase. *Back up the car carefully. Be sure to back up your hard drive. Backup* is a noun often meaning "duplicate of electronically stored data." *Keep your backup in a safe place. Backup* can also be used as an adjective. *I regularly create backup disks.*

bad, badly *Bad* is an adjective, *badly* an adverb. *They felt bad about being early and ruining the surprise. Her arm hurt badly after she slid into second.* See section 13.

being as, being that *Being as* and *being that* are nonstandard expressions. Write *because* instead.

beside, besides *Beside* is a preposition meaning "at the side of" or "next to." *Annie sleeps with a flashlight beside her bed. Besides* is a preposition meaning "except" or "in addition to." *No one besides Terrie can have that ice cream. Besides* is also an adverb meaning "in addition." *I'm not hungry; besides, I don't like ice cream.*

between See *among, between.*

bring, take Use *bring* when an object is being transported toward you, *take* when it is being moved away. *Please bring me a glass of water. Please take these magazines to Mr. Scott.*

can, may *Can* is traditionally reserved for ability, *may* for permission. *Can you speak French? May I help you?*

capital, capitol *Capital* refers to a city, *capitol* to a building where lawmakers meet. *The residents of the state capital protested the development plans. The capitol has undergone extensive renovations. Capital* also refers to wealth or resources.

censor, censure *Censor* means "to remove or suppress material considered objectionable." *Censure* means "to criticize severely." *The school's policy of censoring books has been censured by the media.*

cite, site *Cite* means "to quote as an authority or example." *Site* is usually a noun meaning "a particular place." *He cited the zoning law in his argument against the proposed site of the gas station.* Locations on the Internet are usually referred to as *sites.*

complement, compliment *Complement* is a verb meaning "to go with or complete" or a noun meaning "something that completes." As a verb, *compliment* means "to flatter"; as a noun, it means "flattering remark." *Her skill at rushing the net complements his skill at volleying. Sheiying's music arrangements receive many compliments.*

conscience, conscious *Conscience* is a noun meaning "moral principles"; *conscious* is an adjective meaning "aware or alert." *Let your conscience be your guide. Were you conscious of his love for you?*

continual, continuous *Continual* means "repeated regularly and frequently." *She grew weary of the continual telephone calls. Continuous* means "extended or prolonged without interruption." *The broken siren made a continuous wail.*

could care less   Write *couldn't care less* when referring to someone who does not care about something. (*Could care less* is nonstandard and means that the person described does care.)

could of   *Could of* is nonstandard for *could have*.

council, counsel   A *council* is a deliberative body, and a *councilor* is a member of such a body. *Counsel* usually means "advice" and can also mean "lawyer"; a *counselor* is one who gives advice or guidance. *The councilors met to draft the council's position paper. The pastor offered wise counsel to the troubled teenager.*

criteria   *Criteria* is the plural of *criterion*, which means "a standard, rule, or test on which a judgment or decision can be based." *The only criterion for the scholarship is ability.*

data   *Data* is a plural noun meaning "facts or results." *The new data suggest that our theory is correct.* Except in scientific writing, *data* is increasingly being accepted as a singular noun.

different from, different than   Ordinarily, write *different from. Your sense of style is different from Jim's.* However, *different than* is acceptable to avoid an awkward construction. *Please let me know if your plans are different than* (to avoid *from what*) *they were six weeks ago.*

disinterested, uninterested   *Disinterested* means "impartial, objective"; *uninterested* means "not interested." *We sought the advice of a disinterested counselor to help us solve our problem. Mark was uninterested in anyone's opinion but his own.*

each   See pages 21 and 31.

effect   See *affect, effect.*

either   See pages 21 and 31.

elicit, illicit   *Elicit* is a verb meaning "to bring out" or "to evoke." *Illicit* is an adjective meaning "unlawful." *The reporter was unable to elicit any information from the police about illicit drug traffic.*

emigrate from, immigrate to   *Emigrate* means "to leave one place to settle in another." *My great-grandfather emigrated from Russia to escape the religious pogroms. Immigrate* means "to enter another place and reside there." *Thousands of Bosnians immigrated to the United States in the 1990s.*

etc.   Avoid ending a list with *etc.* It is more emphatic to end with an example, and usually readers will understand that the list is not exhaustive. When you don't wish to end with an example, *and so on* is more graceful than *etc.*

everybody, everyone   See pages 21 and 31.

everyone, every one   *Everyone* is an indefinite pronoun. *Everyone wanted to go. Every one*, the pronoun *one* preceded by the adjective *every*, means "each individual or thing in a particular group." *Every one* is usually followed by *of*. *Every one of the missing books was found.*

except   See *accept, except*.

farther, further   *Farther* describes distances. *Further* suggests quantity or degree. *Detroit is farther from Miami than I thought. You extended the curfew further than necessary.*

fewer, less   *Fewer* refers to items that can be counted; *less* refers to items that cannot be counted. *Fewer people are living in the city. Please put less sugar in my tea.*

firstly   *Firstly* sounds pretentious, and it leads to the ungainly series *firstly, secondly, thirdly, fourthly*, and so on. Write *first, second, third* instead.

further   See *farther, further*.

good, well   See page 39.

hanged, hung   *Hanged* is the past-tense and past-participle form of the verb *hang*, meaning "to execute." *The prisoner was hanged at dawn. Hung* is the past-tense and past-participle form of the verb *hang*, meaning "to fasten or suspend." *The stockings were hung by the chimney with care.*

hardly   Avoid expressions such as *can't hardly* and *not hardly*, which are considered double negatives. *I can* (not *can't*) *hardly describe my elation at getting the job.*

hopefully   *Hopefully* means "in a hopeful manner." *We looked hopefully to the future.* Some usage experts object to the use of *hopefully* as a sentence adverb, apparently on grounds of clarity. To be safe, avoid using *hopefully* in sentences such as the following: *Hopefully, your son will recover soon.* Instead, indicate who is doing the hoping: *I hope that your son will recover soon.*

however   Some writers object to *however* at the beginning of a sentence, but experts advise placing the word according to the meaning and emphasis intended. Any of the following sentences is correct, depending on the intended contrast. *Pam decided, however, to attend the lecture. However, Pam decided to attend the lecture.* (She had been considering other activities.) *Pam, however, decided to attend the lecture.* (Unlike someone else, Pam opted for the lecture.)

hung   See *hanged, hung*.

illusion   See *allusion, illusion*.

immigrate   See *emigrate from, immigrate to*.

immoral   See *amoral, immoral.*

imply, infer   *Imply* means "to suggest or state indirectly"; *infer* means "to draw a conclusion." *John implied that he knew all about computers, but the interviewer inferred that John was inexperienced.*

in, into   *In* indicates location or condition; *into* indicates movement or a change in condition. *They found the lost letters in a box after moving into the house.*

irregardless   *Irregardless* is nonstandard. Use *regardless.*

is when, is where   See section 6c.

its, it's   *Its* is a possessive pronoun; *it's* is a contraction for *it is. It's always fun to watch a dog chase its tail.*

kind of, sort of   Avoid using *kind of* or *sort of* to mean "somewhat." *The movie was a little* (not *kind of*) *boring.* Do not put *a* after either phrase. *That kind of* (not *kind of a*) *salesclerk annoys me.*

lay, lie   See page 25.

lead, led   *Lead* is a metallic element; it is a noun. *Led* is the past tense of the verb *lead. He led me to the treasure.*

less   See *fewer, less.*

liable   *Liable* means "obligated" or "responsible." Do not use it to mean "likely." *You're likely* (not *liable*) *to trip if you don't tie your shoelaces.*

lie, lay   See page 25.

like, as   *Like* is a preposition, not a subordinating conjunction. It should be followed only by a noun or a noun phrase. *As* is a subordinating conjunction that introduces a subordinate clause. In casual speech, you may say *She looks like she has not slept.* But in formal writing, use *as. She looks as if she has not slept.*

loose, lose   *Loose* is an adjective meaning "not securely fastened." *Lose* is a verb meaning "to misplace" or "to not win." *Did you lose all your loose change?*

may   See *can, may.*

maybe, may be   *Maybe* is an adverb meaning "possibly"; *may be* is a verb phrase. *Maybe the sun will shine tomorrow. Tomorrow may be a brighter day.*

may of, might of   *May of* and *might of* are nonstandard for *may have* and *might have.*

media, medium   *Media* is the plural of *medium. Of all the media that cover the Olympics, television is the medium that best captures the spectacle of the events.*

must of   *Must of* is nonstandard for *must have.*

myself   *Myself* is a reflexive or intensive pronoun. Reflexive: *I cut myself.* Intensive: *I will drive you myself.* Do not use *myself* in place of *I* or *me: He gave the plants to Melinda and me* (not *myself*).

neither   See pages 21 and 31.

none   See page 21.

nowheres   *Nowheres* is nonstandard for *nowhere.*

number   See *amount, number.*

off of   *Off* is sufficient. Omit *of.*

passed, past   *Passed* is the past tense of the verb *pass. Emily passed me a slice of cake. Past* usually means "belonging to a former time" or "beyond a time or place." *Our past president spoke until past 10:00. The hotel is just past the station.*

plus   *Plus* should not be used to join independent clauses. *This raincoat is dirty; moreover* (not *plus*), *it has a hole in it.*

precede, proceed   *Precede* means "to come before." *Proceed* means "to go forward." *As we proceeded up the mountain, we saw evidence that some hikers had preceded us.*

principal, principle   *Principal* is a noun meaning "the head of a school or an organization" or "a sum of money." It is also an adjective meaning "most important." *Principle* is a noun meaning "a basic truth or law." *The principal expelled her for three principal reasons. We believe in the principle of equal justice for all.*

proceed, precede   See *precede, proceed.*

quote, quotation   *Quote* is a verb; *quotation* is a noun. Avoid using *quote* as a shortened form of *quotation. Her quotations* (not *quotes*) *from Shakespeare intrigued us.*

real, really   *Real* is an adjective; *really* is an adverb. *Real* is sometimes used informally as an adverb, but avoid this use in formal writing. *She was really* (not *real*) *angry.* See also section 13.

reason . . . is because   See section 6c.

reason why   The expression *reason why* is redundant. *The reason* (not *The reason why*) *Jones lost the election is clear.*

respectfully, respectively   *Respectfully* means "showing or marked by respect." *He respectfully submitted his opinion. Respectively* means "each in the order given." *John, Tom, and Larry were a butcher, a baker, and a lawyer, respectively.*

sensual, sensuous *Sensual* means "gratifying the physical senses," especially those associated with sexual pleasure. *Sensuous* means "pleasing to the senses," especially involving art, music, and nature. *The sensuous music and balmy air led the dancers to more sensual movements.*

set, sit *Set* means "to put" or "to place"; *sit* means "to be seated." *She set the dough in a warm corner of the kitchen. The cat sits in the warmest part of the room.*

should of *Should of* is nonstandard for *should have*.

since Do not use *since* to mean "because" if there is any chance of ambiguity. *Because* (not *Since*) *we won the game, we have been celebrating. Since* here could mean "because" or "from the time that."

sit See *set, sit.*

site, cite See *cite, site.*

somebody, someone, something See pages 21 and 31.

suppose to Write *supposed to.*

sure and *Sure and* is nonstandard for *sure to. Be sure to* (not *sure and*) *bring a gift for the host.*

take See *bring, take.*

than, then *Than* is a conjunction used in comparisons; *then* is an adverb denoting time. *That pizza is more than I can eat. Tom laughed, and then we recognized him.*

that See *who, which, that.*

that, which Many writers reserve *that* for restrictive clauses, *which* for nonrestrictive clauses. (See p. 58.)

then See *than, then.*

there, their, they're *There* is an adverb specifying place; it is also an expletive (placeholder). Adverb: *Sylvia is sitting there patiently.* Expletive: *There are two plums left.* (See also p. 305.) *Their* is a possessive pronoun. *Fred and Jane finally washed their car. They're* is a contraction of *they are. They're late today.*

to, too, two *To* is a preposition; *too* is an adverb; *two* is a number. *Too many of your shots slice to the left, but the last two were right on the mark.*

toward, towards *Toward* and *towards* are generally interchangeable, although *toward* is preferred in American English.

try and *Try and* is nonstandard for *try to. I will try to* (not *try and*) *be better about writing to you.*

uninterested See *disinterested, uninterested.*

unique See page 40.

use to   Write *used to*. *We used to live in an apartment.*

utilize   *Utilize* is often a pretentious substitute for *use*; in most cases, *use* is sufficient. *I used* (not *utilized*) *the printer.*

wait for, wait on   *Wait for* means "to be in readiness for" or "to await." *Wait on* means "to serve." *We're waiting for* (not *waiting on*) *Ruth before we can leave.*

ways   *Ways* is colloquial when used in place of *way* to mean "distance." *The city is a long way* (not *ways*) *from here.*

weather, whether   The noun *weather* refers to the state of the atmosphere. *Whether* is a conjunction indicating a choice between alternatives. *We wondered whether the weather would clear up in time for our picnic.*

well, good   See page 39.

which   See *that, which* and *who, which, that*.

while   Avoid using *while* to mean "although" or "whereas" if there is any chance of ambiguity. *Although* (not *While*) *Gloria lost money in the slot machine, Tom won it at roulette.* Here *While* could mean either "although" or "at the same time that."

who, which, that   Use *who*, not *which*, to refer to persons. Generally, use *that* to refer to things or, occasionally, to a group or class of people. *The player who* (not *that* or *which*) *made the basket at the buzzer was named MVP. The team that scores the most points in this game will win the tournament.*

who, whom   See section 12d.

who's, whose   *Who's* is a contraction of *who is*; *whose* is a possessive pronoun. *Who's ready for more popcorn? Whose coat is this?*

would of   *Would of* is nonstandard for *would have*.

you   See page 34.

your, you're   *Your* is a possessive pronoun; *you're* is a contraction of *you are*. *Is that your bike? You're in the finals.*

Glossary of grammatical terms

This glossary gives definitions for parts of speech, such as nouns; parts of sentences, such as subjects; and types of sentences, clauses, and phrases.

If you are looking up the name of an error (sentence fragment, for example), consult the index or the table of contents instead.

absolute phrase   A word group that modifies a whole clause or sentence, usually consisting of a noun followed by a participle or participial phrase: *Her words echoing in the large arena,* the senator mesmerized the crowd.

active vs. passive voice   When a verb is in the active voice, the subject of the sentence does the action: *Hernando caught the ball.* In the passive voice, the subject receives the action: The *ball was caught* by Hernando. Often the actor does not appear in a passive-voice sentence: The *ball was caught.* See also section 2.

adjective   A word used to modify (describe) a noun or pronoun: the *frisky* horse, *rare old* stamps, *sixteen* candles, the *blue* one. Adjectives usually answer one of these questions: Which one? What kind of? How many or how much? See also section 13.

adjective clause   A subordinate clause that modifies a noun or pronoun. An adjective clause begins with a relative pronoun (*who, whom, whose, which, that*) or with a relative adverb (*when, where*) and usually appears right after the word it modifies: The book *that goes unread* is a writer's worst nightmare. See also *subordinate clause.*

adverb   A word used to modify a verb, an adjective, or another adverb: rides *smoothly, unusually* attractive, *very* slowly. An adverb usually answers one of these questions: When? Where? How? Why? Under what conditions? How often? To what degree? See also section 13.

adverb clause   A subordinate clause that modifies a verb (or occasionally an adjective or adverb). An adverb clause begins with a subordinating conjunction such as *although, because, if, unless,* or *when* and usually appears at the beginning or the end of a sentence: *When the sun went down,* the hikers prepared their camp. See also *subordinate clause; subordinating conjunction.*

agreement   See sections 10 and 12.

antecedent   A noun or pronoun to which a pronoun refers: When the *battery* wears down, we recharge *it.* The noun *battery* is the antecedent of the pronoun *it.*

appositive   A noun or noun phrase that renames a nearby noun or pronoun: Bloggers, *conversationalists at heart*, are the online equivalent of talk show hosts.

article   The word *a, an,* or *the,* used to mark a noun. See also section 16b.

case   See sections 12c and 12d.

clause   A word group containing a subject, a verb, and any objects, complements, or modifiers. See *independent clause*; *subordinate clause*.

collective noun   See sections 10e and 12a.

common noun   See section 22a.

complement   See *object complement*; *subject complement*.

complex sentence   A sentence consisting of one independent clause and one or more subordinate clauses. In the following example, the subordinate clause is italicized: We walked along the river *until we came to the bridge.*

compound-complex sentence   A sentence consisting of at least two independent clauses and at least one subordinate clause: Jan dictated a story, and the children wrote whatever he said. In the preceding sentence, the subordinate clause is *whatever he said.* The two independent clauses are *Jan dictated a story* and *the children wrote whatever he said.*

compound sentence   A sentence consisting of two or more independent clauses, with no subordinate clauses. The clauses are usually joined with a comma and a coordinating conjunction (*and, but, or, nor, for, so, yet*) or with a semicolon: The car broke down, *but* a rescue van arrived within minutes. A shark was spotted near shore; people left the water immediately.

conjunction   A joining word. See *conjunctive adverb*; *coordinating conjunction*; *correlative conjunction*; *subordinating conjunction*.

conjunctive adverb   An adverb used with a semicolon to connect independent clauses: The bus was stuck in traffic; *therefore,* the team was late for the game. The most commonly used conjunctive adverbs are *consequently, furthermore, however, moreover, nevertheless, then, therefore,* and *thus.* See page 63 for a longer list.

coordinating conjunction   One of the following words, used to join elements of equal grammatical rank: *and, but, or, nor, for, so, yet.*

correlative conjunction   A pair of conjunctions connecting grammatically equal elements: *either...or, neither...nor, whether...or, not only...but also, both...and.* See also section 3b.

count noun   See page 49.

demonstrative pronoun   A pronoun used to identify or point to a noun: *this, that, these, those. This* is my favorite chair.

direct object   A word or word group that receives the action of the verb: The hungry cat clawed *the bag of dry food*. The complete direct object is *the bag of dry food*. The simple direct object is always a noun or a pronoun, in this case *bag*.

expletive   The word *there* or *it* when used at the beginning of a sentence to delay the subject: *There* are eight planes waiting to take off. *It* is healthy to eat breakfast every day. The delayed subjects are the noun *planes* and the infinitive phrase *to eat breakfast every day*.

gerund   A verb form ending in *-ing* used as a noun: *Reading* aloud helps children appreciate language. The gerund *reading* is used as the subject of the verb *helps*.

gerund phrase   A gerund and its objects, complements, or modifiers. A gerund phrase always functions as a noun, usually as a subject, a subject complement, a direct object, or the object of a preposition. In the following example, the phrase functions as a direct object: We tried *planting tulips*.

helping verb   One of the following words, when used with a main verb: *be, am, is, are, was, were, being, been; has, have, had; do, does, did; can, will, shall, should, could, would, may, might, must.* Helping verbs always precede main verbs: *will work, is working, had worked.* See also *modal verb*.

indefinite pronoun   A pronoun that refers to a nonspecific person or thing: *Something* is burning. The most common indefinite pronouns are *all, another, any, anybody, anyone, anything, both, each, either, everybody, everyone, everything, few, many, neither, nobody, none, no one, nothing, one, some, somebody, someone,* and *something.* See also pages 21 and 31.

independent clause   A word group containing a subject and a verb that could or does stand alone as a sentence. In addition to at least one independent clause, many sentences contain subordinate clauses that function as adjectives, adverbs, or nouns. See also *clause; subordinate clause*.

indirect object   A noun or pronoun that names to whom or for whom the action of a sentence is done: We gave *her* some leftover yarn. An indirect object always precedes a direct object, in this case *some leftover yarn*.

infinitive   The word *to* followed by the base form of a verb: *to think, to dream.*

infinitive phrase   An infinitive and its objects, complements, or modifiers. An infinitive phrase can function as a noun, an adjective, or an adverb. Noun: *To live without health insurance* is risky. Adjective: The Nineteenth Amendment gave women the right *to vote.* Adverb: Volunteers knocked on doors *to rescue people from the flood.*

intensive or reflexive pronoun   A pronoun ending in *-self* (or *-selves*): *myself, yourself, himself, herself, itself, ourselves, yourselves, themselves.* An intensive pronoun emphasizes a noun or another pronoun: I *myself* don't have a job. A reflexive pronoun names a receiver of an action identical with the doer of the action: Did Paula cut *herself*?

interjection   A word expressing surprise or emotion: *Oh! Wow! Hey! Hooray!*

interrogative pronoun   A pronoun used to introduce a question: *who, whom, whose, which, what. What* does history teach us?

intransitive verb   See *transitive and intransitive verbs.*

irregular verb   See *regular and irregular verbs.* See also section 11a.

linking verb   A verb that links a subject to a subject complement, a word or word group that renames or describes the subject: The winner *was* a teacher. The cherries *taste* sour. The most common linking verbs are forms of *be: be, am, is, are, was, were, being, been.* The following sometimes function as linking verbs: *appear, become, feel, grow, look, make, seem, smell, sound, taste.* See also *subject complement.*

modal verb   A helping verb that cannot be used as a main verb. There are nine modals: *can, could, may, might, must, shall, should, will,* and *would.* We *must* shut the windows before the storm. The verb phrase *ought to* is often classified as a modal as well. See also *helping verb.*

modifier   A word, phrase, or clause that describes or qualifies the meaning of a word. Modifiers include adjectives, adverbs, prepositional phrases, participial phrases, some infinitive phrases, and adjective and adverb clauses.

mood   See section 11c.

noncount noun   See pages 49–50.

noun   The name of a person, place, thing, or concept (*freedom*, for example): The *lion* in the *cage* growled at the *zookeeper.*

noun clause   A subordinate clause that functions like a noun, usually as a subject, a subject complement, a direct object, or the object of a preposition. In the following sentence, the italicized noun clause functions as the subject: *Whoever leaves the house last* must lock the door. Noun clauses usually begin with *how, who, whom, whoever, that, what, whatever, whether,* or *why.*

noun equivalent   A word or word group that functions like a noun: a pronoun, a noun and its modifiers, a gerund phrase, some infinitive phrases, or a noun clause.

object   See *direct object; indirect object.*

object complement   A word or word group that renames or describes a direct object. It always appears after the direct object: The kiln makes clay *firm and strong.*

object of a preposition   See *prepositional phrase.*

participial phrase   A present or past participle and its objects, complements, or modifiers. A participial phrase always functions as an adjective describing a noun or pronoun. Usually it appears immediately before or after the word it modifies: *Being a weight-bearing joint,* the knee is often injured. Plants *kept in moist soil* will thrive.

participle, past   A verb form usually ending in *-d, -ed, -n, -en,* or *-t: asked, stolen, fought.* Past participles are used with helping verbs to form perfect tenses (had *spoken*) and the passive voice (were *required*). They are also used as adjectives (the *stolen* car).

participle, present   A verb form ending in *-ing.* Present participles are used with helping verbs in progressive forms (is *rising,* has been *walking*). They are also used as adjectives (the *rising* tide).

parts of speech   A system for classifying words. Many words can function as more than one part of speech. See *adjective, adverb, conjunction, interjection, noun, preposition, pronoun, verb.*

passive voice   See *active vs. passive voice.*

personal pronoun   One of the following pronouns, used to refer to a specific person or thing: *I, me, you, she, her, he, him, it, we, us, they, them.* After Julia won the award, *she* gave half of the prize money to a literacy program. See also *antecedent.*

phrase   A word group that lacks a subject, a verb, or both. Most phrases function within sentences as adjectives, as adverbs, or as nouns. See *absolute phrase; appositive; gerund phrase; infinitive phrase; participial phrase; prepositional phrase.*

possessive case   See section 19a.

possessive pronoun   A pronoun used to indicate ownership: *my, mine, your, yours, her, hers, his, its, our, ours, your, yours, their, theirs.* The guest made *his* own breakfast.

predicate   A verb and any objects, complements, and modifiers that go with it. The horses *exercise in the corral every day*.

preposition   A word placed before a noun or noun equivalent to form a phrase modifying another word in the sentence. The preposition indicates the relation between the noun (or noun equivalent) and the word the phrase modifies. The most common prepositions are *about, above, across, after, against, along, among, around, at, before, behind, below, beside, besides, between, beyond, by, down, during, except, for, from, in, inside, into, like, near, of, off, on, onto, out, outside, over, past, since, than, through, to, toward, under, unlike, until, up, with, within,* and *without.*

prepositional phrase   A phrase beginning with a preposition and ending with a noun or noun equivalent (called the *object of the preposition*). Most prepositional phrases function as adjectives or adverbs. Adjective phrases usually come right after the noun or pronoun they modify: The road *to the summit* was treacherous. Adverb phrases usually appear at the beginning or the end of the sentence: *To the hikers*, the brief shower was a welcome relief. The brief shower was a welcome relief *to the hikers*.

progressive verb forms   See pages 29 and 46–47.

pronoun   A word used in place of a noun. Usually the pronoun substitutes for a specific noun, known as the pronoun's *antecedent*. In the following example, *alarm* is the antecedent of the pronoun *it*: When the *alarm* rang, I reached over and turned *it* off. See also *demonstrative pronoun; indefinite pronoun; intensive or reflexive pronoun; interrogative pronoun; personal pronoun; possessive pronoun; relative pronoun.*

proper noun   See section 22a.

regular and irregular verbs   When a verb is regular, both the past tense and the past participle are formed by adding *-ed* or *-d* to the base form of the verb: *walk, walked, walked*. The past tense and past participle of irregular verbs are formed in a variety of other ways: *ride, rode, ridden; begin, began, begun; go, went, gone;* and so on. See also section 11a.

relative adverb   The word *when* or *where*, when used to introduce an adjective clause: The park *where* we had our picnic closes on October 1. See also *adjective clause*.

relative pronoun   One of the following words, when used to introduce an adjective clause: *who, whom, whose, which, that*. The writer *who* won the award refused to accept it.

sentence   A word group consisting of at least one independent clause. See also *complex sentence; compound sentence; compound-complex sentence; simple sentence.*

simple sentence   A sentence consisting of one independent clause and no subordinate clauses: Without a passport, Eva could not visit her parents in Poland.

subject   A word or word group that names who or what the sentence is about. In the following example, the complete subject (the simple subject and all of its modifiers) is italicized: *The devastating effects of famine* can last for many years. The simple subject is *effects*. See also *subject after verb; understood subject.*

subject after verb   Although the subject normally precedes the verb, sentences are sometimes inverted. In the following example, the subject *the sleepy child* comes after the verb *sat*: Under the table *sat the sleepy child*. When a sentence begins with the expletive *there* or *it*, the subject always follows the verb. See also *expletive.*

subject complement   A word or word group that follows a linking verb and either renames or describes the subject of the sentence. If the subject complement renames the subject, it is a noun or a noun equivalent: That signature may be *a forgery*. If it describes the subject, it is an adjective: Love is *blind*.

subjunctive mood   See section 11c.

subordinate clause   A word group containing a subject and a verb that cannot stand alone as a sentence. Subordinate clauses function within sentences as adjectives, adverbs, or nouns. They begin with subordinating conjunctions such as *although, because, if,* and *until* or with relative pronouns such as *who, which,* and *that*. See *adjective clause; adverb clause; independent clause; noun clause.*

subordinating conjunction   A word that introduces a subordinate clause and indicates the relation of the clause to the rest of the sentence. The most common subordinating conjunctions are *after, although, as, as if, because, before, even though, if, since, so that, than, that, though, unless, until, when, where, whether,* and *while*. Note: The relative pronouns *who, whom, whose, which,* and *that* also introduce subordinate clauses.

tenses   See section 11b.

transitive and intransitive verbs   Transitive verbs take direct objects, nouns or noun equivalents that receive the action. In the following example, the transitive verb *wrote* takes the direct object *a story*: Each student *wrote* a story. Intransitive verbs do not take direct objects: The audience *laughed*. If any words follow an intransitive verb, they are adverbs or word groups functioning as adverbs: The audience *laughed* at the talking parrot.

understood subject The subject *you* when it is understood but not actually present in the sentence. Understood subjects occur in sentences that issue commands or give advice: [*You*] Put your clothes in the hamper.

verb A word that expresses action (*jump, think*) or being (*is, was*). A sentence's verb is composed of a main verb possibly preceded by one or more helping verbs: The band *practiced* every day. The report *was* not *completed* on schedule. Verbs have five forms: the base form, or dictionary form (*walk, ride*); the past-tense form (*walked, rode*); the past participle (*walked, ridden*); the present participle (*walking, riding*); and the *-s* form (*walks, rides*). See also *predicate*.

verbal phrase See *gerund phrase; infinitive phrase; participial phrase*.

Index

Revision Symbols

abbr	abbreviation **23a**	" "	quotation marks **20**
add	add needed word **4**	.	period **21a**
adj/ adv	adjective or adverb **13**	?	question mark **21b**
agr	agreement **10, 12a**	!	exclamation point **21c**
appr	inappropriate language **9**	—	dash **21d**
art	article **16b**	( )	parentheses **21e**
awk	awkward	[ ]	brackets **21f**
cap	capital letter **22**	...	ellipsis mark **21g**
case	case **12c, 12d**	/	slash **21h**
cliché	cliché **9b**	*pass*	ineffective passive **2b**
cs	comma splice **15**	*pn agr*	pronoun agreement **12a**
dm	dangling modifier **7c**	*ref*	pronoun reference **12b**
-ed	-*ed* ending **11a**	*run-on*	run-on sentence **15**
ESL	English as a second language/ multilingual writers **16**	*-s*	-*s* ending on verb **10, 16a**
frag	sentence fragment **14**	*sexist*	sexist language **9d, 12a**
fs	fused sentence **15**	*shift*	confusing shift **5**
hyph	hyphen **24b**	*sl*	slang **9c**
irreg	irregular verb **11a**	*sp*	misspelled word **24a**
ital	italics **23c**	*sv agr*	subject-verb agreement **10**
jarg	jargon **9a**	*t*	verb tense **11b**
lc	use lowercase letter **22**	*usage*	see glossary of usage
mix	mixed construction **6**	*v*	voice **2**
mm	misplaced modifier **7a–b, 7d**	*var*	sentence variety **8**
mood	mood **11c**	*vb*	problem with verb **11, 16a**
num	numbers **23b**	*w*	wordy **1**
om	omitted word **4, 16c**	*//*	faulty parallelism **3**
p	punctuation	∧	insert
⌃,	comma **17a–i**	x	obvious error
no ,	no comma **17j**	#	insert space
;	semicolon **18a**	⌒	close up space
:	colon **18b**		
⌄	apostrophe **19**		

Detailed Menu